ACKNOWLEDGEMENTS: Though in debt to many, the authors would like to particularly thank the following: Tony Arismendi, Police Chief Lawrence Donahoe, Officer Bob Elliot, Steve Emmett, Dr. Ronald T. Greene, Jr., Eugene Kaili, R.K., Dr. Harold Lerhman, Tim McGinnis, John Pelan, Officer Ed Snydicker, and March 19, 1983.

DEDICATION:

For LS - for chances taken and opportunities missed.
And for Matt Schwartz.

Portrait of the Psychopath as a Young Woman
has been published in an edition of 700 copies;
676 of which are offered for sale in the following manner:

Twenty-six copies, signed & lettered,
deluxe slipcased limited edition hardcover.

One hundred & fifty copies, signed & numbered,
limited edition hardcover.

A five-hundred copy, signed & numbered,
limited edition trade paperback.

Number: ___124___

first edition

PORTRAIT OF THE PSYCHOPATH AS A YOUNG WOMAN
©1998 by Edward Lee & Elizabeth Steffen

Cover art ©1998 Brandy Gill

This edition June 1998 © Necro Publications

book design & typesetting:
David G. Barnett
faT caT Design
PO BOX 540298
Orlando, FL 32854-0298

Assistant Editor:
John Everson

A Necro Publication
PO Box 540298
Orlando, FL 32854-0298

Hardcover	ISBN: 1-889186-10-4
Trade Paperback	ISBN: 1-889186-09-0

Portrait of the Psychopath as a Young Woman

by Edward Lee and Elizabeth Steffen

Chapter 1

(I)

An image flashed. The cat clock.
tick-tick-tick-tick
And unbidden words in her head: It's Sleepytime, Kathy.
She frowned then, blinked it all away, and went to light her hourly cigarette…
The thought came with no volition at all. It never did. The *mail's here,* Kathleen Shade thought. Every day she seemed to sense the approach of the squat, cumbersome white vehicle. Was it premonition? *By the prickling of my thumbs,* she thought, quoting Shakespeare. Ordinarily, she might've laughed, but she never laughed about the mail. The mail provided her only turnstile to the outside terra incognito that was the world.
The world felt removed from her. It honed her oneness, erecting her into shining, crumbly dark. The mail truck, and its singular sound—the way its brakes squealed, the rumble of its muffler—called to her much in a way like lust. The honest urge to touch oneself, for the pleasant yet ersatz sensation. Never to climax. Just for the feeling.
The urge had eluded her these days. Odd comparison, she considered. The mail, and precursory masturbation…
She'd been working on her "Verdict" column.
Dear Kathleen:
My boyfriend, with whom I've been living for three years, recently suggested that we "swap." It was at a work party. I

didn't know what he meant until a friend explained. He wanted us to switch sexual partners with my boss and his wife! When I refused, he (my boyfriend) took me aside and told me it would be good for my career! Can you believe it? I really love my boyfriend, but this suggestion leaves me shocked. What should I do?

Kathleen typed her response:

Dear Shocked:
Any man who needs to "swap" simply offers more proof of his own male sexual defectivity. Not only does he insult your love for him, he offends himself by verifying his lack of real domestic priority. And in his further coercion, i.e. his suggestion that trading partners would enhance your career status, he commits an even less forgivable slight—the traditional male two-faced rationalization: the pursuit of his own kinky pleasure as an excuse. Your boyfriend, therefore, demonstrates his utter unworthiness. He is selfish, immature, and prevaricating.
Dump him.

There. Short and sweet. Kathleen's "Verdict" column had become a hit. She'd merely applied, citing her sociology degree and a few published writing samples. "We like your edge," the senior editor had told her. Besides, teaching had bored her. Though the $600 per month she made from *'90s Woman* didn't pay all the bills, it made her feel she was doing something. It also made her feel... What?
Connected to something.
A moment later she turned to the next letter (she received several dozen per week) and the thought rang: *The mail.* She could even be napping, and would wake to realize the mail had arrived. One man she'd dated years ago had told her, "All women are psychic." *I guess that's how I knew you were an ass before we even met,* she thought now. When she'd caught him sleeping around, he'd claimed, "You gave me no choice!"
She severed the memory. *The mail, the mail,* she thought. In cutoff jeans, an old white Bud Burma men's longsleeve shirt, and barefoot, she went to retrieve the all-important mail. No check this week; God knew she could use the money. Her father always came through, at least. *Because he loves me? Or because of guilt?* It scarcely mattered now. "I'm very proud of you," he'd said when she'd been given "Verdict." "Your mother would be too." *What about Uncle Sammy?* she'd wanted to ask. *Do you think he'd be proud of me? Should I send him the magazine in prison?*

She opened the front door and peered out. Washington, D.C., had a smell no matter where you lived. It wafted up the open stairwell. The hall stood empty. *I haven't had sex in a year,* she thought. But why think that? And why now? Sex often made her feel totally alone; it made her feel unwanted, which never made sense to her. What more proof did she need of being wanted than an erect penis? She sometimes smirked when she saw lovers holding hands in Georgetown Park, or couples kissing in public. Her neighbors infuriated her, their passion raging through the wall. Mr. and Mrs. Bedsprings. *Stop fucking!* she yearned to yell at the wall every night.

The mail. Why did it seem so important today? It whispered false promises to her, as Uncle Sammy had, and many of the men she'd made love to. "I ascend to the blinding light," she whispered, descending the apartment steps. A boot lifted away in the sunlit entrance—the mailman. Before the glare, and the heat shining off cars, it looked like a foot stepping into hell.

The August humidity made her feel pallid and dry. She got her mail out of the gray row of boxes, and went back up. As she climbed, she felt the sensation of descending. Since turning 30—three years ago—she felt choked in a web of opposites: she felt chilled in the heat, she felt bright in utter darkness. *I'm weird*, she thought.

She did weird things sometimes, like eating only peanut butter for days, or looking at the Spiegel catalogue upside-down to see how funny the faces became. She rarely wore clothes in the apartment. Nakedness offered up a reality to her, an encompassing one. She watched TV naked. She read, cleaned, ate, did laundry—she even wrote her column—naked. *Why wear clothes inside?* she reasoned. *No one can see.*

Who'd want to see, Fattie? a darker voice inquired. She insisted she was fat, though she really wasn't. She could stand to drop 10 pounds (maybe 15 would be better) but she wasn't really fat. According to the woman shrink on the radio at night, Kathleen had acquired a "negative self-concept continuum." She had a bad image of herself. It was all childhood, according to the woman shrink. Constancy-hypothesis from Womb-Exit. Reactivity to gender-realization. Connate-impressions during the formative years. Uncle Sammy probably had a lot to do with it, too.

She wore her self-perceptions like a winter jacket, which wrapped her in contradictions. *I'm an unsocialized sociologist.* Frequently she felt phony. "Verdict" required her to apply deft sociological interpretations, as well as solutions, to the love-related quandaries of her readers. The column thrust her forward as an expert on love, when she'd never really been in love at all. She'd loved men, she supposed, but that wasn't the same. *If they only knew!* she thought. God. Womanhood, which her column exalted, often felt like a curse to her personally. She didn't know what to do with it. She didn't really even know what it was...

She closed and locked the door. She took the mail to the kitchen. AT&T bill, WG&E bill, MasterCard bill. A renewal notice for *Cosmopolitan.* A renewal notice for *Allure.* And the weekly carrier envelope from her editor. Readers sent their problems to "Verdict" care of the magazine, and the magazine sent them to her. Several dozen envelopes spilled out of the carrier, most of them the standard 4 1/8 x 9 1/2. And then there was one larger envelope—

The cramp popped in her loins. *Shit!* she thought. Her period always arrived like a sniper shot. Menstruation pissed her off; it didn't seem fair. If women have to bleed from their vaginas, men should have to bleed from their penises. Blood trickled. It felt hot. Just as she would make tracks for the bathroom, though, she caught herself standing still, staring.

She was staring at the larger envelope.

It was 9 x 6, manila. Her name and the magazine's address had been typed neatly on a white adhesive label. Kathleen opened it, wincing at the steady cramp.

First, there was an index card on which had been typed:

```
DEAR MS. SHADE:
    YOU ARE A GREAT WOMAN. IN THE FUTURE I WILL
BE SENDING YOU MY STORY. CONSIDER IT A PROPOSI-
TION. IT IS A VERY IMPORTANT STORY.
    WOULD YOU LIKE TO DO MY STORY?
```

Kathleen's frown turned her face up. There was no return address on the envelope. *What story?* she wondered.

Her fingers delved deeper.

Something else in here.

A thin foil packet wrapped in plastic. Unbidden, she thought of drugs. They wrapped drugs in foil, didn't they? Kathleen had never used drugs herself. Too scary. She'd never even smoked pot because she heard it increased appetite. But she remembered from her college days, kids brought hash into the dorm wrapped in foil, and LSD tabs.

Curiosity throbbed with the cramp. She opened the packet on the kitchen counter, peeling away first the plastic, then the foil.

Initially it didn't seem to be what it undoubtedly was. It seemed flattened, like a twist of raw chicken skin. Kathleen could have sworn that her heart stopped for the full minute that ticked by before she called the police.

(II)

Flesh—gorgeous, shining—shellacked in blood.

It's the image she craves.
It's the truth behind the image.
And The Cross.
She remembers the others, and sighs.
She remembers The Cross.
It's an anticipation: to see the flesh shining in blood.
The Amytal always keeps them out.
I hope you liked the back rub, she thinks. I give good back rubs, don't I?
His face looks childlike in this ponderous unconsciousness.
It's a wonder. His skull seems to glow beneath his face.
Skulls mean death, her mother says.
She Crazy Glues his eyes shut.
She daintily ruptures his eardrums with a Skeele 1.75 mm biopsy curette.
With lovely violet suture and an Ethicon FS-3 radial needle, she sews his lips shut.
She likes that.
Questions kiss her, they lick her.
It's very erotic, these questions.
What do they think when they wake up?
What goes on in their minds?
They can't see, they can't hear. They can't speak. They can't even move.
But they can feel.
She always gives them a lot to feel.
Here he comes.
"You're back," she says.
She caresses his penis.
"I give good back rubs, don't I?" she asks, not that he can hear the question, oh no, not with his eardrums punctured.
"I never lie. I told you I give good back rubs."
She imagines his horror: deaf, dumb, blind, immobile. This imagining arouses her, it lifts her smiling to her tiptoes, swells her perfect nipples, glows between her legs. Soon he's snapping his wrists and ankles against the Peerless Model 26 detention cuffs. It's a lovely, bracing sound, the sharp metallic snap snap snap! Lovelier still: the way his entire face lengthens to misshape, his eyes trying to open, his mouth trying to open, and the frantic swallowed sounds from his throat. "What are you thinking?" She rubs his flexing stomach. "What's going on in your mind?"
She works on him for a long, long time.
He keeps going out, and the hypodermic keeps bringing him back.
"Skulls mean death," she says matter-of-factly.

Portrait of the Psychopath as a Young Woman

Bruns serrated plaster shears. What they are, exactly, is a nine-inch-long pair of angled stainless-steel scissors, designed for cutting off plaster casts. The Miltex version costs $52.50 per pair, not that she had to buy them. "No plaster casts today," she says.

The shears open.
He's still alive.
The shears close.
"There."
His hips heave.
The buried scream rages in his throat.
"Did that feel good?"
To her left is The Box of Souls.
To her right is The Window.
In the Window she sees The Cross, all white in light.
She smiles.
Her surgical gloves are beautiful bright red now.
His blood is on her; it feels lovely, hot, exotic.
And here is the image she's awaited: to see him shine in his own viscid, wet beauty.
She lets him simmer down some.
She looks at what she's done.
She looks at her slick red hands.
She hopes that Kathleen Shade will want to do her story.

• • • • •

Clay-Adams dissecting pin. What it is, exactly, is an 18-inch-long stainless-steel rod, the width of a knitting needle, designed for pushing organs aside during autopsies.

He's numbly convulsing.
He's still alive.
She inserts the Clay-Adams dissecting pin into his left nostril and with her palm very slowly drives the rounded-steel point deep into—
Mother! Mother! she thinks.
—his brain.

Chapter 2

(I)

"Faggot."

Spence was standing in front of the mirror at the HQ bathroom. He was straightening his tie when he turned to face the person who'd just entered.

Some LT from District Four Narcotics; Spence couldn't place the name.

"What did you say?" Spence asked.

"I said you're a faggot. Get that tie nice and straight. You want to look pretty for the boys."

Spence finished his tie. "What's your problem, man? What's your beef with me? You don't even know me."

D4 glared back. "A police department is no place for homos."

Spence, in resolute calm, rammed his fist into the LT's mouth so hard there was an echo in the tiled room, a sound like five pounds of raw sirloin hitting the floor. What also hit the floor was this D4 lieutenant. His eyes crossed at once, and he fell hard.

Spence leaned over to finish the tune-up when his beeper went off. He grabbed D4's collar and gave a good shake.

"Listen, asshole. The only reason I'm not going to flush you down the toilet is because I just got beeped. But don't ever cross my path again, all right? Don't even walk down the same hallway as me unless you want to get aired out like somebody's laundry."

Groggily, D4's eyes focused, blood on his lip. "I—I'm gonna file charges."

"Go ahead," Spence said. "You picked the wrong *homo* to fuck with today. See how far you get filing charges against an MCS officer. See how long it takes before you're spending the rest of your career emptying parking meters."

Spence, then, let him go, checked his tie one last time, and walked out of the bathroom. He was not offended, nor agitated, nor pissed off. He couldn't have cared less.

(II)

"So. You're the feminist writer."

The voice: monotone, dark. He'd identified himself as Lieutenant Jeffrey Spence. His face looked ruddily handsome; he seemed fit, and wore a nice baby-blue dress shirt, suspenders, and a dark silk tie. Broad shoulders, well-styled short dark-blond hair. Kathleen guessed he must be about 30. She also received the immediate impression that he didn't like her.

"I'm a magazine writer," she corrected. "I do a monthly column."

"For a militant feminist magazine," Spence added. "Do you make a living? From this feminist column?"

"It's not a *feminist* column. It's a self-help column."

"Ah. Well. Do you make a living from it?"

"No," Kathleen said.

D.C. Police Headquarters occupied an entire block of Indiana Avenue; it reminded her of a vast above-ground crypt. At the front desk, an old sergeant—with chin-mole that looked like a tumor—directed her down a hallway longer than an airport concourse. *Is this the secret hall?* she thought. It was empty, silent.

She frowned, heels tapping. She'd worn a flowered billowy wedge dress, and she feared now that it made her derriere look huge. *Fattie,* she condemned herself. *Go back on Slim-Fast.*

HQ MAJOR CASE SECTION read crisp black block letters across the blond wood door. It reminded Kathleen of other letters, which now felt stamped across her eyes: WOULD YOU LIKE TO DO MY STORY?

Spence looked like an irked statue behind the desk. To his right a computer screen blinked SYSTEM DOWN in pretty amber. "Do you know a man named Stephen W. Calabrice?" Spence asked.

"No," Kathleen said. "Is he the victim?"

"That's right. Hot shot trademark attorney. Upper-, upper-class bar hound. This guy's bar tabs were more than most people make in a year."

"He's dead?"

"What? Did you think he was recovering? Take two aspirin and call me in the morning? Is that what you thought?"

Asshole, Kathleen thought. "May I smoke here?" she asked.

"No," Spence said. "You live at—" He glanced down at some nondescript sheet. "At 3660 Leiber Street, number 307?"

"Yep."

"Nice place?"

Was there some purpose hidden behind the tangents of Spence's questions and comments? Or was he just a nut? "It's all right, I guess," Kathleen said. "It seems to be one of the safer apartment complexes."

Spence tilted his head. "Insinuating?"

"Pardon me?"

"You're insinuating that other apartment complexes aren't safe because of police negligence?"

"I was making an objective comment."

"Oh. Yes. Of course." Spence pushed back in his seat. Yes, he was very muscular; Kathleen sensed the great girth of his upper chest, his shoulders, and she could easily picture a bodybuilder's physique out of the tailored, quality clothes. All ripples and hard lines, and zero body fat. "Did you know that Stephen W. Calabrice," Spence went on, "had been tortured for an extended period?"

"How could I know that?"

"His body was found three days ago in an underground parking garage near the corner of M Street and 19th. He lived in Georgetown. He was murdered in an unknown location. We believe he was picked up in a bar called Jonah and the Whale, taken to the killer's home, tortured, murdered, then dumped. The killer stole his car, a brown Audi Quattro."

Kathleen remembered a joke, which often rang true. What's the difference between a porcupine and an Audi?

A porcupine has pricks on the outside.

"Do you have any acquaintances in the medical field?"

"No," Kathleen said.

Spence cleared his throat. "We believe that a high-quality cutting tool was used to, uh…you know. A scissor-like implement with one flat blade and one serrated blade. There were drugs in his bloodstream, not street drugs, but pharmaceutical drugs, skillfully administered."

"You think the killer's a doctor?"

"Maybe," Spence answered. His eyes stared. "Do you?"

All right, Kathleen thought. "You think that I know her?"

"Her?"

"The killer?"

Spence put his elbow on the desk. "Why did you say *her?*"

"I…well…" Kathleen looked at her feet. "You think the killer's a man?"

"I want to know why you think the killer's a woman."

"I presumed…" *Presumed what?* she wondered. "You just said he was picked up in a bar."

"Maybe Calabrice was gay. Did you consider that possibility? Gays go to bars too, don't they?"

Spence was treating her like an idiot-child. Kathleen wished she had a drink to spill on him. Then she thought: *Drinks.*

"But Jonah and the Whale isn't a gay bar. It's a straight singles club."

"Ah, so you hang out there."

Jesus Christ! "No," she said. "I don't *hang out* there."

"But you've obviously been there. How else would you know that it's a singles bar?"

"All right, I've been there a few times."

"To pick up men?"

"To have a drink."

"You drink a lot? Writers drink a lot, don't they?"

"That's a stereotype—"

"Is it? Is it really? I just read an article in *Regardie's* or somewhere about occupational dispositions of clinical alcoholism. Guess which occupation hosts the highest percentage of alcohol abusers?"

"Police Lieutenants?" Kathleen joked.

Spence didn't react. "Writers. Creative people in general but writers in particular. Faulkner, Hemingway, Poe, Thomas, Fitzgerald—"

"All men."

"Sure. But also all writers. It was an interesting article. There's even a suggestion that the genetic propensity toward alcoholism is the actual root of one's propensity toward writing, not the other way around. Most people who become writers were born later in the mother's life, after 30. It's amazing—the commonalities in genetics and behavior of those who were born after their mothers were 30. Like night and day."

"Well," Kathleen said, "I just read an article in *Discover* or somewhere about the subconscious motivations of men who gravitate toward police work. It all revolves around the gun, a phallic symbol, which actually reflects deeply rooted sexual inadequacies."

"What does that have to do with your being here?" Spence asked.

"Nothing," Kathleen said.

"I see. In other words you're discreetly implying that my observations about the genetic predispositions of alcoholism have nothing to do with your being here either."

"That's exactly what I'm implying, Lieutenant."

"And that I made those observations, in truth, to discreetly harass you."

"Yes," Kathleen said.

Spence nodded. His face never changed. It seemed to sit there on his skull. Frozen. Blank. "Then you've misinterpreted me completely," he went on. "I raised the topic, not to harass you, or to suggest that you're an alcoholic, but to open an avenue of conjecture that's relative to almost every sexually motivated homicide."

Kathleen didn't know what he was talking about. "Okay, so what you really want to know is do I drink a lot?"

"Yes," Spence said.

"No," Kathleen answered.

When Spence set his chin in the crook of his thumb and index finger, his upper arm bulged to the extent of nearly bursting his shirt. "Do you have any close female friends who hang out in singles bars, or who are alcoholics?"

"No," Kathleen said.

"Is that your natural hair color? Brown?"

Kathleen gawped at the query. "What?"

"Or do you have any close female friends with red hair?"

"Yes to the first ridiculous question, no to the second."

"The reason I ask—" Now Spence moved his chin from one propped up hand to the other. "—is that our technical services crew found several red hairs on the body. Hairfall is quite common in sexually motivated crimes."

"She's a redhead, in other words," Kathleen observed.

"Who?"

Kathleen rolled her eyes. "The killer."

"There you go again. Your absolute certainty that the killer is a woman."

Should I leave? Kathleen asked herself. *Is there any reason why I should put up with this?* "It's not an absolute certainty. I told you, it's a presumption, and a pretty logical one, I think."

Spence nodded again, blankly. "Sure. Oh, and we discerned days ago that Calabrice wasn't gay. I'm just curious as to the basis of your...presumption. But it occurs to me now—" He paused, and tapped himself on the head. "—that it's a pretty stupid curiosity on my part. Of course you presume the killer's a woman. You're a militant feminist."

"I'm not a militant fem—"

"This looks pretty militant to me." Spence withdrew the May issue of *'90s Woman* from his desk, and read off some of the table of contents. "The Man-Trap: Don't Walk Into It; What He Doesn't Know Won't Hurt Him; When He's Lying To You: The Giveaway Signs; Exploitation In The Workplace: How To Survive In A Man's World."

"They're legitimate articles about some very important topics in our society," Kathleen told him.

"Ah, and here we go. 'Verdict.'" Spence looked up. "In four out of five segments in your column, you recommend that a relationship be terminated in, I must say, some highly specialized terms. 'Thumbs down.' 'Give him the ax.' 'Don't punish yourself, his baggage isn't your problem.'" Spence smiled very faintly. "I like this one best of all. 'Dump him.'"

Pea brain, Kathleen thought. "It's a process, Lieutenant, of applying a combination of style and colloquialism that readers can relate to, in response to their relationship problems."

"Oh, is that what it is? Style and colloquialism, yes." Spence put the magazine down. "I just don't understand your refusal to admit that you're a militant feminist."

Kathleen tensed up as she leaned forward. "Listen to me. I'm not a militant feminist—God, that term went out a decade ago. I'm a magazine writer. I'm a sociologist. And that's all."

"Ah. I see. A sociologist. I'm sorry." Spence kept his voice dead flat, to steepen the obvious sarcasm. "And these terms, these terms here— 'Thumbs down, Give him the ax, Dump him' —these are accepted sociological designations?"

"You're an asshole, Lieutenant," Kathleen said.

"I resent that. But I also realize that your opinion of me is irrelevant. Are you left-handed?"

"Wha—" Suddenly Kathleen was squinting. Clouds had moved off, leaving the sun glaring in her eyes. "Would you please close the blinds."

"Sorry, they don't work, I'm afraid," Spence said. "Are you left-handed?"

Now she couldn't see him at all, just an erect smear before the window. She tried to shield her eyes. "Yes," she eventually answered. "Why?"

"The killer's left-handed too. Our hand writing analyst could tell by the note."

"But the note was typed, not hand written."

"We call it strike-impactation. The graphology section has special microscopes that measure the depth, in microns, of any planar impactation. The typewriter, by the way, is a Smith-Corona Coronet. And we know the killer's left-handed because the letters on the left-hand-side of the keyboard made deeper impactations. Of course, we already had a good idea that the killer was left-handed for two other reasons. One, the angle of the...cut."

Only now did the imagery commence, the scarlet fact driving into Kathleen's psyche like a nail driven into new wood: Just exactly what someone had done to someone else...

"What's the second reason?"

"Most sex-killers are left-handed."

Kathleen could not fathom what he suspected. *He can't possibly be that stupid, that rude,* she thought. *No. No way.*

"Let me ask you something," Kathleen said. "What makes you think the killer's a *man?*"

Spence looked fuddled at her. "We don't. We're quite certain that the killer's a woman. The hairs found on the body fusiformally matched a typical female scale-count."

"Then why—" Kathleen stopped to think, to contain her now bristling anger. More quietly she said, "Then how come you've been all over me for my presumption that the killer's a woman?"

"I was merely assessing the motive of the presumption." Spence opened his hands flat on the desk. They were big hands, sturdy. "Most of what I do," he said, "revolves around the simple recognition of inter-personal similarities in homicides. There's always something, you know?"

"No, I don't know."

"What kind of word processor do you use?"

"I don't use one. I use a typewriter."

Spence's brow did a trick over the blank face. "I thought all writers used word processors or computers."

"Some do, some don't." In her eyes, Spence's own computer screen continued to blink in amber: SYSTEM DOWN. "I don't," she said. "I use a typewriter. And, no, it's not a Smith-Corona, it's a Xerox MemoryWriter."

"Hmm. Another... Let me think of the right word." Spence seemed to drift off behind the stone facade, a big hard finger tapping the blotter. "Parity," he said.

"What?"

"Another interesting parity. You know. The killer's a woman, you're a woman. The killer's left-handed, you're left-handed. The killer uses a typewriter, you use a typewriter—"

"This is the most ridicu—"

"The killer was abused as a child, you were abused as a child," Spence finished.

Kathleen's shock seemed to turn her to a pillar of salt.

Spence stared at her. "As far as the killer goes, I'm only making a, to use your word, a presumption based on known-typical psycho-social statistics. It's a very reliable denominator, that most sex-killers were abused as children."

"What about me?" Kathleen's voice croaked.

"I ran your name in the records computer."

"Bullshit. Your computer's down."

"We have more than one computer here."

No, she thought. *Somehow, he knew.* "You guessed, didn't you?"

For the second time, Spence smiled, but this was a sheepish smile, like that of a child caught doing something forbidden. "All right," he admitted, "you're right. I guessed. Or I should say I *deduced.*" He pointed behind him, to his psych degree. "After all, I'm trained as a psychologist."

"If you were trained as a psychologist, why are you a cop?"

"I felt phony. I wanted to act, rather than counsel."

Another cut. It was Spence's way of saying that she, as a trained sociologist writing for a woman's magazine, was phony. *Just what the hell are you driving at?* It was all building up: the policeman's unfounded dislike for her, his insults, his prejudgment, and the preposterous implications...

Kathleen's fists clenched in her lap.

"What kind of car do you drive?" Spence asked next.

Kathleen couldn't resist. "An Audi Quattro, a brown one. I just got it three days ago."

"Funny. But there's nothing funny about any of this, is there?"

"You tell me. You seem to be getting a kick out of it."

"I've never been more serious," Spence said. "Do you think Calabrice is laughing? Now, what kind of car do you drive?"

"Why didn't you just look in your computer?"

"The computer's down." The screen continued to blink: SYSTEM DOWN. "As you have already observed."

"I drive a 1997 Ford Thunderbird."

"Black, probably. Right?"

Kathleen grit her teeth. "Yes."

"And didn't you tell me, shortly after you came in, that you actually didn't make a living as a writer?"

"Your memory is without equal."

"'97 Ford T-Bird. That's an expensive car, isn't it? Twenty thousand dollars, 25?"

"I don't know how much it cost. It was a gift."

"From who?"

"From my father. He helps me out financially sometimes."

Spence remained expressionless as a stone bust of Caesar. "Is your father the one who abused you as a child?"

Kathleen sucked a deep breath. "No."

Spence looked disappointed. "Then who was?"

Her nails dug into her thigh, through her dress. *Don't...let him...do this to you.*

"It's none of your business."

"Technically, none of these questions are my business, so why have you answered so many of them?"

"Because you're a police officer, or facsimile thereof. I've always been taught to cooperate with the police."

"So you've been involved in police matters in the past?"

"Yes."

"Would you elaborate?"

"It's none of your business!"

Spence did not react to Kathleen's holler. He looked at her a moment, then said very quietly, "Don't get hostile. Don't get...militant. I'm only asking objective questions."

"No you're not," Kathleen countered. She felt sweat trickling at her sides, at her armpits. "There's nothing objective about any of this. You've been absolutely intolerable. I came in here because I was asked to; I'm trying to be of some *assistance* to you. And in return, you've interrogated me. You're practically accusing me of cutting off a man's penis and mailing it to myself."

"Now we're way off base," Spence said.

"And you can bet your ass that I'm going to send a letter of complaint to the commissioner."

"Chief," Spence said.

"What?"

"We don't have a commissioner, we have a chief. Address your letter to The Office of the Chief of Police, Metropolitan Police Headquarters, 300 Indiana Avenue, Northwest, 20010."

"You haven't liked me since the instant I walked into this grubby little office of yours. Why?"

Spence steepled his fingers on the desk. "I can tell you that. You want me to be honest with you, right? It's not difficult to figure out. You're an unfulfilled columnist for a militant feminist magazine who doesn't even make a living at it. We have a psycho-killer on our hands, and for some reason, that psycho-killer is very impressed by you, impressed enough to actually write to you, and to send you physical proof of a very heinous crime. The killer's note indicates that she wants to collaborate with you; she wants you to write her story. I'm certain that this idea appeals to you—it's the only chance you'll ever have for real fame. You want to turn this very sick person's life into a sensationalist book that will make you rich and famous."

"You're an asshole," Kathleen reasserted.

"But that's not even my chief complaint. That's not the complete reason I don't like you."

Kathleen stood up, glaring down. "What is?"

"I believe that your selfish, contrived, and very militant magazine writing has directly incited someone to commit an appalling murder, and that because of your written insights, this person will continue to murder people."

"I'm leaving," Kathleen said.

"You're free to do so. In fact, I encourage you to do so because, to be blunt, your presence in my office unsettles me. But before you go, I'd like your permission to put a tap on your phone and to have your mail rerouted to our technical services division."

"If you do either of those things, I'll sue you. I'll also write a feature article about you and your inexcusable treatment of me. *'90s Woman* has a circulation of 750,000. I will nail you to the wall in print, Lieutenant. By the time I'm through with you, you'll be walking a beat in Alaska."

Spence nodded. "And don't get any ideas about concealing evidence."

Kathleen wanted to slap him. She actually wondered what would happen if she did. Would they put her in jail? "As usual, I don't have any idea what you're talking about."

"Yes, you do. Whether you like it or not, you are very much involved in this case. Anything the killer sends you is district evidence, and if you fail to notify us of your receipt of any such evidence, I will have you arrested for misprision of a felony, obstructing a criminal investigation, citizen failure to report the knowledge of a crime, and tampering with evidence." He gave her his card, staring at her, his face forever deadpan. "Anything you even think might be correspondence from the killer you will not open or even touch. You'll call me, and I'll send a forensics technician to pick it up. I'm quite serious about this. Do not tamper with evidence."

Yes, she thought, *I really should slap him.*

"Because," Spence finished, "there's one thing you can count on. This killer, this sick, demented, sociopathic madwoman, is going to be contacting you again very soon."

Chapter 3

(I)

A long drooping banner hung along the front of a Mass Avenue hotel: 75 YEARS OF THINKING OF THE FUTURE.

The future of what? Kathleen wondered as the banner floated by in the windshield. The city commingled with itself, like something pressured together by force: the endless crush of cars, bodies, cement, and heat. Summer wrung sweat out of the air.

The future of what? she thought again, and stopped short. *Pay attention!* Pedestrians plodded sightlessly, their faces wet and pallid under the beating sun. Car exhaust hung in sheets.

In spite of the heat, Kathleen kept the a/c off. Washington felt more real with the windows down; she could taste its clarity and its hot, noxious scents. Her own sweat drenched her in minutes as the T-Bird lurched on, and her period felt like a hot living sponge, tickling her. Did the heat purge her? And if so, what did it purge her of? In the packed, ornery traffic she felt free in open space. The chaotic pedestrian droves made her feel joyously alone.

Perhaps she was alone in her own mind. Her mind hummed.

She passed a row of newspaper boxes; each hosted a plastered sign. SILENCE = DEATH. STRANGE BOUTIQUE/MAGAZINE w/HOWARD DEVOTO at D.C. SPACE! And an old one: U.S. OUT OF EL SALVADOR!

A young man in a business suit read *The Washington Times* before the DON'T WALK light. Kathleen eyed him. He looked successful, handsome in some keen way. A pang of animal lust flared, then abated as quickly. Someone like that, her insecurities calculated, most likely would not even pass the time of day with her, or at best he'd acknowledge her only long enough to hump her and climax. Animal lust was relative, she supposed. *What would the radio shrink say?* she wondered. "Your open negativity, your activated cynicism and distrust of men, has become the fulcrum between your failed romantic experiences and your unfounded low self-concept," she'd accounted to one caller.

"Am I the same way?" Kathleen asked herself.

The image relit: the lust. She gasped for real. The man with *The Washington Times*, now bereft of business suit, was very adroitly pressing her knees back to her face, drawing his penis, which felt long and thin, in and out of her. *He's so attractive,* she thought, catching breath. Her bed felt like clouds, it seemed small. The man didn't say anything in the slow ministrations of his pelvis. Kathleen felt much more secure in silence; she could concentrate more deeply. He parted her legs, grasping the backs of her knees, and she leaned immediately up to watch. She could see his penis going in and out of her, which seemed fascinating. It seemed like proof of something.

"Almost. Almost. Alm— Here," he said.

But the voice could not have been his.

At once something crushed her. Some sad, disillusioning truth. A child's hand reached forward in bedroom daylight...

Behind her, a carhorn brayed. The light had changed, and the image exploded. "Oh, blow me!" she shrieked as the horn behind her continued to blare. The T-Bird jerked through the light. In her rearview, the accosting driver's head jiggled in silent tirade, a black with one of those anvil haircuts. He leaned on the horn. "Inconsiderate anal-retentive type-A *asshole!*" she screamed when the car whipped by. Traffic backed up at the very next street. *You can walk faster in this city than you can drive!* Rows of cars percolated, going nowhere in the still heat.

Was Spence the cause of her bad mood? She didn't think so. One thing she prided herself on was her skill at leaving unpleasantries behind her, or at least so she thought. Up ahead she spied A.V.'s, a wonderful Italian Ristorante where they served delicious, crunchy fried squid. A grad student had taken her there the year she'd finished at Maryland. Kathleen remembered that she'd liked him a lot—a snapping wit, short blond hair, blue eyes, and a well-lined tanned face—yet she couldn't remember his name. He'd been working on his masters in business, at Georgetown, which she'd heard was one of the best schools in the country for that curriculum, and one of the most expensive. She'd slept with him, and he'd never called her back. Months later she'd run into him at the Torpedo Factory Art Gallery in Old Towne. He'd pretended that he didn't know her. *Am I that bad in bed?* she wondered now, in traffic. *Am I that fat and dull?*

Just before the light changed, she saw Uncle Sammy.

Her knuckles whitened on the wheel; blood seemed to tint her vision. In less than a few seconds Kathleen was out of the T-Bird and running down the sidewalk, a flowered billowy blur whose feet pounded with her consciousness. Long, unpleasant looks chased after her.

"Sam! Damn you, Sam! Stop!"

He'd been sentenced to 13 years: Lorton. Though it had been part of a federal sting, Sam had plea bargained out of the longer federal charges, 30 years' worth. One of the bailiffs had told Kathleen's father, "Lorton's one of the worst cuts on the east coast. It's bad time," which was fine with Kathleen. And the prosecutor's office had guaranteed that Sammy wouldn't even be eligible for parole until late next year.

Liars! She wanted to cry she was so mad. She flew down the sidewalk like something on rails...

"Goddamn you, Sam, you goddamn bastard! STOP!"

He didn't stop. Kathleen's shoes flew off. Way behind her a cacophony of car horns lowed like animals dying en masse. Kathleen stumbled, nearly fell, and sprinted on.

She nearly collided with the oblivious back. She grabbed the shoulder, wilting at the contact, and spun him around. Her entire face felt wilted shut as she shrieked "What the HELL are you doing out of pri—"

The incredulous face looked contorted.

"Lady, you must be nuts."

Oh my God.

It wasn't Uncle Sammy at all. The summer-weight suit looked like good material, a plush pinstriped tan. Stuck under a crisp sleeve she recognized in dread *The Washington Times.*

From somewhere faraway, so distant it wasn't even real anymore, a voice said: *Almost. Almost. Alm— Here.*

"I'm very sorry. I—"

The young man jerked a shock of blond hair off his brow. "You better be. I'm a fucking lawyer. You go grabbing people like that in public and you'll wind up getting sued."

"I'm so sorry," Kathleen said. She blushed, then turned slowly white. "I thought you were someone el—"

"Yeah, well next time be more careful."

The man with *The Washington Times* turned crisply and walked away.

Kathleen thought of a child's plastic cat clock, eyes ticking.

The city surged on.

• • • • •

She wanted a cigarette but her rule was only one per hour. More than that she wanted a drink but she rarely kept liquor at home. "I'm losing it," she said aloud. She closed the door and locked it. *Am I hallucinating now? Am I seeing things?*

She examined her mail on the kitchen counter. *New Woman, Vogue, Woman's Day,* and a junk ad selling special cylindrical lightbulbs that cut your electricity bill but cost $15 each.

That was all.

She turned on the radio—*Sports Talk*—and turned it back off. She'd already finished this month's column; there was nothing to work on, and the lady shrink's show wouldn't be on for hours. She took off her dress and bra and sat on the couch. The TV fizzed on: soap operas. Their progressiveness, or degeneration, (Kathleen wasn't sure which) amazed her. No more neo-victorian love/anguish stories; soap operas, today, rose with the times. Hackneyed plots of ransom schemes, murder, blackmail, sex scandal. Here was one fatally attractive man revealing to his bride that he was gay, while the astonished woman burst into tears, wearing skimpy purple and black lace lingerie. On another channel a young couple lay in bed, trying to figure out who kidnapped Candice's baby? Was it her estranged husband? Her bartender boyfriend Carl? Or Sally Ann, her true love? Yes, television had come a long way. The woman was obviously nude beneath the sheer bedsheets. Kathleen turned off the set and closed her eyes.

The killer was abused as a child, you were abused as a child.

Spence.

How had he known?

The bitter anger had drained. Spence was just an obnoxious, typical policeman, an annoyance. *If I let him bother me, he wins,* she realized. She could feel the perspiration dry up on her skin. She wished she could lose some weight, start exercising, help herself look better. Her inability to do so made her feel envious, and Spence had implied the same thing, hadn't he? He'd implied that she was a smalltime writer looking for the bigtime. The words tapped out in her mind again, in bold film-ribbon print:

WOULD YOU LIKE TO DO MY STORY?

Would I?

The answer fell on her, like bricks dumped out of a wheel barrow.

Yes.

Spence was right, on the wrong grounds. *He can go to hell,* she dismissed. Of course she wanted to do the story. What writer wouldn't? Spence branded her as a phony opportunist looking for any chance to get out of the rut. *But I'm not in a rut,* she reminded herself. If a story did come out of this, then she'd do it only because it was a story that deserved to be told.

Ick, she thought. She hated wearing clothes when there was no reason, and her panties qualified as clothes. She couldn't very well take them off now—she needed them to hold the Always pad in place. At least nature had graced her with little periods, not the great red tides that many women complained of. She seemed, though, to sense them getting even smaller as she aged. *Disuse,* she thought. Perhaps her psyche had given up on the prospect of her ever having children and her reproductive system was drying up as a result. Once a reader had written to her, a paraplegic. *I feel atrophied,* she'd said. *I feel like rotting fruit.* The radio shrink commented one night about tubal ligation, citing essentially the same thing. "Sex drive will often diminish, as the body realizes that the capacity for reproduction no longer exists." *I'm rotting fruit,* Kathleen thought now. She envisioned her ovaries as desiccated plums, their seeds old and dead. Her vagina felt like a shriveled flower. No taproot to give it fleshy life, just unrequited desire dry as salt. She rarely even masturbated, which seemed pointless and just as dry. It only bottled up her lust, pressing the cork deeper. The red circle on her calendar caught her eye. *Oh, Jesus.* Tomorrow she had a speaking engagement, a local writers group. TWAW, they called themselves: The Writer's Association of Washington. Kathleen wondered if there was a similar group in Tucson, and hoped not, considering the initials. Suddenly, she didn't want to do it. *I'd rather think,* she thought.

Think about what? some other voice asked.

The bizarre query letter reformed in her mind.

YOU ARE A GREAT WOMAN. IN THE FUTURE I WILL BE SENDING YOU MY STORY. CONSIDER IT A PROPOSITION. IT IS A VERY IMPORTANT STORY.

WOULD YOU LIKE TO DO MY STORY?

Kathleen stared.

Should she feel guilty? Was she really just a sensationalist? Something awful had happened, after all. Something unspeakable. Something disgusting.

But the idea of doing this story excited her. It excited her to no end.

And in her mind, the cat clock ticked, its plastic tail and eyes switching back and forth...

Chapter 4

(I)

She bites down hard on the towel.
She needs to be careful.
Her beauty is her power.
Her teeth are beautiful, and she doesn't want to break them.
The pain is extraordinary.
The needle sinks again.
She thinks of The Box of Souls.
The sad, little pile sinking into itself.
Newspaper clippings turning yellow like jaundice on the old people at the hospital.
She thinks of her mother.
She thinks of Daddy.
She thinks of Daddy's Room.
Go ahead, Rocco, give 'em both a pop.
It hurts so much.
But the pain absolves her.
In pain there is truth.
The pain makes her beautiful.
The needle sinks again.

She still has the book. *Bizarre World,* it's called. Warning label: NOT FOR SALE TO MINORS. She'd found it in Daddy's Room. It's black, hard-bound. It makes a little crunching noise whenever she opens it, sort of like the crunching noise when she stuck the Yale 13-gauge biopsy needle into that U Street guy's brain stem to see how long he could live with a subdural membrane full of motor oil. He hadn't lived long. It was still fun, though.

The book whispers many things.
Secrets.
It's all tribal.
INITIATORY RITES is her favorite chapter.
Even today, society is a tribe, no different in function than the Uru-Wau-Waus, the Kushites, or the Druids of eons ago...
Pain presses tears from her eyes.
She looks up in the mirror. She's placed her feet against the warm glass.
She sees her face there, between her pretty legs, looking back.
Her face so red from pain it's nearly purple.
In the mirror she sees her fingers poised.
In the mirror she sees her sex.
In her eyes she sees The Cross.
Of course! Her story!
This will be the first part of her story!
She'll begin it tonight.
She'll share her secrets.
After all, they're both women.
They're both from the same tribe.
She'll share her secrets with Kathleen Shade.
But for now...
The needle sinks again.
She rests awhile. Minutes or hours. Time means nothing to her. She looks at her pretty, bare feet against the mirror, wriggles her pretty, painted toes.
She's very smart.
She knows lots of things.
She's like the tribes. They knew lots of things, too—secrets. But who told them the secrets?
God?
"It's absolutely unbelievable that your grades are so poor," the lanky counselor said. Years ago. She barely graduated. She couldn't concentrate. "You have an IQ of 177. Do you know what that means?"
"That means I'm a genius."
"Yes, it does."
She thinks that she would like to put a pencil in his eye.
"You have an eidetic memory. That means that if you applied yourself, if you buckled down to your studies, you could write your own ticket."
She would like to buckle him down, with shackles. She would write *his* ticket. She would like to aspirate all of his spinal fluid. She would like to scrape his face off with a Red Devil razor. Just a fantasy. "Skulls mean death," she whispers.
Sometimes she walks in her sleep.

Portrait of the Psychopath as a Young Woman

Sometimes she sees her mother.

She's the midnight mopgirl at the hospital. She has no aversions to the job, she enjoys it. When patients excrete in their beds, she likes to clean it up. When patients vomit on themselves, she likes to clean it up and look at it later.

Mopping up blood in the ER is her favorite. Seeing the flesh writhe in gunshot agony, or gilled by knife-slits. Innards quivering in opened abdomens. Faces smashed flat by baseball bats. She likes to watch the doctors operate. She likes to see the doctors cut people open.

It must be wonderful to get paid to cut people open.

Sometimes she rushes to her closet, to masturbate.

She lives in a little box of memories, a little box of nightmares.

Daddy's House. Though it's really her mother's.

Daddy's House is in a little town called Cottage City. Just down from the district line.

The old house sits back on the corner, in darkness.

No one bothers her. No one can hear.

Sometimes she forgets things. Sometimes the lights go out because she forgets to pay the bill. Sometimes she forgets to have the grass mowed, and the neighbors complain.

Once she left the garage door open all night. The car—a bright green Ford Pinto—could be seen from the street 'til dawn. No one said anything, though. Once she forgot to close the window in Daddy's Room. She'd been cutting a man's belly open, to feel his insides, and he'd been screaming. He'd screamed even more when she'd begun to take his insides out of him. How could she forget something so important? No one heard anything, though.

Now she sews their mouths shut so they can't scream.

She keeps the prostitute down in the basement. Out of the light. Mother gave her the idea. She needs to be very careful. She needs to be smart, like the counselor said she was.

The prostitute is secured to Daddy's old workbench. Wrists chained to the hook on the wall. Waist tied down. Ankles chained to the table legs. She's cut a gap in the table, so the prostitute can excrete into a bucket. She's read all about it in the books she ordered from Thomas and Elsevier. Radio-immune assay. SEM radiography. Cuticular microscopy. There's no other way.

"I'm sorry," she says to the prostitute. "There's no other way. Please understand. You must understand."

The prostitute, of course, cannot reply. Her lips, too, are sewn shut by high-grade vicryl surgical suture. The suture is a bright pretty violet color. It comes in sterile packets, like condoms.

"Vanilla?" she asks.

The gap between two stitches leaves enough space for her to feed the prostitute with a convalescent squeeze bottle. She feeds her a nutritional drink called SEGO. It comes in several flavors: vanilla, strawberry, chocolate, and Dutch chocolate.

What are you thinking? she thinks. What's going on in your mind?

The prostitute's green eyes are dull. She's rack-thin stretched out like this, and her ribs show. Nipples so pale they're almost invisible. Nearly invisible marks inside her thighs, where men have burned her with cigarettes. Her throat makes muffled animal gulping noises as she sucks the SEGO through the squeeze bottle's flexible straw.

"I'm saving you. Did you know that? I'm saving you from yourself. You give them power over all of us when you let them use you for their devil. Mother called it the Devil's Horn."

The prostitute's throat wobbles as she gulps.

"I know. You couldn't help it. Neither could Mother. Sometimes we have to do things we don't like."

She smiles down.

"Let's get you pretty now."

She brushes the prostitute's plush hair. She sponges her off and empties her bucket. She clips her nails. She shaves her legs and her armpits.

"There. Better?"

The prostitute's head lolls against the wood.

· · · · ·

Back upstairs she drinks cold wine called Mouton-Cadet.

It makes her feel good. It rounds off the hard edges of the pain.

Cricket sounds come in through the kitchen window.

It's hot out.

She likes hot nights.

When she's in bed, she can see The Cross in the window. Sometimes she walks all the way down Bladensburg Road at night, to look at it up close. The Cross stands huge and beautiful in the middle of the road, in a ring of white light, and it reminds her of something, but she never knows what.

It reminds her of something but she never knows what.

It reminds her of something but she never knows what. Once she saw the town police shoot a retarded man in the subshop across the street. The man was drooling. The man was having a fit, a seizure, or epilepsy, and a knife fell out of his pocket, and when he reached, drooling to pick up his knife, the police shot him.

July's *'90s Woman* is opened on the table. "Lose 10 Pounds In 14 Days And Keep It Off!" reads one article before "Verdict." Folded back next to it is *The Washington Post BookWorld.*

When she closes her eyes she sees beautiful blood.

The flesh writhing.

Their smothered screams are the herald.
To her? To her mother? To The Cross?
Later she will type.
CALENDAR OF LITERARY EVENTS reads the *BookWorld* caption.
The Writer's Association of Washington, American University, Pickman Fine Arts Center, 7:30 p.m., lectures by abstractionist poet Maxwell Platt and feminist columnist Kathleen Shade.
Tomorrow she will go and see Kathleen Shade.

(II)

Midnight in the city was yellow, an endless shroud of pallor lain by innumerable sodium lights. Spence thought of lost worlds. Metropolitan Police Traffic Branch occupied a pie-wedge of 100-year-old asphalt where New York Avenue crossed L Street, a high, shabby brick building stained by age. The desk sergeant, a young black man, seemed enthusiastic, sharp, yet on an instant edge. Spence was no stranger to this regard. Anyone from Major Case Section got it: glints in the eye like subtle terror. They were spooks. The Department Occupational Designation was classified. Nobody really knew who they were or what they did. If you made even an insignificant error in front of any Major Case personnel, you were reassigned.

Poor kid, Spence thought. *Don't shit in your pants on account of me.*

"It was a priority system flag," the sergeant said. "I hope I didn't disturb you, sir."

The sergeant had called Spence at home. "If you *hadn't* disturbed me, you'd have been transferred to Warehouse Division in the morning," Spence said, trying to make a joke.

The sergeant didn't laugh. "I diverted them en route on their way to impound. What is it?"

"GTA," Spence said. He was looking at the printout. AUDI 4DR, GR. WT. -3700, TYPE: A, STEPHEN WILLARD CALABRICE.

"GTA? How come it's not on the hot sheet?"

"You ask too many questions, sergeant. It's a GTA."

"Yes sir."

Through the smudged window he could see the tow truck from District Impound lowering the car off the ramp.

Traffic Branch had picked up Spence's priority code on the computer when the vehicle's plates had been run. They'd found it blocking a hydrant in front of a gutted Northwest rowhouse. Parking Section, thanks to budget cuts, didn't even get near that area until after dark now, and—*A prostitute would know that,* Spence considered. Lots of prostitutes shacked up out that way, in the deeper blocks. And no one would fuck with the car—an Audi Quattro—fearing it might be a pimp's. *Hmm,*

Spence thought. Had the car been parked there deliberately, or for convenience's sake?

"When did your guys tag it?"

"About 40 minutes ago," the sergeant said. He restrained his obvious curiosity. What was the big deal? Cars parked in front of hydrants weren't rare in this city. "PS's tied up all night these days."

"Thanks for moving on this," Spence said. "And call Mobile CES, will you?"

"Yes sir."

Spence walked outside. He wore tailored shirts from a Korean clothier on Connecticut Avenue, 80 bucks a pop. He had broad shoulders, well-developed arms. Keeping fit and wearing good clothes let him feel vividly separate from the city that was falling in on itself. He'd been promoted two years ago—he was 36 now—from 2nd District Homicide, after solving a rash of crack-related murders. "Major Case Section needs men like you, Spence," his deputy chief had told him. "And I presume you'd prefer to work alone—you know, because, uh, because—"

"Because I'm gay, sir?" Spence asked.

"Well, uh, yes."

"I don't prefer to work by myself because I'm gay, sir," Spence explained. "I prefer to work by myself simply because I get more work done."

"Excellent. And, well, I want you to know that...well, here you're only judged by your performance record, not by, well, you know, any sexual, uh, preference you may have."

Spence didn't like to be patronized. He'd merely left, and thanked the man for the promotion.

But the new assignment pleased him only because it granted him a professional solitude. He got to work, essentially, alone.

Spence was gay. He was also celibate for the last decade due to a steepening anti-sociability. Eighteen years ago, when he'd joined as a cadet, gays weren't allowed on the force. Now they had support groups and monthly meetings. Spence had driven a sector beat and gone to night school throughout his twenties, and once he'd gotten his psychology degree, he'd found that the world had changed without him. He saw many tragic things which, over time, cauterized him. He looked at death as a clinician. By now he wasn't even the least bit interested in looking at himself.

One night several winters ago, a stool had set him up. Spence wound up killing three guys in an abandoned textile factory near Brentwood. They took shots at him, so Spence hunted them down and killed them. Simple. Then he did the paperwork, went home, and caught the last two minutes of a Redskins/Giants Monday Night game. The Skins lost, and Spence was pissed.

A flashback, then, a whisper of memory. Too many years ago to remember, his last lover had broken up with him on a night in the middle of May. The man's name was Reginald, and Spence had loved him.

"You don't love anyone, Jeffrey. Your job eats you up. You're still half in the closet, pretending."

"No, I'm not," Spence said. "I don't give a shit what anyone thinks about me."

"You don't care about me. You don't even care about yourself."

"That's not true!" Spence bellowed. Then his voice cracked, like wood splintering. "Please don't leave me." It was the first plea he'd ever made in his life, to anyone.

"Be real, Jeffrey. There's nothing left."

"I'll do anything for you," Spence croaked.

"Whatever it is you're looking for," Reginald said, "I truly hope you find it. Good-bye, Jeffrey."

Spence punched holes in the wall when he got home. He bit his tongue 'til he bled, tears in his eyes like hot acid. *Goddamn it! You can't do this to me!* he thought. *I love you! I love you!*

But the next day it was all gone. He knew he had no choice but to make it go away, like he always had.

Reginald was right.

(III)

The yellow sodium light looked like gas. The tow driver, in Fleet Management overalls, disconnected the Audi from the ramp hook.

Spence showed the driver his ID. "Has this vehicle been inventoried?"

"Nope. Dispatch rerouted me on my way to the impound lot."

"Good," Spence said. "Have you touched anything inside the vehicle?"

"Nope. Don't need to on a ramp tow." The driver was tall and lanky, with disheveled blond hair.

"Sliphammer the trunk."

The driver's mouth formed some silent objection. He scratched his head. "Let me slimjim the door. There's probably a trunk button in the glove box."

"I don't want anybody going inside the vehicle. Sliphammer the trunk."

"You want me to do a couple hundred bucks' worth of damage for no reason? It's private property. You're telling me to bust up a $40,000 car. All he did was park in front of a hydrant. It'd be easier if I slimjimmed the door and used the trunk but—"

"Take my word for it, the owner won't file a complaint. I don't want anyone but CES people inside the vehicle, for reasons that are none of your business. Neither of us have time to stand here and argue. The Metropolitan Police Major Case Section is fully authorizing you to sliphammer the trunk. So do it."

The driver scratched his head again. He wasn't a cop, he was just a car jockey. He returned in a moment with a sliphammer and screwed it into the Audi's trunk lock. "Look," he said, "I'm not going to be held responsible for any dam—"

"Sliphammer the fucking trunk!" Spence yelled.

Two hard strokes on the metal sleeve tore the lock out of the trunk. The night swallowed up the sound, and at the same time a mobile unit from the Criminal Evidence Section pulled into the pie-shaped lot. The grotesque sodium light made the brown car look green. As if covered with pollen, or mist.

Spence, for whatever reason, thought of his mother.

"Jeffrey, how come you don't go out with friends?"

I don't have any friends.

When the trunk lid raised, the towman turned away. Spence gazed down into a trunk full of body parts.

(IV)

At 3:15 a.m., Kathleen Shade, naked and drenched in sweat, lay deep in REM sleep.

She was dreaming.

This is a dream, she thought, as though it were of paramount importance that she acknowledge that fact. It made her feel safe.

She was dreaming that she lay awake in her bed late at night. The moon gazed in at her like an eye behind the window. Darkness hung about her in strangely precise angles.

One of the angles was a figure.

Was it a ghost? Kathleen didn't think so; she didn't believe in them. *I'm in bed dreaming,* she thought, *and I'm dreaming that I'm awake in bed.* She was naked on the mattress, having kicked the sheets fully off. Her nipples, inexplicably, stood erect.

The figure, standing to her side, leaned over. It seemed to be holding something out, offering something.

What are those? In the moonlight, Kathleen's skin looked dead. The sweat all over her felt like warm slime.

"Who are you?" she asked.

The figure didn't answer.

"What's that in your hand?"

"Pictures," the figure said.

It was a woman's voice, one Kathleen didn't recognize. It sounded clement, soft in care. Kathleen's eyes tried to focus upward…

Pieces of the darkness itself composed the figure's form. Its hands were black bones. Its face was an abyss.

The hand opened. A stack of pictures, Polaroids, fell into Kathleen's naked lap.

"Embrace your hatred," the figure said.

Kathleen didn't know what that meant. She squinted at the pictures, but it was too dark to make any of them out.

The cat clock ticked...

"Would you like to do my story?" the figure asked.

Chapter 5

(I)

It was disappointment that had dogged her all day, and that made her wonder. The only mail today had been a credit card solicitation and a Neiman-Marcus catalog. Nothing forwarded from the magazine. Nothing from the killer.

Her cramps were fading. The weatherman said today had almost broken records: 103 degrees. Kathleen had turned the a/c off and opened the windows and the slider, and had sat around all day in her panties. She was thinking about "the story," hoping the heat would incite her. She didn't even know if a story existed. What if the killer never contacted her again? And even if she did, how could Kathleen make a story out of it?

What do you look like? she wondered. *What's your name? What do you do?* She closed her eyes, lax on the couch, and tried to visualize this red-haired human cryptogram who'd seen fit to mail her a severed penis. The red hair was as far as she got. The rest stood upright in her mind as only black smears, like a charcoal sketch. Red hair atop a faceless head. A body of shadow. Hands like black bones.

The Dream. Of course. The figure in the dream symbolized the killer. You didn't have to be a psychiatrist to figure that one out. And the photographs? Kathleen vaguely remembered. Quite a bit had been booked as evidence at Uncle Sammy's trial. One exhibit had been a King Edward cigar box filled with snapshots of naked children. That's what the nightmare had been about: backwash of her past colliding with her horrific speculations regarding the killer. *Embrace your hatred,* the figure had said. Kathleen hated Uncle Sammy.

She smoked one cigarette per hour; it was a long road. She'd gone from Salems to Merits to Nows, which were the lowest tar she could find. She'd tried cold turkey several times, and had been miserable. Weaning herself slowly made more sense. She discovered, oddly, that anticipating the next hour's cigarette kept her on a sparkling creative edge. It gave her something to look forward to.

But that's my life, she thought. Not much ever happened now. All her hopes seemed to exist in the future. She'd lose weight in the future. She'd have a lover in the future. She'd become famous as a writer in the future.

I want something now.

The sunlight through the sliding-glass door made her feel dark. The heat chilled her. She attempted to masturbate on the couch but gave up after a diligent 20-minute effort. Images of male models left her unimpressed; they weren't real to her. Her fingers dawdled over her pubis for nothing. Often she'd picture herself in bed with past lovers, and would moisten. But then the desire shut down like a power failure when the memory elucidated her own body. It wasn't the men, because Kathleen was much older when Sammy was caught. There was one guy she'd dated in her freshman year at Maryland. He was the only one she'd ever told about Sammy. After a mixer at the Student Union, they had gone back to his dorm and begun to make love, but suddenly, well into the act, Kathleen had gone dry as pumice. She'd had to stop, gushing apologies. "It's all right," the guy had said. "It's that goddamn uncle of yours, isn't it? I'd like to strangle the bastard." But that wasn't it at all. Thanks to a private counselor her father had sent her to, Kathleen was cured of Uncle Sammy's horrific memory within a year. "Rape-Conclusion-Substitution," the technique was called, and it worked. She knew it wasn't Sammy who sabotaged her sexual desire. She knew it was herself. The image she had, and the concept she had, of—

Myself, she thought.

At 6 p.m., she turned on the radio shrink. "...and it makes me feel dirty," a caller was confessing. "It makes me feel absolutely perverted. It can't be normal for a woman to become excited while she's breast-feeding her baby. I'm so ashamed." "Don't be," the radio shrink replied. "Sexual excitation during breast-feeding is not only normal, it's a clinically acknowledged component of primal genetic motherhood. Cave women had a lot of perpetual worries—worries that make the stresses of our own lives seem quite paltry—such as starvation, predators, inclement weather. Today we worry about our next pay raise; our ancestors, however, had to worry about getting eaten by saber-toothed tigers. Its part of the cerebro-chemical design of motherhood to feel sexual pleasure while breast-feeding. It's an inducement, an additional reason to feed our babies when we might otherwise be worrying about more dire things, and it's not to be confused with any sexual aberration. It's normal and it's healthy and it's nothing to be ashamed about. Many women, in fact, experience minor orgasmic spasms while breast-feeding. Think of it as your body's way of reminding you of the importance of keeping your baby well fed..." This seemed interesting to Kathleen, yet grossly disconnected. She didn't like to hear about babies because it reminded her that she didn't have one, and probably never would. *Who'd want to have a baby by me?* she asked herself. Her thighs spread on the couch, and her spreading buttocks stretched her panties. When she leaned up, a roll of fat at her waistline looked like a seam in dough. *You're a Fattie, Kathleen. You've got to lose weight.* But there she went, slamming herself again, doing exactly what she advised her own readers not to do. How many times had readers written in, depressed because their boyfriends had left them for slimmer women? Kathleen always told them that they were better off without men like that, and that better men awaited them. *Hypocrite. Fattie.* She looked at the clock. Ten after seven.

The lecture! Holy shit!

• • • • •

"Isn't it wonderful?" the group president elated. She was an elderly, pale woman, quite misdressed in a shiny black evening gown. Kathleen sat with her in the back of the auditorium, at a table where tickets were sold. "We sold over 200 non- member tickets tonight," the older woman said.

Kathleen had arrived late. *Thank God there's a speaker before me.* A voice echoed hollowly, amplified through the PA system. Rows and rows of people in chairs faced a long draped stage. The first speaker, a long-haired blond man, looked tiny behind the distant podium.

"He must be pretty well-known," Kathleen remarked, noting the packed auditorium. *There must be 300 people here tonight,* she realized.

"Who? Platt?" the older woman said. "Oh, no. He's just a local poet. Usually we don't even sell *50* non-member tickets. All these people, Ms. Shade, are here to see you."

Kathleen felt remotely flattered. She'd spoken at writers groups before but never to a crowd this large. Had all these people really come just to see her?

"He'll be done in a minute," the older woman said.

The voice echoed on. Kathleen fidgeted. *I hope I don't smell,* she fretted. She'd skipped showering. She'd fixed her hair as best she could and had jumped in her car. She couldn't imagine how embarrassed she'd have been if she hadn't made it.

She looked on, over a plethora of heads. The poet, whose name was Maxwell Platt, had read several poems and then broke into a commentary about the function of aesthetics. "...and I can think of no better way that humanity defines itself than through its art. All art really is, after all, is the decryption of our feelings and our views into creative terms, and poetry, the ultimate art form, best discharges this function. Where would we be without it? Where would we be a million years from now when our ruins are discovered and all we have to show for our existence are sitcoms and Schwartzenegger movies? I thank God we have better than that. We have Shelley and Stevens and Pound. We have Owens and T.S. Eliot. We have Shakespeare. But more important than that, we have you. We have all of us, mindful people in chaotic times, the new poets of the new dark age..."

This sounded insightful, but the words kept shifting away. Kathleen scarcely knew what she would talk about when her turn came. These people had paid money to hear her talk. *What am I going to give them back?* she thought.

Now Platt was saying, "...and I'd like to finish by reading you my latest. It's called 'Exit.'"

The crowd hushed. Kathleen was thinking about the dream. She was thinking about the killer, and the things Spence had said...

Platt began, "Cenote or ziggurat, so shall it be, to end this riven hatred which beckons me, like torture into the light of the past. The dreams of some are the nightmares of others, blessings assigned or black lots cast, in the most wretched adieu. I glimpsed the light, the light went out. All my dreams come true."

Dreams, Kathleen thought.

Applause rose. Platt smiled behind the long blond hair that hung in his face. He held up a finger and said into the microphone: "Thank you all very much. And let me add one more thing... We are all the progeny of creation. I bid you to create."

Kathleen's heart fluttered. *It's my turn now,* she thought as the older woman said at the same time, "It's your turn now."

The poet came off the stage as the applause subsided. *I must look fatter than Roseanne in this dress,* Kathleen feared. The lavender crepe swished behind her as she followed the older woman up. She sensed her heels on the waxed wood sounded like mallets pounding.

The older woman tapped the microphone, a formality. "It's my great pleasure," she said, "to introduce our next guest, the renowned columnist from *'90s Woman*, Ms. Kathleen Shade."

Kathleen addressed the podium. The applause deafened her and seemed to go on and on—her propped up smile made her feel like Arsenio Hall. *Stop clapping!* she thought. *Let me start, even though I haven't got the slightest idea what I'm going to talk about.* She felt sorry for the poet; he'd received only half the applause. When they finally died down, Kathleen began, "I'm grateful for the opportunity to be here tonight—" At the edges of her vision, though, at the back of the auditorium, she noticed two men in suits standing by the door. Another similarly dressed man stood at the forward entrance, arms crossed as if bored.

Kathleen began her talk, which occurred to her somewhat unconsciously. Words flowed from her lips without her really hearing them. The crowd stared up raptly. "Feminism has evolved in many unique ways over the past decade," she was saying, "and what I'd like to talk about tonight, among other things, are the ways in which we, as critical writers, can assert…"

And while she was talking, her eyes drifted across the crowd, and there, sitting in the middle of the front row, was Spence.

(II)

She's thinking of blood.
She's thinking of cutting off skin.
Don't go in. You shouldn't go in.
Her mother's a ghost. Her mother sits beside her in the little car. She's waiting in the lot for 7:30, to go in and see with her own eyes, the Great Woman, when her mother says, *Don't go in.*
"But why?"
They could catch you.
Her eyes want to explode.
Sometimes she just doesn't think.
"I'm sorry. I wasn't thinking."
That's all right, honey.
Her mother dissolves.

For a moment she wants to cry. The sun is an orange, bright ball creeping past the edge of the city. She presses a fingernail into her palm until blood comes out.

Then she feels better.

No, she mustn't go in. She's about to back out of the parking lot, which is full of cars all coming to see the Great Woman. It's 8:15 now.

A big car whips into the lot.

A big black Ford Thunderbird.

The Great Woman is late.

She watches the Great Woman get out in a fluffy lavender dress and rush toward the pillared building.

She writes down the tag number and leaves.

Bright lights buzz over her head. Tiles shine.
She hears screaming.

A man screaming.

It's a sweet sound. It makes her want to go to the custodial closet and touch herself.

On her way to work, she drove past The Cross.

She sees The Cross now, in her head.

The screaming lets her see The Cross.

The body on the crash table convulses under the bright lights. A black man. Multiple knife wounds to the throat.

"Cut down!" one doctor yells. "Stat!"

"Clamp it!" yells another.

People yell in the ER a lot.

The black man's feet kick.

Blood flies across one doctor's face as if shot from a squirt gun.

Another squirt hits him right in the eye, like Daddy.

Her head lightens. The image: licking the blood off and sliding an Arista #24 scalpel up his crotch at the same time. Several times a month she sneaks into the prep station a night to watch the charge nurse fucking one of the interns. The nurse is on her belly, her white skirt pulled up and her white pantyhose off, on a transport gurney with the rails down gritting her big white teeth in a mindless grin. The intern always slaps her big flabby buttocks as his hips thrust. She always fantasizes sneaking up behind them and snipping off the intern's testicles while he fucks the fat nurse, with something nice, like Westcott umbilical scissors, or the shiny Bruns serrated plaster shears.

But it's only a fantasy.

Instead she sneaks away because this is the best time to steal, while the charge nurse is busy fucking the intern. The other nurses are on their bed checks so she can go into the supply room and take what she needs. She can also go into the med station for pharmaceuticals of lower control classifications. The barbiturates like diazepam and Amytal, and the amphetamines like Desoxyn and methamphetamine HCL are strictly controlled and inventoried, so she can't steal those. She gets those instead during the post-ops in the ER where things are always very hectic and everybody's going in different directions.

She takes what she steals out in a gym bag since all custodial personnel are required to bring a complete change of clothes every shift in case someone throws up on them or bleeds on them. She steals all kinds of neat things. Tissue forceps, hemostats, brain spatulas, rib-cutters, disposable S,K,&F packaged tourniquets.

The ER doctors disperse, snapping off their gloves, when the black man dies.

She leans over to wring a clean mop.

Pine-smelling water spurtles through plastic holes.

Her vagina hurts.

She smiles at the truth of the pain.
She sees The Cross.
When they've all left the ER cove, she starts to mop up all the beautiful blood.

Chapter 6

(I)

Was Spence smiling? His blatant, arrogant blank face seemed to mock Kathleen throughout her speech. It provided a distraction she didn't need. Maintaining eye contact with the audience was important during a lecture, yet as she spoke, and wherever she looked, she could feel the cold police-face gaze on her.

She was so mad she wanted to shriek.

Her speech seemed to go well, however. She began with a short biography of her life and credentials—leaving out, of course, Uncle Sammy—and then she spent the rest of her time proposing insights and speculations about the woman's market in general and the new feminist philosophies in particular. Psycho-social dynamics, counter-subjugation, interpersonal domestic designs of the '90s, etc. When she was done, the auditorium tremored with applause. Several women actually asked her for an autograph.

The older woman, who turned out to be the treasurer of the writer's group, gushed gratitude, as did many of the group's other officers. Then things began to thin out.

"I thought you gave an excellent talk," a male voice came up along her side. It was Maxwell Platt, the poet. He had dressed neatly in jeans, a midnight-purple shirt, and a black tie.

"Thank you," Kathleen said. "So did you."

"I read your magazine regularly. It's much more diverse than a lot of the others, and much less sexist."

Kathleen wasn't sure what he meant by that last clause. She lit her hourly cigarette, which by now she was dying for. "That's a little unusual, isn't it? I mean, a man reading a women's magazine?"

"Why?" Platt said. "What better channel can men have to the feminine mystique?"

Kathleen could've laughed. She hadn't heard that term in years. She was about to ask him about his poetry when another, less welcome voice rose at her other side.

"You are an absolute hallmark of civil irresponsibility."

She knew it was Spence before she even saw that blank, arrogant face of his. She could feel his bulk shadow.

"I'm not surprised," she said, "that I have no idea what you're talking about."

Spence smirked stolidly. "I can't believe your incognizance. A public speaking engagement. An *advertised* public speaking engagement. And you didn't even tell us."

"Why on earth would I tell you?" Kathleen sucked her cigarette, hoping the kick of nicotine might quell her rage. "Am I supposed to notify you every time I go somewhere? To the library? The mall? The toilet?"

"Fortunately I caught the announcement in *BookWorld—*"

"Oh, you read?" Kathleen interrupted.

"—and was able to get some men down here."

"Why?" Kathleen asked. "What's the big deal?"

"The big deal is—" Spence lowered his voice, honed his glare "—there's a certain person who's taken quite an interest in you. And that person could very easily have seen one of the advertisements for this little talk of yours. In other words, that person could be here right now."

Kathleen opened her mouth, then closed it. She hadn't thought of that at all. Had the killer attended the lecture? But then she dismissed it, if only to save face. "That's ridiculous, like everything else I've heard you say..." And then her rebuttal trailed off. Past Spence's shoulder she saw some of the men in suits at the back of the auditorium questioning five or six women with red hair. "You've got to be kidding me. You're harassing women just because of their hair color?"

"We're following a normal investigative protocol," Spence said. "And the next time you decide to give a lecture open to public, you will notify me first. At least then we'll be able to give you some protection."

Protection, she thought. Is that what she needed? Did they actually think that this woman might try to kill her?

Spence adjusted his tie for no apparent reason. At least he dressed well. "Have you had any further contact with our friend?" he asked.

"No. I only get a carrier from my editor once a week."

"What about the normal mail channels?"

"I'm unlisted. So don't worry."

"Oh, but I am worrying. Your obliviousness amazes me, as does your outright refusal to acknowledge the gravity of this matter. And, by the way, I thought your lecture was heinously biased, unrealistic, self-serving, and ideologically useless." Spence let his stare soak a moment. Then he added, "I'll be in touch."

Eat shit, Kathleen thought. She winced at him as if shooting a gun. She would have liked to kick him in the pants as he strode toward the back of the auditorium to further his harassment of the red-haired women. *What nerve,* she thought.

"Wow," Platt remarked. "What was that all about?"

"Long story," she excused. What could she say? *Well, you see, the other day a female killer mailed me a severed penis, and that guy is the cop investigating the case. And he doesn't like me because I happen to be a woman.* She felt like a dissident in some totalitarian regime, shadowed by policemen. Spence's audacity was outrageous, unconscionable.

"You want to go somewhere and have a drink?" Platt said.

Kathleen wasn't sure if he wanted to have a drink with her or just wanted a ride home; Platt didn't have a car. She didn't care, though. The innocuous talk helped get her mind off Spence, and she found something comfortable about chatting idly with another writer, despite how little they had in common creatively. She drove downtown in somewhat of a daze; then they were sitting in a bar. But only after her first drink did she realize exactly what bar it was. Jonah and the Whale, the same bar where Stephen W. Calabrice had made the last pickup of his life.

"I kind of lied," she admitted. "I didn't really hear much of your talk; I was really late. But I liked your poem."

"I've written better," Platt said, "and I've written worse, a lot worse. Poetry's weird; it never succeeds unless the poet realizes its utter failure."

"That sounds like something a poet would say." She sipped her Cardinal. Platt on the other hand ordered the cheapest beer they had on tap, which seemed appropriate for a poet. "I guess none of us succeed as real people," she theorized, "unless we realize all our own failures."

"What do you mean?"

"Well, like your poem, 'Exit.' It was about failure. It was an acknowledgment of your failure with a woman."

Platt nearly spat out his beer. "How did you— I mean, what makes you think that?"

Did I touch a nerve? Kathleen hadn't meant to. "I only assumed... That's not what the poem was about?"

"That's another thing about poetry. It's about whatever the reader perceives it as being about."

Yeah, I touched a nerve, she thought. The first drink went frightfully fast. Platt was nursing his; he mustn't have much money. The bar seemed fairly full for a week night: legs flashing beneath sleek dresses, guys in expensive suits checking the time to deliberately show off their Rolexes. *Mecca of Yuppies.* Her thoughts felt split like logs. She ordered another drink, chatting and thinking. Then she ordered another drink. Music droned: some dismal song by *The Cure.*

"Do you make a living writing poetry?" she asked.

Platt threw his head back and laughed, a bit too loudly. "I teach a couple classes at GW. There's no money in poetry but that's how it's supposed to be. It wouldn't be real if you got paid for it. Whenever I get offered money for a poem, I send the check back. If it was an article, or an expository piece, that would be different; I'd take money for that." Platt sipped his beer. "This may sound corny, but poetry comes from my heart. And my heart is not for sale."

It didn't sound corny only because of the indifference with which he'd made the statement. *At least he has convictions,* Kathleen thought. She wondered what her own convictions were and couldn't think of any. *My hormones are skewed tonight.* Images and thoughts sideswiped her; she listened to Platt but often didn't hear him over her own ponderings. The music and the voices and bodies around them coalesced to gentle chaos. The macabre question titillated her: Exactly what had the killer done to Stephen W. Calabrice? Spence said he'd been tortured.

"What?" she said.

"I said you should order some food."

"Not hungry." She'd ordered another Cardinal without really realizing it. Platt's suggestion was a polite reminder as to how much alcohol she'd consumed. *I'm not drunk, am I?* she thought. She almost never drank to excess; getting drunk made her feel stupid. She often found a silly joy in watching others get drunk in bars. They knew they'd get drunk, they knew they'd make asses of themselves eventually, yet they continued to drink. "Have you ever thought," she said to Platt (and for the life of her she couldn't remember his first name), "about the actual social symptomatology of drinking? It's absurd. It's like bars are places where people go because it's acceptable to make jackasses of themselves."

"I've, uh, I never thought of it that way," Platt said with a brow tightening.

"I mean, look at this. People would never act like this in other public places, would they?" Behind them, three young guys in baggy Dockers laughed uproariously. One of them chugged a full bottle of dark brown beer in less than 15 seconds. At another table, two girls giggled as their dates conversed loudly about their jobs. A girl at the end of the bar shouted to the barkeep, "Hey, Craig, can I have your kids?" It was an arena of silliness. An overdressed dolt with a face like Chris Isaak squeezed next to her and ordered a Stoplight shooter as his friends cheered him on. *Chaos,* Kathleen thought.

"I guess we better go," Platt said.

"Why?"

"You seem pretty bored."

"I'm sorry," she said. He must think she didn't like him. "I'm not bored, I'm thinking. I have this habit of thinking about lots of things at once."

Platt at last ordered a second beer. "What are you thinking about?"

"I... Well..." But what *was* she thinking about? She scanned the long bar for redheads. She wondered where the killer had sat, what she'd worn, what type of drinks she'd had. What had Stephen W. Calabrice's last drink on earth been? *I hope it was a good one,* she thought. Eventually, she answered Platt, as more overdressed patrons squeezed past, "A project."

"You mean a writing project?"

"Yeah." She caught Platt's brow ticking again when she ordered another Cardinal. "You're a writer. Have you ever considered writing a book?"

Finally she'd given him something to talk about. "Oh, sure," he said. "I'm always toying with the idea of writing a novel, but I know I never will. I prefer poetry. It seems to me—I mean for my own creative purposes—that even the best novel can never be more truthful creatively than a poem. You never know what your motives are with a novel."

"What do you mean?"

"Is the novel motivated by money, by status, or by aesthetics? You never know," he said.

"Why can't it be all three?"

"Well, it can, but that doesn't appeal to me. I know a lot of novelists, and most of them are just prostitutes. Soon they're writing books based on the needs of the market instead of the needs of their muse."

Kathleen thought about that. These were more of Platt's convictions. She remembered what Spence had implied at the police station: that she was looking to sensationalize a tragedy. That wasn't it at all. Maybe she just wanted something to do.

"What about you?" Platt asked. "Are you considering writing a novel?"

"I'm not sure if it's a novel. It might be, or it might not be, or it might be something in between." The Cardinal was making her buzz a little. "All I know is that it will be a book."

"What's the book going to be about?"

"A killer," she said. She sipped the rich drink, closed her eyes. "It's about a female psycho-killer."

Chapter 7

(I)

When Kathleen woke, at about 6 a.m., she had to pressure her brain to give up the memory. *Where am I?* she thought at first, and then the headache reminded her. She lay seeping with sweat; Platt's apartment, an efficiency off of P Street, was not air-conditioned. Morning light poured in from the balcony—as if caught off guard, Kathleen quickly pulled the sheet up over her. Platt lay asleep beside her.

You bad girl, Kathleen. What would the radio shrink say about this? That she'd gotten drunk on purpose as a ploy to sleep with Platt? *And we did more than sleep,* she reminded herself.

Extended periods of inactivity in your sex life, the radio shrink would say, *have imbued rigid feelings of self-doubt. Not having sex makes you feel unwanted. In becoming intoxicated, you have manufactured a situation which will increase the potential of a sexual encounter.*

Is that what I did? she wondered now. She only vaguely recalled Platt's insistence that she not drive home. "You're too drunk," he'd said. "I'll call you a cab, or I'll drive us in your car back to my place. I'll sleep on the couch." Platt had not taken advantage of her by any means. Kathleen supposed the opposite, that she took advantage of him. She took a cold shower, checked herself to see that her period had stopped. Her pubic hair looked a little straggly so she stood there ludicrously over the toilet trimming at it with a little pair of scissors she found in the cabinet. It was all so calculated that she scarcely believed it of herself.

He was lying on the couch, as promised, under a sheet, when she emerged wrapped in a towel. A small lamp glowed; he was reading a book of Anne Sexton poems called *The Death Notebooks.* For a moment his long straight blond hair made him look girlish. *Maybe he's gay,* she considered. P Street and Dupont was certainly a gay area. But the poem he'd read was about a girl; she felt certain of that. He looked up at her then and said, "The bed's right over th—"

"I'd rather sleep here," she said. She turned off the light, let the towel fall, and climbed on top of him, squeezing Anne Sexton between their chests as they kissed. At first Platt was stifled, not quite sure what to make of this. In the dark she felt completely unrestrained; she felt like someone else, someone she was watching in a dirty movie, or someone people gossiped about. She knelt beside the couch, pulled the sheet off, pulled off his briefs. His skin felt smooth and cool as she ran her hands up and down his right side. She let her hands be her eyes in the dark, and was content by what she saw. *No, he's not gay,* she concluded; his penis—average length, thin, and uncircumcised—had already become erect before she even touched it. She squeezed it gently; Platt stifled a moan. *I have a man's penis in my hand,* she realized, *and I don't even remember his first name!* How embarrassing. She leaned over and began to fellate him; he stifled another moan. She let her tongue glaze over the glans, wiping away small drops of salty, precursory fluid. His hand slid up and down her back as his legs stiffened. "Kathleen," he whispered. "You better stop. I'm getting ready." *At least he's a gentleman,* she thought. She didn't care; in fact, she was flattered, remembering the old joke about a man's three biggest lies: I love you, I was just about to call, and I promise not to come in your mouth. His testicles, caged in her fingers, drew up. She noticed with some fascination that the right one drew up farther than the left, and that it was minutely larger. Her mouth sucked harder, increasing the wet friction, and there he went again, whispering in panic, "Kathleen, Kathleen..." "Um-hmm," was all the reply she was able to make at the moment. She could sense with her lips a nervous throbbing building up. When he began to ejaculate, she squeezed his testicles; the right one by now had all but constricted into his groin. She'd only done this a few times before. *I hope I'm doing it right. Is it the same for men?* Even her own past could attest: of the times when men had gone down on her—not many times—there were an array of ways to do it wrong. You practically had to read off a list of guidelines. She flinched at the first few spurts which launched to the back of her throat. His fingers ranged in her shower-wet hair. When she was done, she let the fair volume of semen fall out of her mouth onto his stomach.

"Let's get you cleaned up," she said. She felt around in the dark for a Kleenex but found none. Would it be rude to wipe him off with his sheet? *Maybe I should have swallowed it,* she thought, but she really didn't want to do that. "There's no tissues here," he said, and suddenly there was a tearing sound. Kathleen laughed. "It that how poets smite each other?" she asked. "Actually," he said, "it's sort of an esoteric compliment. I wouldn't consider it an insult at all, creation merging with creation." He wiped himself off with a page he'd ripped out of the Anne Sexton book.

He brought her to her feet in the dark. She was glad for the dark—he couldn't see her fat. She felt deliciously hot in the un-air-conditioned apartment. "Come on," he said, leading her toward the bed. "The condoms are over here."

• • • • •

After another cool shower, she sneaked around the efficiency, draped in the sheet from the couch. Platt snored slightly, brazenly naked on the bed. Nearly as brazenly herself, she stepped onto the balcony in the dawn light and smoked a cigarette. Below stretched an ugly pay parking lot beside P Street. The man in the booth looked like Uncle Sammy until she blinked and saw that he was black. Another man walking briskly down the street with a briefcase looked like Uncle Sammy too. She blinked him away. *Retrograde shock jags,* the counselor had called them. Not hallucinations but tricks of memory. She hadn't had them in years. *Why now? What's Sam doing now?* she asked herself. *Masturbating in his cell? Thinking of me?* she wondered. Then she thought about the killer, who, according to the all-knowing Lieutenant Spence, had also been sexually abused. Who had abused the killer? And how? At what age and how many times?

She would have to know all these things for the book. And if the killer never wrote to her again, there'd *be* no book. Spence's threat loomed: "Do not tamper with evidence." She made a mental note: *Call New York, ask about mail.*

Back inside, she perused Platt's work space, which was much less organized than her own. A little Brother electric typewriter sat on a big desk with a fake-woodgrain top. A piece of paper hung out of the platen like a tongue. Creative people often had quirks. Weird superstitions about new work. Territorialism. Was she violating some poetic law by looking? But Platt remained asleep, now curled into a naked ball. On the paper, he'd typed:

EXIT by Maxwell Platt

Maxwell! Kathleen celebrated. Now at least she knew his first name. But hadn't "Exit" been the title of the poem he'd read at the writers lecture? This was different.

> Through twilit nights
> my love still soars.
> I am forever
> and ineffably yours.

One the desk rested a manila folder. *Dare I?* she thought. She had no right to look at his work without his permission. She looked at it anyway; poets intrigued her, especially poets who gave her orgasms. The first poem in the folder read, again:

EXIT by Maxwell Platt

Did he title all his poems "Exit?" *An exit fixation,* she thought. *Like my killer fixation.* The poem, dated December 12, 1990, read:

> Ah, love—it leaves us bleakly blessed,
> either that or sweetly cursed.
> I watch you take your heart from me,
> you watch my heart burst.
> But upon this night, exactly one year ago,
> I remember: you and I were kissing in the snow.

Kathleen closed the folder. She felt ashamed, even though Platt would never know. *My God,* she thought when she looked down. Leaning against the corner of his work area stood a stack of publications, four feet high: magazines, newspapers, trade-sized digests, small-press and literary journals—all the places Platt had been published. It was literally a pillar of poetry. She picked up the top magazine, *The Annapolis Critique,* and thumbed the contents.

EXIT by Maxwell Platt... page 8

Yet another poem called "Exit." This began to fascinate her. She turned to page 8 and read:

> I always got less
> than the least from you.
> Now I hope that the rats
> come and feast on you.

Platt the altruist finally shows some bitterness. Yes, it was obvious to her: these poems were about women from Platt's past; he was a love-poet. This seemed totally real to her, totally honest, not corny. Too much of today's poetry dismissed love as a trifle. They deemed it more "important" to write about politics or nuclear weapons. *But such a bitter poem,* she thought. Bitterness didn't seem to suit Platt. As for herself, when men had stopped seeing her, or stopped calling, Kathleen never felt bitter. She felt fat and disillusioned but never bitter. Or maybe she'd never loved anyone enough to feel bitter over a relationship's demise.

But this is just sexual, she pointed out to herself. Platt, though not a physical specimen, looked trim and enticing. *There's no way he could ever love a Fattie like me.* This impression of herself did not depress her at all; it made her feel proudly objective, not weighing, of course, the hypocrisy. When readers wrote in, fearing rejection due to being overweight, Kathleen reassured them that looks meant nothing in a real relationship. *Dump them,* she'd advise.

Still draped in the sheet, like a disheveled statute of liberty, she padded to the bed to look down at Platt. Every few minutes he shifted positions in sleep. Now he lay arms out and spread-legged on the mattress, his face covered by blond hair. Her headache was dissolving. *Should I just leave?* she wondered. She really did want to call her editor and ask if any letters had come in for her. On the floor lay three condoms tied in knots, their reservoir ends laden with proof that Platt could rise to an occasion. Her memory unreeled like clippings of film: he'd made love to her voraciously, constantly concerned for her pleasure. It got to aggravate her to a point. He'd ask her "which way feels the best for you?" or "does it feel better this way or that way?" She felt like saying, *Look, Platt, I haven't been laid in a year. Any way feels good, so be quiet and just do it.* She'd had several bouts of orgasms, but the best came when he finished her off. He'd slid her buttocks to the edge of the bed and knelt on the floor, laving her clitoris with his tongue while two fingers stroked in and out of her vagina. She'd shrieked as her climax spasmed, then purred grinning in the dark as the lovely pulses drew on.

Platt kept his condoms—a brand called Sheik—in an odd little cup with a hinged lid atop the nightstand. She took one and very carefully crouched at his hips. The deflated penis lay across his pubic patch like something exhausted. She touched its underside very gently—she didn't want to wake him—then leaned forward and began to lick it. She could smell her own musk laced with the scent of the condom lubricant and sperm.

It came erect fast as a spring popping. She rolled the condom over it, then shook him.

"Maxwell?" she said. Or did he prefer to be called Max? *How do I know?* "Maxwell? Wake up."

She leaned up and kissed him on the mouth as his eyes slowly opened. Her fingers gently kneaded the sheathed penis. "Maxwell? I have to go soon."

"Hmm?" he said.

"I have to go home soon. But can we do it one more time first?"

He leaned up and groggily glanced down at his groin. "It looks like the decision has already been made," he remarked.

(II)

Earlier that morning at the CES morgue, Kohls told Spence, "What we've got here, Lieutenant, is a little of the old Human Jigsaw."

Spence was familiar with the jargon; he'd seen stuff like this before. This was what crack dealers did to stools, or other dealers moving on the wrong turf. Bodies taken apart with chainsaws or axes. Parts often stacked up like cordwood.

Kohls, the MCS evidence tech, had lain the body parts found in the Audi's trunk onto three stainless steel dissection tables. The tables came complete with run-off gutters and filter traps. "Three bodies," he said. "We'll call them One, Two, and Three. One"—he pointed—"has been dead about a week according to the potass levels in the humor. Two and Three several weeks, maybe a month. T.O.D. is always tough to pinpoint this time of year, the heat and all. Depends on where the parts were kept."

"Where are the heads?" Spence asked.

"In the fridge. You want to see them?"

"Uh, no. All I want from you now is the quickest read you can give me. I want any significant similarities and differences."

"You mean between these three and Calabrice?"

"That's right."

Kohls always seemed full of some weird downplayed vigor, which was not what Spence would expect from a man who made his living histologizing human brains, weighing organs, and forensically analyzing carnage. He drank a can of Coke. "Similarities? Lips sewn shut with hospital-spec suture, eyes Crazy Glued, eardrums pricked."

She's shutting down their senses, Spence realized. *Why?* "That's all?"

"Pretty much. Extreme genital violence, of course, but you can see that for yourself."

Yes, Spence could. Weird, rawish ovals. "What about the genitalia?"

"She kept them, sir. Not a pecker in the pile."

Spence, a strong man, felt his knees wobble for a second.

"The differences are much more significant," Kohls went on. "Calabrice's hands and feet were intact. These three she severed all of them, burned them, and put them in the pile. I'm not even sure if I've got the right hands and feet with the right bodies. Spectrometer reads reduced carbon and commercial Naphtha. Know what I think? I think she burned the hands and feet up in a barbecue. Point is she did a good job—don't expect an easy ID on any of these guys."

"What about their teeth?"

"That's another significant difference. These guys all had their teeth pulled out first, unlike Calabrice, before she sewed their mouths up. The dental extractions are all pretty clean, so she must've done it while they were still unconscious from the sodium-am. She didn't want these three ID'd, but she obviously didn't care if we ID'd Calabrice. It's almost like…"

It's almost like she wanted us to know about Calabrice, Spence considered.

"You sure you don't want to see the heads?"

"No thanks," Spence said. "I gotta drive."

"Histo data's all in the prelims. There's your big difference between these guys and Calabrice."

"What do you mean?"

"Calabrice was a well-nourished white male. Moderate drinker, sure, low B-6 and mag, but he was healthy. He had good guts."

Good guts, Spence echoed.

"These guys?" Kohls flicked his hand. "Low economic histo spectrums. Lot of arterial plaque, first-stage liver sclerosis, lot of lipofusial rancidity, low body-fat. These guys were malnourished."

"Bums?"

"No, not bums. Just nutritionally deficient, players."

"Players" meant hustlers, street hawks, city people whose incomes were erratic and who didn't eat right. "In other words," Spence asked, "Not the kind of guys who hang out in high-class bars."

"Exactly," Kohls said. "Compared to Calabrice, these three guys were phantoms."

Phantoms, Spence thought.

He considered this on his drive back to Headquarters on Indiana. He had an appointment. The autopsy reports were dicey this early but Kohls had given him enough up front to get him thinking.

Spence had been doing a lot of thinking.

Now he sat in the office of one Dr. Ian Simmons, who quietly read over the forensic preliminaries. Simmons, sixtyish, goateed, and with a paunch, was the department's forensic psychiatrist. He'd recently had an article published in a British medical journal called *Lancet* ("Criminal Behavioral Differences of Ipsilateral Males"), and had been nominated for some award.

"So you're looking for someone with medical knowledge. A doctor, perhaps." Simmons' eyes widened in amusement. "Me, perhaps."

"You're not a woman with red hair," Spence observed.

"Ah, but couldn't the hairfall be from a wig?"

"Not with intact hair-root sheaths. Not with shaft cuticles full of unoxidized dihydrotestosterone. All the pubic hairs microscopically match the head hairs. Fusiformal lineament and scale-count are female positive."

"Good, good," Simmons said, still scanning the prelims. He was just testing Spence, as always. "Who's doing the radio-immune assay?"

"McCrone Associates. They're expensive but they get the work back a lot faster than the Bureau."

"You should've saved the taxpayer's money," Simmons said. "The r.i.a results will indicate a long-term drug or alcohol abuser, malnourishment, megalopsis."

"How do you know?"

"If I'm wrong, I'll buy you dinner."

"I hope you're wrong," Spence said. "I haven't been to a good restaurant in ages."

Simmons chuckled. "No doubt you've instructed Background Programming to cross-reference red-haired females with recent psych ward releases?"

"Yes," Spence said. "And hospital employment."

"Too bad there's a Privacy Act, hmm?"

"I'm telling them to go back four months."

"Tell them to go back a year," Simmons corrected. "This is something more evolved than your typical unsystematized reality break. Take my word for it, Jeffrey. That's what they pay me for."

Simmons' mien always captivated Spence. The doctor regularly spoke with great animation and facial inflection yet rarely looked up from his reading, as though the preliminaries were Spence's face. Simmons was perhaps Spence's only real friend.

"Sagittal fusion, fusion of the mastoid process...all four of your victims are late-'20s to early-'30s, yet the first three clearly come from lower economic backgrounds."

"That's right," Spence said.

More reading. Then Simmons' brow furrowed. "Your friend is quite tribal—" Simmons always amusedly referred to killers as Spence's "friends." "—and probably very smart as well as very well read."

Spence backed up. "What do you mean tribal?"

"She collects physical symbols of adversarial power. Use the Bantis of lower Africa as an example, or any number of pre-colonization Filipino tribes. They collected the heads of their enemies because they believed it would give them power. You've got vou-dou cults in the deep south doing the same thing today. Similar tribes collected penises for the same reason." Simmons fell into a bemused pause. "And your friend here is definitely collecting penises."

Collecting penises, Spence thought. It was perhaps the strangest thought of his life.

"Calabrice, Stephen, W. Your friend mailed Mr. Calabrice's penis to a magazine writer?"

"That's right. A self-help columnist."

"Idolatry," Simmons said, still smiling vaguely at the reports. "Objects of abuse serve as objects of power to be envied—hence, the missing penises. In Calabrice's case, your friend decided to share that object of power with another woman. More tribalism."

This was too strange. This entire conversation was too strange. *What would the average person think, overhearing this?*

"She probably lives in a house, in a secluded community," Simmons continued. "She was sexually abused, probably quite heinously, and probably by her father or other prominent male family figure, from a very young age. She's obviously bipolar enough to function in public."

But Spence had considered all of this already. Preliminary deductions that any investigator would make. Simmons added: "And she has no close acquaintances. No friends."

A flash of memory. Spence's mother. *How come you don't go out with friends, Jeffrey? How come you never go out with—*

Spence frowned the memory away. "I'm thinking maybe she's a prostitute. Calabrice's vehicle was ditched just off the red-light corridor."

"Maybe, maybe not," Simmons said. Finally he set down the CES prelims and looked at Spence. "We have some oddities here, most paramount of which is that she's probably also very attractive."

"Because Calabrice was attractive?"

"Of course. And wealthy, and successful. You can't catch quality fish without quality bait."

"Why is it an oddity?"

Simmons stroked his silverish goatee. "Most acute stage psychopaths are uniformly unattractive. The sexual traumas of their childhood enforce a repugnant self-image. But of course most psychopaths, contrary to popular belief, don't kill people either."

"I thought we were looking for a stage sociopath," Spence said.

"No no no no," Simmons replied. He said "no" a dozen more times. "I thought your degree was in psychology, not onanism. Your friend here is uniquely psychopathic, and it was only very recently that she suffered the first major reality break of her life."

"On what do you base that?"

"The four victims. Aren't you curious as to why she went to extremes to obstruct the potential identification of the first three victims, yet not Calabrice?"

"That's the chief reason I came to see you," Spence said.

"Oh, and all this time I thought it was my invigorating persona. It's rather typical in serial-killer scenarios that are psychopathically rooted, as opposed to sociopathically rooted. The first few victims are frequently discovered after later victims. No difference here. One, Two, and Three had no fingerprints, no teeth. Calabrice did. Why?"

"You're the clinical psychiatrist."

Simmons laughed in his throat. "All psychopathies eventually assume an objective purpose in the psychopath's mind. The initial crimes are always unformed. It is only until well after the reality break that the crimes pursue a solid focal point."

"Well then what's the focal point?" Spence asked.

"I should think it would be obvious. It's this magazine writer. This—" Simmons reglanced at the Calabrice summary. "—this Kathleen Shade."

They walked down to the automat, for Macke coffee. "But why?" Spence inquired. It bothered him. "Why Kathleen Shade?"

"I have no idea," Simmons answered. "I don't know her, nor have I read her. But I suspect that's the key—it has to be. A psychopath's active delusions almost always cling to a physical symbol. For some reason, your friend relates to Kathleen Shade. I'd love to know exactly why."

You're not the only one, Spence thought. "In her first correspondence, she referred to Shade as a 'Great Woman.'"

"Not surprising. Shade's an idol, and you can probably count on the keystone of the idolatry as being quite subjective, or even invented. On one hand it may be something as simple as a physical resemblance; or it could be something so complex via the delusion that no sane person could grasp it... How are you handling Shade?"

"I think I summed her up pretty quick," Spence said. "She kind of strikes me as a fractured personality type. Smart, independent, but diced up from insecurities."

"And she's trying not to show those insecurities," Simmons guessed rather than asked.

"Yeah, that's what it looks like. So I'm playing Bad Guy with her, and it's working. You know, the stone-face, rigid body language, deliberately rigid speech patterns, and all that. Objective rudeness; she thinks I'm a male chauvinist pig. It really pisses her off."

"Good, good. She sounds like the type you'll have to keep pissed off in order for her to remain perceptive herself. She has to feel the necessity to compete with you, otherwise she won't be of much help. And there's probably something in Shade's writings that have set off the idol-concept. I suggest you read everything she's published."

Spence nodded. "I already got Research pulling it all up."

"And find out if Shade was sexually abused."

"I did," Spence said. The coffee was terrible. "I ran a prelim background on her; she was abused by a family member a long time ago. The guy got busted, and she testified against him. I'll be getting more info on that soon." Spence half-smiled. "She thinks I guessed. I kept her antsy by using all those great kinetic and kinesthetic gestures you taught me in school. She practically thinks I read her mind."

"Good, and make her *keep* thinking that. Is she lesbian?"

"No. Her advice column is hetero-sexual. And last night she spent the night with a man she just met."

"You're a bad boy, Jeffrey. Discreetly psychoanalyzing citizens, following them, invading their privacy."

Spence shrugged. "Hey, I'm a cop. That's what cops do, isn't it?"

Simmons' nose crinkled over his coffee. "You should've been a psychiatrist. Then you could invade people's privacy even more."

"The killer seems to want Shade to write a book about her," Spence said, "or a story of some kind. 'Would you like to do my story?' she asked Shade."

"Of course. Shade's the key; the killer relates to her. More proof that the purpose of the delusion has solidified. That's why she left the first three bodies in Calabrice's car. She *wanted* you to find them. She *wants* you to know what she's doing now. Without that, the purpose has no actualization, and no meaning. And if Shade publicizes her crimes, the purpose will assume even more meaning for whatever the killer's delusion is based upon. She thinks Shade will sympathize, will view her as a colleague. More delusion. Actually, it's wonderful that your friend is a stage psychopath."

"Wonderful?" Spence questioned. He couldn't think of a word more inappropriate.

"Because unlike sociopaths, psychopaths always make mistakes," Simmons asserted. "You'll probably catch her soon, probably through some very unelaborate means."

"Unelaborate?" Spence could've laughed. "She manually extracted the teeth of the first three victims to prevent a dental-record ID. She burned up their hands and feet. And she hasn't left a single latent, not in the car, not on any of the bodies. My guy at CES says she's wearing double pairs of surgical gloves, for God's sake. In other words, she's so well-informed about modern criminalistic procedures that she knows about the resin applications that can ID latents left through a single pair. Christ, she's knocking these guys out with sodium amobarbital."

"Fine, fine. She's intricate. But what you're under-rating is that she's a chronic stage bipolar. As more time passes, the delusional stage becomes more apparent. Psychopaths are notoriously forgetful. They have outstanding long-term memories but almost no short-term memories. They can have human body parts going karyolytic in their bedrooms and not even be aware of it. When enough time passes after the psychotic event, they become convinced of their delusions. They become monomanic, oblivious. They begin to think in fragments and visual splices. They hallucinate. They'll drive to the store naked and think there's nothing wrong with that. I had a man last year who actually buried a bag of garbage and left a body out by the curb. It doesn't matter that they often have higher IQs than you and I. When their delusions overtake them, they become prone to outrageous, and even comedic, acts of stupidity." Simmons sipped his coffee and grimaced. "Don't worry, your red-haired friend will start making mistakes. But that doesn't mean you don't have quite a lot to worry about in the meantime."

"What should I *expect* in the meantime?"

"More bodies," Simmons said. His mouth hooked up, then he dumped his coffee in the wastebasket. "You remember your basic psychiatric terms from school. Do you remember what a nascent is?"

Spence dumped his coffee out too. "An object or ideation that causes a delusion to become real to the afflicted. Or something like that."

Simmons held up a finger. "Exactly. And Kathleen Shade is the link to the nascent." Simmons' bizarre smile seemed to radiate. "Find the nascent, Jeffrey, and you will find your psychopath."

Chapter 8

(I)

She's at the kitchen table.
Late morning.
She can see birds hopping on the cracked patio outside.
She'll have to remember to mow the grass.
She's naked beneath a silk, purple robe.
She doesn't like mornings.
Mornings make her remember things.
Memories, she thinks, drinking wine.
But her memories are what make her important.
Memories are what make her story…
She begins to type.

• • • • •

CHAPTER ONE
CHILDHOOD MEMORIES

Your father is a memory. Your mother is a ghost. The Cross reminds you of something but you never know what. Your mother died when you were about 15. She was a prostitute and took heroin. Daddy beat her up a lot because he had friends who liked to have sex with women who were beaten up or unconscious. You loved your mother very much. You wish there was some way you could find all the men who had sex with your mother so you could kill them all. Daddy made you watch sometimes. He made you touch him while he watched the men in Daddy's Room through a trick mirror in the closet. He first started molesting you when you were four or five. Whenever he came back from his job, he'd take you into the den, which you only think of as Daddy's Room, and he'd fuck you. He'd make you do things to him. He was never mean like he was to your mother. He'd do mean things but he'd never act mean. And lots of times his work friends would come to the house and Daddy would let them do things to you and your mother, sometimes at the same time. All those nights for all those years you remember being fucked on the couch or on the table or on the floor, and you remember looking up into The Window and seeing The Cross.

The Cross glows like huge beautiful white fire.

It's The Cross that saves you. It's The Cross that gives you your power. Your mother's ghost told you that.

Sometimes Daddy and his friends would tie your mother up and stick things in her. They'd all laugh as she quivered on the floor.

You look at The Cross and decide that one day you'll tie them up and stick things in them.

Later she mows the lawn.

She used to pay neighborhood boys to do it, but then her mother told her that they might find something in the yard.

Places where she's buried things.

After that she drives to work to pick up her paycheck.

She's driving the little blue car. Her mother isn't with her today.

Maybe she's with Daddy.

Maybe she's cutting the devil off of Daddy.

In Daddy's Room.

Again and again and again.

She wishes she were a ghost like her mother so she could cut off Daddy's devil too.

Sometimes she sees skulls beneath people's faces.

"Skulls mean death," her mother told her once.

It's The Cross that lets her see the skulls.

She wonders if Kathleen Shade sees the skulls too.

• • • • •

She gets her paycheck at the hospital's physical plant office.

Her supervisor says "Hello," and gives her her check.

Nobody talks to her very much.

They all think she's weird.

She smiles at that.

She goes up to the 4th floor where most of the ICU coves are.

A candy-striper at the nurses' station says "Hello," and she says "Hello" back.

"You're working four to twelve today?"

"No, I don't work again 'til tomorrow night," she tells the candy-striper. She wants to warn the young girl, about the devils, and about all the horrible things that men would like to do to her, but of course she can't. "I forgot to finish my shift log from last night."

"Oh, okay."

While she's finishing her shift log, a doctor comes around the corner and starts yelling at the candy-striper. "Carrington, not Carrolton!" he yells and slaps down an aluminum folder that they keep the ICU records in. It makes a sound so loud she jumps.

"I'm sorry, doctor," the candy-striper apologizes.

"Do you have any idea, *any idea at all*, what could happen when you order the wrong records!"

"I'm sorry, doctor. I thought you said Carrolton."

"I thought you said Carrolton," the doctor mimics her. "Jesus Christ, girl, a patient could die because of your stupidity!"

The candy-striper starts to cry.

The doctor jerks around into the station, to get the records himself. "If it were up to me, you'd all be fired," he mutters, rummaging. "Incompetent, the bunch of you."

She feels sorry for the candy-striper, but she smiles. "Don't worry," she consoles when the doctor stalks off. "I heard that a patient went comatose last year because he administered the wrong beta-blocker. The patient almost died."

"He's such a prick!" the candy-striper half-sobbed. "He's always acting like that. It's not my fault he can't say a patient's name right."

"Don't worry."

A fantasy blooms, like a light turning on.

Hold him down, she's saying to the candy-striper, *while I get him cuffed.*

He's jerking and screaming as she cuts off his face with a Gradle-Miltex post-mortem abdominal knife.

See what I'm doing for you? she says to the candy-striper. *You can learn from me.*

She slices off his ears like the ends of a loaf of bread.

She clips off his nose with Knowels cartilage shears.

She places the shears in the candy-striper's hand and holds up the doctor's penis so the candy-striper can cut it off.

"That asshole," the candy-striper says, dabbing her eyes with Kleenex. "I could kill him."

Yes, she thinks.

All the while she's been putting the tag number into the computer. All hospitals have an uplink to surrounding motor vehicle administrations for car-wreck victims who are brought in with no IDs so they can run the plates and get a print-out of the owner's driver's license and see if the car-wreck victim matches the face on the license.

"If I wasn't in school, I'd quit this damn place," the candy-striper is saying. At least she's calmed down a little now. "I don't deserve to be treated like that."

"Nobody does."

She doesn't print out the information because she knows that if she does the computer will out-index it.

Instead she memorizes what appears on the color-graphic monitor.

HEIGHT: 5-6
WEIGHT: 135
SEX: F
LIC. TYPE: R
KATHLEEN MARGARET SHADE
3660 LEIBER STREET #307
WASHINGTON, D.C. 20005

Chapter 9

(I)

"I'm sorry I missed your lecture, honey," Kathleen's father said over the phone. "I completely forgot about it."

Kathleen had never expected him to show up in the first place. "It went pretty well," she said. She was looking out the window, into sunlight. "I met a nice man."

"Oh, really?"

"His name's Maxwell. He's a poet."

She could nearly hear her father's frown. "A poet?" he said. "Do poets make money?"

"He also teaches college, but he's off for the summer."

"Hmm. A poet."

Her father called every few weeks, either from his house in Alexandria, or from his company office. He was a millionaire. From his own father, he and Sam had inherited a mining company, coal and tin, in Allegheny County. He made several 100,000 per year in what he called "Schedule E Mineral Royalties," which, over the years, he'd converted to millions through real estate deals and the stock market. Sammy sold his shares to her father and put the money in the bank. It infuriated Kathleen, that a pedophile should be allowed to be wealthy.

"I want to meet him when I'm back in town," her father went on. "How old is he?"

"I'm not sure. Late twenties, early thirties."

"We'll go to a nice restaurant, 21 Federal maybe, or how about Duke's? Maybe we'll see Ted Kennedy again."

"Anyplace'll be fine, dad. You'll like him."
"Who? Kennedy?"
"No, dad. Maxwell. He's really nice."
"He better be. Nobody's too nice for my little girl."

What a trip, Kathleen thought. *I'm a 33-year-old little girl.* She didn't even consider telling him about the killer. As far as over-reactive fathers went, her own father was outdone by no one. He'd have her moving out of state. He'd send her on a vacation for a year.

"Do you need any money?" he asked.
"No, dad, I'm fine."
"You're sure."
"Really, dad. Things are great."

And it dawned on her then, that things really *were* great. Even if her conception of Maxwell was an over-reaction of her own—she'd met him less than 24 hours ago—her life suddenly felt bristling with excitement and reality. *What's different about it now?* she wondered. Was it the credibility she had as a writer? Was it Maxwell? *Is it the killer?* she wondered.

She felt complete. She was a complete woman in, basically, a man's world, and she knew she always had been. So why was she only realizing that now?

The moment darkened, though. *Almost, alm— Here.* Kathleen shriveled. She knew she shouldn't ask, but...

"Dad? Sam's still in prison, isn't he?"

The pause unreeled like something dropped into an abyss.

"Honey, oh Jesus. Of course he is. Are you having problems with that again?"

Kathleen wasn't quite sure how to answer. "A little, or...something," she said. Late morning sun glared in the window, an inferno. "Just lately, for some reason..." She didn't bother finishing. The cat clock ticked in her head.

She knew how guilty her father felt about it. Sam was his brother, his blood. Worse was that he'd found out only years later, when Sammy had been caught. "You remember what the prosecutor's office said," her father recounted as though it were some unimpeachable assurance. "Even when he's up for parole he'll be turned down. Don't worry about him."

"I won't," she said, then hastened to correct: "I'm not... Well, be sure to call when you're back home."

"I will." The voice sounded ruined. "'Bye."

"'Bye."

Well, Kathleen, you sure screwed up his day. Why had she even brought it up? The radio shrink would say she'd done it on purpose, that subconsciously she blamed her father more than Sam. To a 9-year-old,

Father was God, Father was Protector. Kathleen's mother had died the same year; Sam, the weak link in the family business, had looked after her constantly while her father was on the job, or away on business. *He looked after me, all right,* she sourly reminded herself. And all those years afterward... For so long she hadn't even suspected that something was wrong. *Don't worry, Kathleen. I'll take good care of you while your dad's away.* Years, yes. Years. Such was the precision of Sam's diabolical ability to brainwash her. The counselor had told her this was a common trait, the pedophile's talent for gaining the child's absolute trust and then converting it to his own end. Kathleen had never said a word until she was 27. Sammy had been caught in a Justice Department sting. *All those years, all those years,* she thought now. "It's part of the offender's overall strategy," the counselor had informed her. "You never said anything to your father about it because you were expertly programmed not to. And as you gradually became an adult, and gradually realized that your uncle's behavior had been criminal, you remained silent out of a retroactive shame-fixation. This is a typical complex in these situations."

It had been an honor to testify against him, however after the fact; the evidence had been heinous. Sam had probably molested over a 100 children, male and female, in his two decades of pedophilia. He'd been in some of the films himself, and in some of the magazines, with a beard or mustache. She'd never forget the titles: *It's Playtime, Stomper Room, Cum To Jeannie's Birthday Party, Uncle Dick Comes to Visit.* The defense attorney had actually tried to have Kathleen's testimony dismissed, since she'd been recounting experiences that had taken place when she was a minor. *What a joke. How could anybody deny all those films and magazines?* A plea bargain had reduced Sam's sentence; he'd wound up testifying against all his associates. But 13 years in Lorton, she'd been told, was worse than 50 anywhere else.

She had no qualms with her rage. She hoped Sam was being sodomized every night in his cell. She hoped he was being treated as the object he'd treated all those children as. "I hope you hang yourself," she told him as the bailiffs escorted him out. He'd only looked back at her dolefully, which felt strange.

The memories hadn't bothered her for years. She'd been trained by the private counselors—by backward association techniques, and memory-links—to recreate in her mind her own endings for the images. "There are times when it's perfectly healthy to redirect the pain in our lives. To transform it into someone else's pain." The method worked very well. Whenever a memory popped up, whenever she remembered the cat clock or heard Sammy's hypnotic words *Almost, Almost—Here,* she simply murdered him in her mind. "Rape-Conclusion Substitution is what we call it," the counselors had said. Often rescuers would barge in at the last moment, policemen usually, and shoot Sammy as he attempted to flee. Sometimes children would barge in, and cut him up into pieces. Sometimes she'd shoot him herself, watch his sweating, intent face explode before the muzzle flash. Sometimes she'd let him be eaten by monsters...

Her editor at *'90s Woman* wasn't in, so she took a nap for an hour or two. The August heat embraced her, it made her feel dreamy and cool; the sunlight in the window seemed to drape her in darkness. Wisps of the dream kept brushing back: the darkened figure showing her pictures she couldn't see. It aggravated her, so she stopped trying to sleep. She wanted to see the pictures, and she knew the dream would never let her.

Later she took a cool shower, and caught her sudsy hand lingering over her pubis. The cool torrent made her breasts feel dully electrified. She remembered what Spence had said, about... What word had he used? *Parity,* she remembered. Similarities between herself and the killer. The whole thing had been a set-up, but why? *The killer was abused as a child, you were abused as a child.* So what? *Does she look like me?* she wondered. *Does she have a body like me? A face?* Kathleen smiled to herself. *Does she touch herself in the shower?*

What was Spence driving at?

Suddenly she felt bursting with quirks, with silliness. She didn't dry herself off but went at once out to the couch. In a moment she was lying down, eyes closed. She was masturbating. She was thinking about Maxwell. She fantasized saying the dirtiest things to him, things she would never say for real. She blushed as her fingers goaded her.

Her bare feet kneaded the couch end when she came; it didn't take long. For some reason, unlike ever before, touching herself seemed to bring all the parts of her closer together—spiritually, not physically. It attuned her to herself, this upfront granting of pleasure by her own hands. It seemed honest. Perhaps that was it. She often felt hypocritical and contradictory, smothering the real woman that she was in the vagaries of the age.

She snapped up the phone before the end of the first ring, as if caught doing something she shouldn't.

"Kathleen? This is—"

"Maxwell!," she recognized the voice at once. She blushed again, noticing her still-shiny fingers. "I was, uh, just thinking about you."

"I've been trying to call—"

"Oh, I'm sorry. I was on the phone for awhile, with my father. Then I took a nap."

"Well, listen." He sounded reserved, or discomfited. "Something kind of weird happened. This morning, just a few minutes after you left."

"Yeah?" Kathleen said, crossing her feet on the couch.

"There was a knock on the door, so I open it and there're two city cops standing there. And they ask me if I'm all right."

"All right? Why wouldn't you be?"

"I don't know," Maxwell said. "Then they started asking me about you. Like how long I've known you, and if I noticed anything unusual about you, stuff like that."

"I can't imagine wh—" She bit the rest of the sentence off. It hit her all at once, like walking down the street and having a flower pot land on her head. *Spence,* she realized. *That son...of a...bitch.*

"Are you there, Kathleen?"

"Yes, I, um..."

"They also asked me if I knew about any book projects you might be working on."

"What did you say?" she asked, perhaps too quickly.

"I told them I didn't know what they were talking about. It's none of their business anyway. This isn't a police state."

Kathleen lolled in relief. Of course, Maxwell was a poet; most poets were liberals, even radicals.

"They even asked me if you dyed your hair, or if I knew of any friends of yours who were redheads."

But Spence knows I couldn't be the killer, she fumed to herself. *Does he actually think I'm in some sort of complicity?* The idea was too absurd. No, Spence was just sending his boys around to harass her. *I'm going to sue him so help me G—*

"It was kind of strange, at any rate," Maxwell went on. "Are you in some sort of trouble with the police?"

"No, no, nothing like that." *At least not yet,* she thought. "I'll tell you all about it sometime."

Silence drifted. "I was just worried a little."

"Don't be. It's really silly if you want to know the truth."

Another pause. "Okay. Good. So when can I see you again?"

The abruptness of the question stifled her; it made her feel pretty, it made her feel demanded. Not "Can I see you again?" but "When?" *Don't push things, Kathleen,* she told herself, aware of all the times she'd advised her readers likewise. It seemed all too prevalent: women, after even a single sexual encounter, would go nuts for a man. They didn't give it time. Universally, men freaked when pressured toward commitment. The best recommendation was to take things slow, and that's what Kathleen regularly prescribed to her readers. *Take your own advice for a change, Kathleen,* she insisted to herself. *Don't move too fast. Give it a week. Or at least give it a few days.*

"How about tonight?" she said. She frowned at herself. "I'll pick you up at eight. I'll even spring for carry-out Chinese."

"Sounds great," Maxwell said. "See you then."

Kathleen hung up, thinking of the old axiom: Don't Do As I Do, Do As I Say. She knew she could ruin everything by pushing; at this early stage, in fact, she didn't even know what there was to push. *I can't help it!* she thought, as if arguing. *I want to see him. What could be wrong with that?*

She was about to light her hourly cigarette when she felt the familiar rumble of the mail truck. Even though she knew her carrier from the magazine would not arrive 'til next week, she hauled on old clothes—ratty red sweat pants and a JUST SAY MOE T-shirt—and rushed ahead.

She opened the front door. She was about to go down the steps. Something caught her right eye, a tan flash. A rectangle.

A 9x12 envelope had been taped to the front door.

On a white label someone had typed:

MS. KATHLEEN SHADE

That was all.

Chapter 10

(I)

"—'s it really," Maxwell was explaining in the Thunderbird. "The only thing I hate is hatred. The only thing I'm negative about is negativity." His face looked placid in some stoic satisfaction. "The only thing, in the whole world, that I have ill will toward is ill will."

"Eat shit and die, dickhead!" Kathleen barked as a black Fiero cut her off at Sheridan Circle. "Can you believe these people? Learn to drive!" she yelled out the window and honked. The man in the Fiero gave her the finger.

"I'm not religious," Maxwell continued, "at least not in any classic sense, but I suppose I'm what most people would consider spiritual. Christians, for instance, believe that life is a gift from God. Well, even if it's not from God, it's still a gift from somewhere. A gift from providence, perhaps, or fate. It's a gift from the pure positive potential of the human spirit. I don't believe in the 'Cosmic Soup' theory—it can't be true. Life really is a wonderful, joyous thing. It really is a gift."

"*Fuck*brain!" Kathleen honked, stopped behind a double parked plumbing van that read MR. ROOTER! on the side. "Oh, right, like it's my fault this idiot's double-parked!" she yelled. The line of cars behind her blared their horns in unison.

"Take the fundamental nihilists." Maxwell's hands shaped things in the air as he spoke. "They believe that there is no objective basis for truth and, hence, no objective basis for beauty. But how can this be? It's easy to see the world as nothing but a sphere of ugliness, despair, and lies when we're bred to believe that. I, on the other hand, reject that, most adamantly. If you open your heart when you look, the world really is a beautiful place."

"This is such infuriating shit!" Kathleen commented. "Where do all these cars come from?" Her fists clenched on the wheel as she squeaked by MR. ROOTER! and nearly got clipped by a Red Top cab.

"You should calm down," Maxwell said.

"Yeah, well, I've had a bad day." Now a commuter bus pulled in front of them, excreting blue, soot-laden smoke.

"But that just goes back to what I've been saying," Maxwell went on. "We should examine our ideals more closely, I think. By what standards do we define a bad day? I prefer to look at the matter through a veil of jubilation. So what if the rent goes up? So what if we don't have enough money for all our bills? So what—" He raised a finger. "—if we're stuck in traffic? Whenever I'm in a bad mood, I try to shake myself and take a good hard look at what life really is. Any day that I wake up and the sun's still shining and the world's still turning and my heart's still beating—now *that's* a good day."

Bugger philanthropy, Kathleen thought. She supposed he was right, but that didn't matter, not today. The traffic, and the ugly, sooty, mephitic city was just a catalyst. Stark, rust-stained buildings made a canyon of Massachusetts Avenue. The descending sun glinted like lava in windows.

"Is everything all right?" Maxwell inquired.

"Of course," she said a bit too testily. Now the sinking sun shot spikes of glare across the windshield. "Jesus Christ!" she yelled. "How am I supposed to see?"

"You don't seem like yourself."

"You've only known me for two days, Maxwell," she replied, very unglamorously lighting a cigarette as she spoke.

"Oh."

What a dumb thing to say, she lamented. But how could she be cheery knowing that a psycho-killer had discovered her address?

"I'm sorry," she said a moment later.

"You shouldn't apologize for how you feel."

She grit her teeth. The light changed and traffic hitched on. Her address was unlisted. The killer had gotten it somehow.

The killer had actually walked up her apartment steps and affixed the envelope to her front door, no doubt while Kathleen had been inside. *She was just feet away from me,* she realized. *A killer.*

Maxwell had dressed laxly in faded jeans, sneakers, and a blue T-shirt that read THE TAIT LITERARY REVIEW. He didn't complain that she had not turned on the air-conditioning. Perhaps he was as content in smothering heat as she.

"How's your story coming along?" he asked.

It was the worst thing he could ask just then, or perhaps ever. What could she say to him? Anything? "I'll be right back," she said, and pulled over. She hopped out of the car and went into Berose Liquors. Long reach-in coolers hosted unique beers. She didn't particularly care what she got; she just wanted something cold. "Is this wine?" she asked the proprietor, holding up a big bottle. "It's Blue Heron Ale," he said. "You can't do better."

Why did she need a drink all of a sudden? It wasn't like her. As she paid for several of the large bottles, not really even knowing what she was buying, she felt some sort of dread, like mystic pressure. Of course. She would be home soon. And the killer's manuscript was waiting for her.

She had read it all and quailed.

You asked for it, Kathleen, and you got it. And now you're going to have to deal with it.

"Come again," said the proprietor.

"I thought we were getting Chinese food," Maxwell said when she got back in the T-Bird. An ambulance passed with its siren off, lights throbbing. Pedestrians moved on obliviously.

"Well, we can. I'm suddenly thirsty." She pulled one of the large, pretty bottles out of the bag and placed it between her legs, noting for the first time her ratty sweat pants.

"Isn't it, like, socially irresponsible to drink and drive?"

"Goddamn it!" she exclaimed in sudden turmoil. "These aren't twist-offs!"

Maxwell, frowning traceably, got out of the car, walked around to the driver's side, opened the door, and pushed her over to the passenger seat.

"What are you doing!"

"I'm driving," he insisted. "You're weird today."

"Thanks a lot."

He pulled out, craning his neck. He kept blowing the long blond hair out of his eyes, waiting for a gap.

"You can tell me what's wrong when we get home," he said.

The ale was delicious but it was too strong. Half the bottle left her calmly sluggish on the couch. Maxwell didn't say anything for quite a while; she sensed he was giving her time to cool off. *Men. What schmucks,* she thought. He was watching a baseball game.

Somebody was hitting lots of home-runs. "I don't know why the Yankees don't just disband. There's no reason for them to even be on the field," Maxwell said as if she cared. "The only difference between what that pitcher is throwing and regular garbage is that regular garbage generally comes in a can. Christ, I could pitch better than this guy."

She'd hidden the manuscript in her desk, along with the Xeroxes, which were apparently from a book. INITIATORY RITES, the passage had been entitled. Never in Kathleen's life had she even guessed that such things could exist...

...in an array of unique, and often repugnant, examples. At a tribal level, such customs functioned in one of two ways: fashion, or rite. Hierarchs of empiric China thought it fashionable for their women to have small feet—hence, foot-binding. This process, generally begun at about the age of four, severely inhibited the formative growth of the bones of the feet. Mothers insisted upon it, however; it was status to marry off a daughter to the upper-class. The smaller the feet, the more feminine, it was considered. The fact that this technique crippled tens of thousands for life was quite immaterial. It was culture. The same too for African "lip-plating," thousands of years old yet still prevalent today. Upon puberty, girls would receive their first plates, and from there the race for fashion began. Lip-plates were considered the epitome of female desirability, the larger the better (the largest were often 18 inches in diameter!), and any woman without a lip-plate was laughed at. The idea was to stretch the incised upper lip to such an extremity that women could encompass their breasts when bedding a man. If a married woman was ever found guilty of adultery, she was forbidden to ever wear her lip-plates again, upon the penalty of death, consigning them to spend the rest of their lives with slack ropes of flesh dangling from their faces. Even stranger was the technique of nipple-elongation, of the Chinese Han Dynasty (206 B.C. to 220 A.D.). For an hour each night, prepubescent girls were made to stand with weights suspended by strings which were threaded through their pierced nipple-ends. By the time they were of marrying age, they sported grossly elongated nipples, regarded as an ultimate attraction. Nipples were often stretched to the length of eight inches.

But so much for fashion; tribal mutilation exceeds itself in its ritual designs. Foremost is circumcision—originally the clipped foreskin served as an offering to God. Much less known, however, is the similar rite of female circumcision, i.e. the partial or complete removal of the labium minus. Regrettably, careless or unknowledgable tribal doctors often removed the clitoris as well, by accident. Most interesting, however, and utterly extreme, was the practice of full vaginal closure. Many female-dominant societies actively utilized this technique, as an ultimate offering to the object of their spiritual beliefs. Throughout history, countless female-dominant sects and/or societies have existed, some for protracted periods of time. Chief among them, the notorious "Amazonians" of central and upper South America; the Bengalian Camu sects of the 10th Century, who worshipped the female goddess

Camunda; and the countless female-superior societies of the Polynesian and Melanesian archipelagoes. Perhaps history's earliest feminists, these societies were actively ritualistic in their hatred of the male of the species. Men were uniformly enslaved for labor, secluded for reproductive roles, or cannibalized for religious purposes. The most noteworthy example exists in the Loknas of pre-Druidic northern England, who worshipped a common "mother goddess." First-born males were sacrificed upon birth, while first-born females were viewed as partial incarnates of the mother goddess. So zealous were the Loknas in their loathe of men that the notion of any subcarnate first-born being even touched by a male was unthinkable, and even less thinkable was the notion of sexual congress. Hence, ritual vaginal closure, or the sewing shut of the vaginal channel, which served as an oblation to their goddess. Cured animal gut provided the suture, blessed fishbones were used as needles. Initiants were expected, by codices, to perform the act upon themselves...

My God, Kathleen thought. Stodgily written as it was, the text winded her, crushed her as inquisitors crushed suspects with pallets weighed by rocks. The images raged in her head...

She stared at the TV, through haze raised by the ale. A batter with a bird on his hat hit a homerun. Maxwell swore under his breath. As the batter rounded the bases, he looked like Uncle Sammy.

All those memories were resurfacing now. Why? *Memories,* she thought. Then she thought further: CHILDHOOD MEMORIES.

She wondered if anything could be worse, anything in the world. A prostitute for a mother, and a pedophile for a father, who apparently shared her with his sick friends. In the manuscript, she said she'd been molested since the age of four or five...

Maxwell turned off the set with the remote. "We can talk now if you want," he said.

"That's all right. You can watch your game."

"There is no game, not when the Yankees are playing. Anyway, I really think you should talk about what's bothering you."

She felt like a slug on the couch. "I don't want to now."

"Okay."

"But I want to ask you something..."

But what could she really ask? This was now an intricate problem as well as a legal one. Spence would be furious that she even touched the envelope much less read it. Did the killer expect her not to notify the police? *She knows where I live, and she knows I know that.* Was this a proposition of some bizarre kind of trust?

Maxwell sat on the edge of the couch, his eyebrows propped up as if to say "Well?"

"Never mind," she said. What she really wanted to say, though, was *Maxwell, should I conceal evidence from the police?* Spence could put her in jail, she supposed, and with good reason. By not showing him what the killer had sent, she was hindering the investigation.

"Can they find fingerprints on paper?" she idly asked.

Maxwell frowned. "I think so...but that's not what you were going to ask, is it?"

"No," she feebled. "How's the poetry coming?"

"Fine. What were you going to ask me?"

She couldn't ask. She couldn't even think about it, not any of it. It wasn't the ale that weighed her down as much as the imagery. *He must think I'm a pouting, flighty airhead,* she realized. Suddenly she felt so desperate for distraction she was nearly shaking. She jumped up off the couch and walked away.

"Where are you going?"

"Wait."

The windows framed the city's dark. She walked around the apartment turning off all the lights one by one.

"Kathleen?"

"Just wait, you'll see. You might like this," she said. *Then again you might not. You might just think I'm some horny weirdo.* She'd left the radio on in the bedroom, the volume way down. It was the radio shrink's show. A female caller was saying, "...but I keep going back. I don't know why, but I keep going back every single time. Sometimes I go back even before the bruises go away." "Battered-Wife Syndrome," the radio shrink replied, "is all too evident in most developed societies. Psychiatrists believe its symptoms—the repeated willful return to physical abuse—are deeply rooted in the wife's uncentered concept of identity. Sadly, on a subconscious level, being beaten is a reinforcement of identity, which is why such a great percentage of battered wives never press criminal charges and always return to the abuser. I've counseled many women who claim that they'd rather be beaten than be alone."

Kathleen frequently received letters herself about the issue, and she always strongly advised the reader to escape the brutal spouse at all costs. Was loneliness that powerful? *If I were married and my husband beat me,* she thought, *I'd hit him in the head with a brick.*

But she turned the radio off. It reminded her too vividly of the killer's dizzying first chapter. She remembered the exact words: *Daddy beat her up a lot because he knew men who liked to have sex with women who were beaten up or unconscious.*

"Kathleen?" Maxwell called out. "It's dark in here. What are you doing?"

"Just one more minute!"

Yes, she needed distraction badly. Was that all Maxwell was to her?

A physical object? A distraction? She lit the candle on the dresser. She turned out the bedroom light and quickly skimmed off her clothes.

She walked back out to the living room, holding the candle. She needed it to be dark. She didn't want him to see her.

"What the—" he said. "You're naked."

"Um-hmm." She took his hand, led him away. The candlelight roved eerily on the walls. When they were in the little bathroom she set the candle down and turned on the shower. "I'll be waiting," she said and got in.

The candlelight turned the bathroom to a shifting grotto. Moments later a naked Maxwell stepped in with her. When he embraced her, and kissed her, she felt he was already erect. "Why can't we have the lights on?" he said. He was fumbling for the soap. "I want to see you."

"I don't want you to see me. I'm fat."

"Kathleen..." He turned her back to him, was sliding the bar of soap over her breasts. "You're not fat..."

The slick suds and cool water felt delicious.

"...you're beautiful," he finished.

Was he just saying that? *Don't be insecure,* she ordered herself. She just closed her eyes and let him wash her. Soon he had slickened her into a lush suit of lather, his hands sliding slowly everywhere.

This was the distraction she needed. It plucked everything from her mind and left only the moment. In the flickering orange light, and in the hiss of water, she forgot it all: the killer, Spence, the excerpt of tribal rites, and the heinous first chapter of "the story."

He turned her around again, and knelt. He picked up each foot and soaped it. Next his hands were sliding up and down each of her legs. And next—

He lathered her pubis. She looked down and saw a nest of suds. His face hovered down there, and then the bar was sliding back and forth between her legs as attendant fingers played with her sex. She parted her feet to the edges of the shower floor. One hand came around, received the bar, and guided it up the cleft of her buttocks. When she was sure he wasn't looking, Kathleen caressed her breasts, rolled her nipples between her fingers, which pushed a gust of sensation like something electric to her loins. Meanwhile, one of Maxwell's fingers rubbed up and down over her anus. This felt strange, even mildly shocking—she'd never been touched there before. The hot gust quadrupled then, a luscious tenseness, when the tip of Maxwell's tongue began to very tenderly probe her clitoris. "Mmmmmmmmm," she went.

Each time an ugly image tried to surface, she obliterated it with a sexual thought. When words of the killer's narrative began to appear, she concentrated on the feel of Maxwell's mouth, and then the words were gone. When Spence's face threatened to form, she thought of sucking

Maxwell's penis, of letting him come in her mouth, and the face dissolved. She thought crudely and pornographically: *Eat my pussy like you did last night. Stick your tongue all the way up my pussy. Stand up now so I can suck your cock, etc.* When the first digit of Maxwell's pinkie entered her anus, and when his lips took her clitoris into his mouth, she stopped him. She didn't want to come yet. "Stand up now," she said, "so I can..."

Now she knelt before him, soaping his groin. His fingertips tensed on her shoulders. She rinsed his erection off quickly; she could taste soap when she began to fellate him. One hand rubbed the soapy testicles, the other stroked up and down the back of his thigh.

More words tried to rise, the killer's narrative—

Daddy made you watch sometimes. He made you touch him while he watched the men in Daddy's Room through a trick mirror in the closet.

—so she shut her eyes, sucking harder.

And lots of times his work friends would come to the house and Daddy would let them do things to you...

"Kathleen," Maxwell moaned.

...and your mother, sometimes at the same time...tie her up and stick things in her...

Kathleen's eyes squeezed she shut harder, tried to let Maxwell's erection go all the way into her throat, but she gagged, thinking *Go away!* She relaxed, and tried again, then found her lips pressed against his wet pubic hair. "Oh, Kathhhh..."

It glows like huge beautiful white fire.

"Come on," she whispered.

She didn't bother turning the shower off. They stumbled out, clumsily embracing and kissing, to the bed.

You always see it in Daddy's Room.

She lay back on the bed gritting her teeth. She spread her legs as wide as she could. "Maxwell, please—" His mouth was right on her sex; her buttocks lay in his hands. His tongue slithered down, flicked over her anus.

It reminds you of something but you never know what.

She pinched her nipples so hard it hurt. "No, I want..." She was pulling him up. "Ffffff...now. Oh, please—" She heard the packet tear open. She felt rigid, locked up by the words. Tears squeezed out of her eyes.

There. He was in her. Her nails clawed his back. She wrapped her legs around him. "Harder," she insisted into his ear. Her legs wrapped tighter.

It's The Cross that changes you.

"Harder!" He was hammering her. His testicles slapped her.

It's The Cross that changes you.

"Jesus, Kathleen." His thrusts slowed, then stopped. "You're crying. What's—"

She burst into open sobs, convulsing.

It's The Cross that gives you your power.

"I'm so sorry, Maxwell," she sobbed. She felt like something in the sky falling apart into pieces. She could barely speak through her sobs. "I don't know what's wrong with me."

Maxwell withdrew from her at once. He put his arms around her, rocked her, tried to comfort her.

She was shivering, her throat hitching. Tears ran down both sides of her face.

"It's all right, it's all right—"

She turned her head to one side. The words were gone.

"Everything's fine, Kathleen."

She swallowed, tried to nod.

The candlelight flickered in the bathroom.

The water hissed like rain.

She was staring into the bathroom doorway.

Uncle Sammy was staring back.

Almost, almost. Alm—Here.

The cat clock's eyes switched back and forth.

Kathleen screamed and passed out.

Chapter 11

(I)

The Dome was just the way Brad Weston liked his hunting grounds. Cavernous. Jammed. Chaotic music pulsed around blood-colored, dark throbbing lights. In baggy gray slacks, a black phony-silk shirt and black tie, Brad looked into the pit and immediately thought: *Meat market.*

In the bathroom some guys were doing cocaine as they traded jokes. "What's the difference between Michael Jackson and potato chips? Michael Jackson comes in a can." In the stall, Brad did a line of his own toot himself, to perk up. *It's a jungle out there*, he thought. The blow shot an instant spark into his brain and groin. On the wall someone had written:

> *One last ride before the end of it all*
> *—JOY DIVISION*

Brad was hopping. He was ready to go. He prowled the outer circle of tables and spotted a few. A blonde with a bad complexion smiled at him, but he pretended not to see her. *Forget it, Craterface.* A lot of girls in black, slim, with long hair. A lot of guys trying hard to look like Mickey Rourke. Brad danced to Faith No More with one girl who must've thought she was Morticia on the Adams Family. She had a snitty smirk he didn't like so he bagged her. Depeche Mode beat out "Master And Servant"; Brad spotted some class cleavage, a brunette in sequins with earrings that looked like shower curtain rings. Once he got out on the floor with her, though, he noticed she was fat. She might be good for some head, but... *Not tonight,* he determined. He wanted *tough* stuff tonight. *Are those thighs,* he thought, dancing, *or pontoons?* He bagged her after the next cut.

This was fun. It was like tasting wine. Did these girls actually think they were going to meet Mr. Right on a dancefloor of a singles bar? It was a farce that he could exploit, and he had many times. Brad had quite a sexual resume: 42 one-night stands since he quit college a couple years ago. He discovered that playing the right game, and playing it well, could get him just about any girl he gunned for. It was all lines and looks: wearing the right clothes in the right place, saying the right things...

He had no problem coming to terms with himself and his desires. *I'm going to fuck a girl tonight.* Barring technicalities, it was that simple. You did what everyone else did. You lied. You made false gestures. You feigned common interests. It was easy.

Here came a tall one—huge hazel eyes, slim like Julia Roberts in a tight white dress and black fishnet stockings. Brad wouldn't mind licking up those long legs right to her snatch. *Do you shave your pussy?* he wanted to ask. *I'll bet you do.* He shouldered off the dancefloor past a group squeezed together, and ran his finger right up some streak-blonde's crack from behind. "Hey!" she yelled, jerking her gaze back and forth. "Who the hell—" Brad smiled. *Thanks for the feel.* He wished he could just walk up to any girl and yank her tits out, or rub his cock against their asses. "Wanna dance?" he asked a trim honey-blonde leaning against the middle bar. She'd decked out in a gorgeous strapless silk dress, fiery orange. "Oh, no thanks," she said. *Then I guess an ass-fucking is out of the question, huh?* he thought. *I wouldn't fuck you with a dog's dick anyway. Bitch.*

The Dome had an anteroom just off the entrance, a small figure-eight shaped bar. People came out here either to get a break from the loud music, or because they were sick of striking out on the floor. A barkeep was juggling shot glasses for three spellbound flirts. *Too bad your brains aren't a big as your tits,* Brad thought, *or your asses.* He wanted to laugh out loud. *Christ, baby, you got a pair of feedbags under that dress?* The coke had him sharp; it focused his senses and his cynicism to a razor line. It had his cock feeling like raw current. *Down boy! Down! You go busting out of my slick slacks and all these girls'll think Godzilla just walked into the joint.* A pair of yups were trading jokes. "You got 25 women with PMS, and 25 women with yeast infections," one guy asked. "What have you got?" "What?" the second guy asked. The first guy burst out laughing. "A whine and cheese party!"

"Hey," Brad cut in. "What would Cindy Crawford be if she was dead and buried?"

"What?"

Brad shrugged. "Worth digging up."

That got a charge out them. Two drunk fat guys drinking Heinekens were blabbering over Redskins preseason. Something about Ferrotte having a bag of pasta for an arm.

But the only playing field Brad cared about was the female body. Women weren't people to him, they were arrangements of sexual parts. They were warm things with an array of places for him to put his penis. He slapped down four bucks for a Coors, tapped his foot to the distant music— "If Love Was A Gun" by the diVinyls. The coke made his grin feel carved onto his face. As he watched more women saunter through the brick-arched medieval entrance, his thoughts remarked upon each. *You, Blondie, I'd fuck you dog-style on the floor, and you there in that silly-ass-looking parrot-green dress, I'd yank that shit off you and give it to you sideways up the ass while you frigged yourself with your finger and—hey!—Leather Pants! How 'bout I pull that sleazy halter over your empty head and fuck those Dolly Parton-sized tits of yours, huh? Blow a big Brad-The-Man wad all over your neck and spunk up that bargain-rack herringbone necklace, yeah, spunk it up real good and then maybe wipe my cock off in your fucked-up-looking hair...*

And then he noticed—

Jesus Please Us!

—the splittail standing by herself on the other end of the bar. Brad Weston's coke-locked grin transmuted to an intent incision. The girl stood erect over a glass of wine, something dark like port. The music out on the floor changed— "Dancing Like A Gun" by John Foxx. *An angel with tits and a cunt,* Brad mused. *Who needs wings?* He idled around for a better gander. The closer he got the more electrified he became; he was thrumming. She looked tall, real tall, like maybe even six feet. A sideglance afforded him the most erotic silhouette he'd ever witnessed. *This dish makes Elle MacPherson look like the back of a gorilla's balls.* Black heels, black stockings, short suede black-leather skirt. Her blouse was white veil, see-through—it was like looking at her topless in fog. *Her tits belong in the National Gallery,* Brad thought. High, large, like a primo implant job, only he could tell they weren't implants by the way they minutely jiggled as she tapped her foot to the John Foxx oldie. All that kept her nipples from being revealed to the world were dual white embroiderments which descended from her shoulders...

This is the best-looking hunk of girlflesh the Bradster has ever seen in his fucking life, he realized.

You don't ask, you don't get...

The distant music changed again— "The Girl At The End Of My Gun" by ASF. He finished his beer quickly, an excuse to order another, drawn by densest and most mystical enticement. The girl stood sleek and trim as a wild beast; it was beckoning: the line of her back, the lines of her shoulders and neck, and the long perfect lines of her legs. A power seemed to rage in the air, a force... He saw her face in slices, as though it were too beautiful to look at all at once. Lightly glossed, perfectly formed lips. Crystalline, liquid eyes, huge, greenish, bluish, perfect in their indefinability. And the perfect cheekbones, the perfect angles and lines of her face.

He could calculate her in no other way.

She's...perfect, he thought.

And as he walked the rest of the way around the bar, he noticed that she was looking right at him, and she was smiling.

(II)

"...like he was looking right at me, and he was smiling," Kathleen muttered into the crook of Maxwell's neck.

He stroked her hair, held her. "You don't have to talk about it any more if you don't want. Jesus, Kathleen, I had no idea."

She'd told him everything about Uncle Sammy. Everything.

"The counselor called it retrograde memory jags or something like that. She said it was normal after a long-term trauma. Sometimes I'd think I was seeing him when he wasn't really there. But it went away years ago."

"And now it's back?" Maxwell asked.

Kathleen nodded. Tears dried to crust on her face. "I don't understand. Why? After all this time, why?"

"There must be something in your life, something that's happened recently, to trigger it."

The killer, she thought. But it was really no surprise. *The killer was abused as a child, you were abused as a child.* But she knew she could not tell Maxwell about the killer. She knew she could never do that...

"Sammy's still in prison. Christ, I even asked my father to make sure."

Maxwell cradled her, gently rocked her. "You should try and go to sleep now," he said. "You'll feel better tomorrow."

But she didn't want to go to sleep. She couldn't. "It went on from the time I was nine 'til I was about 17 or 18. And I never said anything, I never told anyone, until years later when he got caught. I still don't understand that."

"It's just what the counselor said. Your uncle was able to secretly abuse you for all those years because he'd developed himself as a symbol of trust to you. You were just a child then, Kathleen. Children are totally vulnerable to their impressions of adults. Your mother was dead, your father was always away on business. The only person you had to look up to—to trust—was your uncle. Of course you never told anyone. You'd been brainwashed into believing that nothing bad was happening."

That's just what the counselor had said. She'd even said it was commonplace in similar situations. The most naive question touched her then: *How can people be like that? How can an adult, any adult, do something like that? To children, for God's sake? To children?*

"Sometimes people can be very evil," Maxwell answered, as though he decrypted the thought by her eyes or the look on her face.

Eventually she drifted into sleep, Maxwell gently rocking her in his arms. The dream came back the instant she closed her eyes: Naked, shivering in sweat, she lay paralyzed atop the bed. The figure leaned over her in tinted darkness. The moon stared at her.

"Embrace your hatred," eddied the woman's voice.

Kathleen could not reply.

The stack of Polaroids dropped onto her stomach. The joints of her fingers clicked as she picked them up. She squinted. She could see them this time.

The first picture showed a cigar box, like the one booked as evidence at Uncle Sammy's trial. But it was closed. The second picture showed Kathleen exactly as she was in the dream: naked on this same bed, her legs parted, paralyzed. Her skin looked garish in the light of the flashbulb. Her sweat glittered like sprinkles of crushed glass.

Third picture: The cigar box again. This time, however, its cardboard lid stood open.

Something dark was in it. Something stout, coiled.

A snake, Kathleen realized.

Now the paralysis bolted her down, plucked her eyelids open. The snake seemed huge despite the confines of the box. It seemed jammed into it.

The fourth picture showed the snake being dumped out onto the bed between her legs.

A black plastic cat clock on the wall ticked hypnotically. Eyes and tail switching back and forth. Its hands moved backward.

"Embrace your hatred," eddied the woman's voice.

In the fifth picture the snake was slithering forward.

In the sixth picture the large, pointed head was about to enter Kathleen's vagina.

(III)

"Can I blow you?" she asks.

He chuckles. "What am I gonna say? No?"

He's naked on the bed.

She's naked next to him, legs crossed.

She feels electric.

"But let me give you a back rub first. I promised you one, didn't I?"

His erection throbs. "How about *blowing* me first?"

They're in Daddy's Room. It's different now, it looks like a bedroom. "All good things to those who wait," she says. "Come on, turn over." He turns over on his belly. Sometimes she'd cry when Daddy was doing it to her, or when he let his friends do it to her. But she always cried the most when he made her watch through the mirror. His friends did horrible things to her mother. "Fire her up first," one of the men said and then they held her mother down while Daddy injected heroin into a vein in her breast and then they'd beat her mother up and all take turns fucking her and then Daddy would take her into the closet and make her watch the men and he'd put his finger into her vagina after he was finished fucking her.

—but no man will ever touch her there again.

Now she looks up at The Cross in The Window.

He's lean and muscular, a Spa Boy.

She gets up to get the massage oil.

He doesn't see her slip on the double pair of Becton-Dickinson vinyl examination gloves.

She straddles him at the small of his back, squirts on the oil.

The squirting reminds her of Daddy.

Behind her is the cabinet, the Box of Souls.

She can feel The Cross on her back.

She feels sexy and beautiful.

You're beautiful, her mother says.

"I know," she says.

"What?"

"Shhh."

She rubs the oil into his back.

Her fingers knead the slick skin, mold his shoulders, run up and down his spine.

"Does that feel good?"

"Yeah," he drones.

Her vagina is rubbing against the small of his back.

She wants to touch herself but not yet.

You're such a smart girl, her mother says from somewhere. *I'm so proud of you.*

Later, he starts to fade.

"I'm really tired," he drones.

Now she turns him over and climbs off.

"God, I'm so—"

"Try to get up," she says, her eyes earnest, inquisitive.

It's funny watching him.

He tries to lean forward, then slumps.

He tries to slide off but his legs barely move.

"What...did...you..."
She walks over and opens the closet to get her things.
She comes back with the stainless-steel tray.
"Look," she says.
She slaps him hard across the face.
His eyes are slits but she can see the terror there.
The gorgeous terror...
"Look."
The tray contains a biopsy curette.
A length of Vicryl suture.
A radial needle.
Bruns serrated shears.

Chapter 12

(I)

Maxwell wondered what she wanted out of life. *What are her dreams?* he thought. *What does she see in the future?*

He felt poisoned by the past, one relationship gone bust after another. It was part of life. He'd almost gotten married twice, but almost meant nothing at all.

His poetry was how he defined his life, and life in general. It was impulse. Without it he'd have no purpose.

He remembered saying to her last night: *Sometimes people can be very evil.* This was true. How could a person live with that? How could she trust anyone ever again?

He didn't dare wake her. All that she'd told him, her own poison spilling like a dark cascade, must've exhausted her. He got out of bed as quietly as he could, took up his clothes, and slipped out to the living room.

This was where she did her writing for the magazine, instead of the second bedroom. He wondered why. *Maybe she doesn't like enclosed places.* Or perhaps the smaller bedroom reminded her of her past.

He glanced at some papers on the desk.

> Dear Kathleen:
> When I was in college I had a lesbian affair with my roommate. I always considered it an experiment so I never gave it much thought. A year later I married a man, and I

never had any reason to question my heterosexuality. Recently we divorced, though, after 10 years, and suddenly I've become attracted to a woman at my place of work. Now I feel very disoriented about myself. Am I a lesbian?

Dear Very Disoriented:
The best way to determine your true sexuality is to first isolate the motives of your divorce. If your marriage disintegrated because of a lack of sexual interest on your part, then you may well have been repressing genuine lesbian urges for the entirety of your marriage. On the other hand, you may be using a lesbian tendency to merely escape the possibility that your marriage failed for other reasons. When love relationships fail, we often seek escape rather than acknowledgment. See a psychologist.

Maxwell wondered what it must be like to counsel others on their problems and uncertainties. He was glad he was a man; it seemed far less complicated. He felt secure that he was living as honestly as he could. His poetry wasn't an escape, but a recognition...

He put on his pants and went out on the balcony. A nice building and complex, clean; the maintenance fees must be sky-high. Even this early—8:30—the heat and humidity smothered him. He thought about Kathleen.

He didn't know what she wanted. He didn't know what she liked or disliked. He didn't know anything about her political views, her social views, her philosophy or religion. At least not really. And he didn't know how she felt about him. But he loved her.

So at least he knew something.

Am I an idiot? he wondered. His hands gripped the railing as he looked out. Yes, he loved her, he knew that. *I love Kathleen Shade,* he thought in increments. *I've known her—what?—three days?* He didn't care. It didn't matter to him. He'd fallen for women very quickly in the past and knew it was a mistake. But something told him this was different.

Providence? he wondered.

No.

Resplendence.

He rushed back into the apartment. He must get rid of everything from his past—now, right now. Poetry was his exorcism. For years he'd been seeking to write the one poem that would release him from the failed love of his past and invite him into the future. *I've got it!* he celebrated. *It's here!*

He'd never been more excited.

If he severed his past, then he could really be in love.

He could really be in love with Kathleen Shade.

The past was a crush of feelings, mostly bitterness, rage, and despair—all negatives. He believed that negativities were evil; they could never be constructive and therefore they could never make him a better person.

Resplendence! he rejoiced.

He sat down at her desk and turned on her typewriter. She wouldn't mind. He had to write it now, right here, before the moment, and its truth, evaded him.

He typed the poem, entitled "Exit," in four quick lines. He looked at it, or past it, or through it. *This is it,* he thought very slowly. His dedication to all the loves of his past. *We're all trying to escape something,* he realized.

I'm free now, he thought.

He took the poem out of the typewriter, took it out onto the hot balcony, and burned it. It would seem weird to anyone but a poet. Creating it, then burning it, made it real.

I love Kathleen Shade, he thought almost giddily.

He typed I LOVE YOU on a piece of paper in the typewriter. He put on his shirt and called a cab. He left the apartment.

Twenty minutes later the cab picked him up. When the cab dropped him off, he had no idea. How could he?

He had no idea that he had been followed all the way home by a dark blue Ford Festiva.

(II)

Brad Weston's remains had been found at 6:30 in the morning by a D.C. parking officer, a young black woman named Judith Mullins. She worked the 11 to 7 shift; her supervisor, the night before, had reassigned every Parking Section beat without explanation. "Scourge the whore blocks," he'd said at shiftchange. "Write up everything you see, regardless of the time, and call Traffic Branch immediately." "Why the change?" someone had asked. "Just do it," the supervisor had replied. So Judith Mullins did it. She wrote up every single illegally parked vehicle she could find in her new grid, a total of 16. Generally at night the mobile Parking Section officers only tagged vehicles in bus lanes and rush hour lines. These new orders didn't make much sense...

"Nissan Sentra, red," she called in on her Motorola. "Good plates." She read off the tag number. "Dave and Lee's Parking Lot, 14th and L. Nose in entry."

Judith generally cut slack on a nose in entry, so long as the entrance wasn't blocked, but orders were orders. She filled out the fluorescent-orange TB tag and was about to fix it to the car door when she noticed the puddle of blood going pasty just under the trunk.

(III)

Spence carried a Smith & Wesson Chief, a standard five-shot snub, while most everyone else carried Glocks now. The Chief was tiny, light; Spence preferred it to today's larger pieces for an absurd reason. A big gun worn under a suit jacket would bulge. He didn't care about being made, he simply didn't want his suits to look bad on him. To Spence a gun was a gun. It fired bullets. If you hit a bad guy with the bullets, the bad guy stopped doing whatever bad thing you were shooting him for. He didn't need to be lugging around some big 19-shot boat anchor and ruining the lines of his suits. *If I die because of inferior fire power,* he reasoned, *then I'll die because of inferior fire power.* End of story.

"Any run down yet?" Kohls asked.

"Another bar punk. The guy got more ass than a toilet seat. Worked for an ad firm. Some friends at his office said he was going to The Dome last night. We're grilling all the keeps and waitresses now."

Spence didn't look at the body on the slab; he didn't need to. Kohls had told him it was all the same. "She's knocking them out first," he'd said. "Doing the lips, eyes, and ears while they're unconscious, then bringing them back with Desoxyn. Tricky. She's also scrubbing their backs with isopropanol."

"Why?"

Kohls shrugged. "What's funnier is Calabrice's tox screen showed some traces of isopropanol in his blood. It doesn't figure. We're still waiting on the fourth pass from chromatography."

"Red hairs on the body?"

"Yep. One head strand, two pubes. Same broad." Kohls took a step back in the workup section. He smiled, sipping coffee. "You ready for the good news?"

"Sure," Spence said.

"Kid's wallet was wiped down, just like Calabrice. But she fucked up."

"What do you—"

"I got a latent off the wallet."

Spence stared a moment, then broke for the phone.

"Relax, Lieutenant," Kohls said. "I already called Ident, and I gave them your MSC priority. They'll call you."

Spence had never been one to show much positive emotion. He had to contain himself. *Simmons was right,* he thought. *He said she'd make a mistake, and she did.* A fingerprint could be meaningless if her prints weren't on file, but if they were...

A name, an address...a face, he thought.

"I got TSD doing the Nissan right now," Kohls added. "We'll let you know the minute we get anything."

"Thank you," Spence said. He felt…happy. There was a corpse lying beside him but he felt happy.

"She's very meticulous," Kohls went on. He set his coffee down on top of a SYSTEM 350 helium laser, which could detect fingerprints and even perfect latent pore schemes on human skin. "It's almost like a religion with her, the extremes she goes to inflict pain."

"She's a clinical psychopath," Spence said.

"You know what she did to this guy?"

Spence didn't really want to know.

"She stuck needles in his eyes. After she glued them shut and brought him back…needles, right through the eyelids into the optic nerve. Can you imagine not being able to see but feeling something like that?"

"No," Spence said. "What do you think about the Skins firing Turner? Christ, I think we need him."

"They're long needles too, like dissection pins. She's sticking them all they way down the optic canal into the brain."

Spence's mouth went dry.

"And God only knows," Kohls added, "what she's doing to their cocks before she cuts them off."

(IV)

CHAPTER TWO
NEEDLE-WORK

Deaver's Sharp/Sharp epidermal scissors. You clip open the scrotum, a 1-inch lateral cut. Through the cut you pop out the raw testicles. There's very little bleeding. It's strange to look at. You expect the colors to be different. The exposed testes are whitish because they are covered by a fibrous sheath called the tunica. The epididymis looks like microscopic angel hair pasta. The remaining subcutaneous tissue looks off-yellow, a pale squash color, with tiny dark lines like threads. The entire mass glistens hanging out of the scrotal sac. He's still quite alive. His hips shiver steadily but that's all they can do is shiver. His wrists and ankles are handcuffed to the bedposts. His back, shoulders, and waist are secured by restraints to a field traction board made of fiberglass. And in addition to that you've immobilized his hips with leather Bard-Parker pelvic restraints. You're very thorough. The 100mgs of Desoxyn will make sure that he doesn't pass out from the pain. You will make him feel everything. He must feel everything. He must. It's all hanging there right in front of your face. It shivers. You gently squeeze the raw left ball in your fingers. It feels warm, wet. The network of tiny blood vessels make it pulse. Ethicon makes a lot of different kinds of needles. Most of them are small and curved for sewing up incisions. But they also make one called a KS. The KS is long and straight like a hat pin. You have a whole box of them. *Make him feel,* your mother tells you. Your mother is standing by The Window. Behind her you can see The Cross. "Okay," you say. You methodically push about a dozen of the KS needles through the left testicle. Each time you plant a needle, he screams. Each scream is like an explosion in his throat that goes nowhere because his lips are sewn shut. You let him lie there smothered in pain, roaring. Then you take all the needles out. You wait 10 minutes and have a glass of wine. You let him think it's over. Then you stick the needles back in all over again. Now there's blood but still very little. You leave the needles in the left testicle. It looks like a weird porcupine. But there are still plenty of nerves left. There are still plenty of things left for his devil to feel. You go on to the right testicle. You clasp it in a pair of Ballenger tonsil forceps. Then, with an Arista #11 scalpel, you begin to dissect it. Very little blood oozes out. The pain sounds like a muffled engine in his throat. The inside of the ball looks grayish like cooked meat. Suddenly this is dull. You slice many long grooves into the testicle, stick some KS needles into it, then leave it alone. The balls are finished so you go on. *Do his devil now,* your mother says. The pain and terror have shrunk the penis to a nub like it's trying to retreat into the groin. "You can't get away from me," you say. You hold it up with forceps, stretch it out straight, and begin sticking needles into the shriveled glans. You stick one all the way down the urethra. Each insertion causes a sound in his throat like a dog barking. This is beautiful, giving his devil so much to feel. *It's beautiful!* your mother says. You're getting hot now. You want to touch yourself, but not yet. You snip off all the topical skin from the shaft with the little Deaver's snippers, then you stick more needles into the shaft, up under the rim of the glans, anywhere. You stick needles under his fingernails and toenails. You stick needles into his nipples, and into his navel. He won't last much longer so you straddle his chest. You're sitting on his chest. You stick needles into his eyes through the sealed eyelids, hunting for the optic ingress. You know when you've found it because the needles sink in much deeper and go deep into his brain. A little while later he dies. Then you have some more wine. You walk around in the quiet room, Daddy's Room. Your mother is gone. You look out The Window and you see The Cross. It reminds you of something but you never know what. Later you take all the needles out. You sterilize them in the little autoclave. Then you cut off his cock and balls with your pair of Bruns serrated plaster shears.

She reads it one more time to make sure it's good.
She's sure she got rid of him good.

She thinks her tricks will work so she can go on and on.

She wonders what Kathleen Shade will think when she sees this new chapter.

I hope she likes it, she thinks.

This morning she drove by Kathleen Shade's apartment and she saw a man with long blond hair standing on her balcony.

A little later a cab came by and picked him up.

She followed the cab.

She can't let Kathleen Shade be corrupted.

Now she knows where the blond man lives.

I'm so proud of you, her mother says.

"I'll visit the blond man soon," she says.

Chapter 13

(I)

Spence's office seemed smaller, and he seemed larger: a well-dressed, dispassionate giant. His eyes reminded Kathleen of chips of ice. *It's like being in a room with a golem,* she thought.

"This is disgraceful," he said.

"Look, you're the one who told me to bring in anything from the killer," Kathleen objected.

"No, I told you to call me. I told you I'd send an evidence technician to pick it up. I told you not to touch anything you think might be from the killer. Not only did you touch it, you opened it, you handled it, you got your fingerprints all over it. This is ruined."

"I have a right to open my own mail," she countered. She had to lie a little, didn't she? "How am I supposed to know if a letter's from a killer or not? I have my column to write. It's my job. I don't have time to call you every time I get correspondence, Lieutenant. I don't have time to wait for some *evidence technician.*"

"When did you get this?"

"Yesterday."

"From your carrier in New York?"

"No," she said.

"What do you mean no?"

"The word denotes a negation, denial, or disagreement," Kathleen told him. "It's an adverb."

Spence's jaw set like a brick. He closed his eyes for a moment. "You're telling me that the killer mailed this to your home address?"

"She didn't mail it. She taped it to my front door."

"My God." Spence tapped his blotter, a Morse code for his thoughts. "You told me your address was unlisted."

"It is," Kathleen said.

"Then how did the killer get it?"

"I don't know. Ask her."

"I should bust you," Spence said. "You've withheld critical investigative data for over 24 hours."

"And let me tell you something," she went on. She knew his threats were idle. He couldn't touch her. "I don't appreciate you harassing my acquaintances."

"Acquaintances? You mean Maxwell Platt? A man you slept with only hours after meeting him?"

"You have no right to invade my privacy and sabotage my romantic life."

"It sounds like a one-night stand to me, a cheap pickup."

He always did this. He always went out of his way to rile her up, to offend her, to insult her. Now he was implying she was promiscuous. *Don't react,* she thought.

"And it's interesting that you chose Jonah and the Whale to take him for drinks. Research, right?" Spence smiled. "For your book about the killer?"

"I can't believe you had me followed," Kathleen evaded the remark. "They don't even do that in Russia anymore."

"It was for your protection." Spence creaked back in his chair; his white dress shirt stretched across the enormous chest. "You seem to keep forgetting that the chief function of a police department revolves around the protection of citizens. I want you to find someplace else to live for the time being. I'm going to put a female decoy officer in your apartment. What's your dress size? 12? 14?"

Kathleen's teeth ticked together. Withholding her rage felt like trying to reel in a huge fish on high seas. Was there no limit to Spence's insolence? "You're a prick, Lieutenant," she said. "Do you know that? You're an absolute prick."

Spence blinked in confusion. "Did I say something wrong? I need to know your—" Then he paused. "Oh. I wasn't implying that you're overweight. Is that what you thought? No, no. I have to assign a decoy officer who's similarly proportioned to you. That's why I need to know your dress size."

Kathleen's size, incidentally, was 8. "That's crap, Lieutenant. And it doesn't matter anyway because you're not putting anyone in my apartment."

Spence sighed. "Maybe it hasn't occurred to you, but you're in a quite a bit of danger. Read my lips. The killer knows where you live. She could come to your apartment and kill you."

"She won't kill me," Kathleen felt assured. "She needs me, remember?"

"Of course. For the bestseller. And due to that you're convinced she'd never want to harm you? How intelligent a conclusion is that? She's pathological."

"Forget it. No way. I won't permit it."

Spence shook his head. "Look, I'm going to have an undercover officer in your parking lot anyway. There's going to be someone watching your building round the clock. If you let me put somebody inside your apartment, we have a much greater chance of apprehending the killer."

"No," Kathleen said flatly. "I'm not going to be forced to move out of my home because of a nut. It's that simple."

Spence smiled again. It was unnerving the way he smiled; the gesture seemed inhuman on the already inhuman, blank face. Kathleen wondered if he had ever smiled in genuine good will in his life, and doubted it. "You don't put on a very good show," he said. "The reason you're not going to cooperate is obvious. You don't want us to catch her, not yet. Not until she's given you enough profile material for your book."

Kathleen thought of landslides, of cliffs falling. Her outrage, her absolute loathe, felt like a high fever. "You're so ignorant I'm not even going to respond to that," she said.

"It's true and you know it." He withdrew a thin cardboard box from his desk and slid it over to her. The box read CRIMINAL RESEARCH PRODUCTS, LTD. Sample Pair, Size Medium. "Do you think you could at least cooperate to the extent of wearing these whenever you open correspondence from the killer? Would that be too much trouble? They're polymer evidence gloves, so you won't get your fingerprints all over the evidence and further disrupt our efforts."

Kathleen put the box in her purse. She wished she could put Spence in her purse, and button him up. "I'm happy to oblige," she mocked.

"Use the gloves, photocopy the material, and bring it to me immediately."

"You should read that material," she suggested, pointing to the Xerox of *Initiatory Rites* and *Childhood Memories*. "In all your harping about evidence, you haven't even looked at it."

"You think it will distress me, unsettle me."

"I know it will, Lieutenant."

"I've seen floaters pulled out of the Anacostia. A floater is a water-bound corpse. Maggots and putrefactive gas make them buoyant. I've seen crack stools hung upside down and gutted like deer. When I was a cadet, a porno theater on Vermont Avenue burned down with about 40 people inside. The exit door was chained from the outside. The bodies were essentially a single congealed mass. They were cooked together. It was my job to separate them."

"Should I stand up and applaud?" Kathleen asked. "Just read the material, Lieutenant. I'll wait."

Spence's CRT screen blinked amber rap sheets. Behind him a picture of a young man in a police hat hung on the wall. The boy looked youthful, innocent, but Kathleen immediately recognized the stoic stare. It was Spence. She wondered if he had a wife, a family, yet she doubted he had either. *Solitude incarnate,* she thought. *The existential triumphant.*

What does he do on Christmas? she wondered, adjusting her hem. *What does he do for fun? Does he go out with friends?* She could not picture a man like Spence with friends. He would consider friends a weakness, wouldn't he? His only friend, she guessed, was his job. His function.

"Jesus," Spence whispered.

The golem quails, Kathleen thought.

The whisper had sounded stark, desperate. He read on through the killer's manuscript, blanching. Every so often he'd wince, though she knew he was making every effort not to. Spence was not a man who felt comfortable revealing his humanity.

"Interesting," he eventually said. He set the sheaf of papers aside.

"That's all? Interesting?"

"It should be very helpful in determining the details of the killer's psychiatric profile," Spence went on. "Our forensic psychiatrist should have a hay day. I'll admit, though. It's probably the most disgusting thing I've ever read. But it's also quite sad."

"Yes, it is," Kathleen agreed. "How is the investigation coming? Any leads?"

"No," Spence said.

Kathleen's nose crinkled as if at a funny smell. She'd been looking right at his face when he'd replied. "Why do I have this odd feeling that you're lying?"

"Because you're a renegade militant feminist," Spence answered. "It is your intractable opinion that all men, uniformly, are liars. That's sad too. Everybody, everybody in the world, has insecurities. It's sad that you've let yours ferment into an unrelenting, distrustful philosophical hostility."

"May I leave now?" Kathleen said. "I mean, is there any reason why I should continue to sit here and be insulted by you?"

"No," Spence said. "There's no reason at all."

Kathleen grabbed her purse and stood up. Her dislike for Spence made her feel clammy. "Have a good day, Lieutenant," she said with no real meaning at all.

"Are you going to mention me in your book?" the policeman asked.

"Oh, you can rest assured I will."

"How are you going to embark?"

"What?" she said, now weary just hearing his voice.

"I mean how are you going to put the book together? What, you're going to publish the killer's writings and then make your own commentary?"

These were surprising inquiries. "I'm going to characterize the killer by a sociological, psychiatric, and subjective analysis, and yes I'll also publish her writings in conjunction. When you catch her of course I'll interview her. My book will show all of her facets. The objectified woman, the innocent abused child, and the demented psychopath."

"And, naturally, the parities," Spence added.

"What?"

"The similarities between yourself and the killer. The book would never be complete without that, right? And it would certainly never be honest."

Kathleen made no reply. She stood in the doorway, her purse dangling—looking at him.

Spence looked back at her for an irreducible moment. Then he picked up a pen and proceeded with his paperwork as if Kathleen weren't there at all.

· · · · ·

She left in a haze of feelings, none of which were positive, a drone in her head. No, there were no limits to Spence's concerted efforts to injure her. *Why?* she wondered all the way out of the huge building. *It's not logical.* Spence was trying to catch a killer; he was not maintaining a constructive relationship with Kathleen. And why had he lied earlier? The reason eluded her, yet Kathleen felt certain he'd lied in response to her question about leads. Men frequently lied open-faced—Kathleen's romantic past provided an indisputable testament. Thinking further back, all of Uncle Sammy's promises had been made with an identical expression. Spence's arcane strategy irked her. Did he think that subtle harassment would make her more eager to cooperate with him? *Oh, he'll be in the book all right,* she vowed to herself. *You can bet on that, Lieutenant.*

Traffic jammed Indiana Avenue; it would take forever to get out. *Spence, Spence,* her thoughts continued to tap at her. *Parity,* she thought. The steering wheel baked in her hands, nearly too hot to hold. A great swordblade of sun glared across the windshield. What had Spence said? *And, naturally, the parities... The similarities between yourself and the killer.* Spence obsessed over reminding her of the part of her past that she needed to forget in order to remain whole. He felt driven, for some reason, to sufficiently hurt her, to rub her face in the facts that both she and the killer were sexually abused as children.

Was she beginning to see his psychology? Spence steeped insults and accusations on her, and then pitted her against them. A good example was his implication that her book would not be honest without her own admission of being sexually abused herself. Spence's cruelty was diabolical. Suddenly she realized, *He's going out of his way to accuse me of being a phony because he knows the accusation will keep me involved.*

Was it that simple?

Crossing 6th and C Street, a quick glance showed her the District Courthouse. Uncle Sammy, in a cheap brown suit, loped down the stone steps until Kathleen blinked at the wheel. There he was again, walking into a toy shop. Down the next block a brunette with snow white teeth smiled on a poster ad for Salem Lights, plastered inside a bus portico. A person sitting on the bench lowered a *Washingtonian*: Uncle Sammy. The heat stuck his thin brown hair to his forehead. He stared at her...

Almost, almost. Alm— Here.

Kathleen blinked the mirage away and drove on. *Sleepytime,* Sammy had always called his visits to her childhood bedroom. *It's Sleepytime, Kathy.* It was always from behind, so she couldn't see him, nor his genitals. This struck her oddly now: in the innumerable ways he'd penetrated her, she'd never fully seen his erection. She'd glimpsed it only once; when she was little she'd had a stuffed toy rabbit named Horace, and she remembered seeing Uncle Sammy wipe his penis off with it one night when he thought she'd fallen asleep.

Heat hung in the air; she could see it. Spence's distractions had made her forget all about Maxwell. *Is it over already?* she wondered. Somehow the question seemed coldly objective. He'd left this morning without waking her, without even leaving a note. She hated to think how uncomfortable things must've been for him last night. Yet he'd seemed so caring, so interested in helping her. *I freaked out right in front of him,* she reminded herself. How could she expect Maxwell to be at ease with all the baggage of her past?

The phone began to ring when she stepped into her apartment; she rushed to it. *Maxwell!* she thought. "Kathleen?" came a familiar female voice. It was her editor at *'90s Woman*. "Oh, hi," Kathleen said.

"Is there a problem?"

"Well, no."

"You're usually a week early with your column," the editor told her. "The next issue goes to press in three days. It's in the mail, right? Please say it's in the mail."

The phone felt numb against her ear. *Oh, no,* she realized. "It's not in the mail," she confessed. "I'm sorry. I forgot."

The long silence revealed her boss' disappointment. "We pride ourselves here at *'90s Woman* on being a very professional publication. I realize your column is quite popular but that does us little good if your miss your deadline."

Quit harping, she thought. *I haven't missed my goddamn deadline.* "I'll Express Mail it to you in the morning, okay? It's all done, I just kind of forgot. I've had a lot going on the past week."

"I see. Please make sure it's on my desk by deadline."

The connection severed. *Your magazine would be squat without me,* Kathleen told herself, or at least tried to. She didn't blame herself, she blamed Spence, Uncle Sammy, the killer—every negative distraction. She kicked off her shoes, shrugged out of the hot dress, and went to her desk to get the submission together. She looked down, then, and noticed the index card in her typewriter.

Maxwell left a note after all. The thought elated her, until she reeled it out of the platen and read it.

I LOVE YOU

The three words terrified her.

Chapter 14

(I)

Kathleen deliberated for hours. Men had said they'd loved her in the past, and she knew they were lying. In bra and panties she sat baking in the hot apartment. Her typewriter hummed. She couldn't figure it. *Why am I mad?* she asked herself. *Just because all those other men lied doesn't mean Maxwell is.* This was a fair judgment. *How come I don't feel fair?*

She knew she'd have to call him, to talk, but she pursued any excuse not to. Work on the book for a little while. She wasn't fooling herself, she was only trying to. Not calling Maxwell was an escape, an exit.

Unbidden, she pushed the REPRINT code on the typewriter. He'd typed the note—perhaps he'd typed something else. The $1000 typewriter had a small memory for making line corrections. As suspected, the machine typed out by itself:

EXIT by Maxwell Platt

Resplendence is truth, yet it's escaped me somehow,
and I don't even remember what you look like now.
But in the trees, in the clouds, in the heavens above
even the angels are burning up with all my love.

Another poem entitled "Exit." Kathleen read it over and over. *It's not about me,* she thought. That much was clear. *It's about someone else, or* a lot of people. It was about the love in his past. A moment ago she'd been thinking about escapes, about exits. *Is this his escape?* Yes, she thought it must be. Was Maxwell, through his poetry, making an exit from his past so that he could proceed into the future?

Why can't I do that? she wondered.

She picked up the phone, dialed at once. "Maxwell, this is Kathleen."

"Hi," he said. "How was your day?"

"All right."

"I hope you're feeling better."

At first she didn't know what he meant, but then she remembered the debacle of last night. "Yes," she said. Her thoughts hovered. "I read your poem."

The pause gaped. "That's impossible," he claimed. "I burned it on your balcony."

She glanced out the slider and noted ashes on the cement. She frowned. "My typewriter has a memory for corrections."

"Oh," he said.

Another gaping pause. "It's not about me, is it?"

"No."

I guess I know him better than I thought. "I also read your note."

This third pause seemed to drip. "You don't sound very happy."

"We need to talk," was all she said.

"Okay, we can do that. I'd like to."

"Not on the phone. We'll go out to dinner or something, and we'll talk. I'll pick you up at 7:30."

"Okay," Maxwell said.

"'Bye."

The driest phone conversation of my life, she concluded. And how must he feel? She felt even drier showering and then getting dressed, her arms and legs like putty as she put on her underthings. The sun blazed in the slider, a face of fire. How could she possibly nail down her feelings? *I don't even know what my feelings are.*

She sat and waited for time to pass. She smoked her hourly Now 100, listening to the radio shrink's show. *More parity,* she realized. She and the radio shrink had essentially the same jobs: counseling the desperate, the confused and the disillusioned. Yet Kathleen could only relate as a listener. "...I've been dating him for over three years," another listener was saying. Their voices always sounded distant, despairing. "I've always loved him, and I've always wanted to be married to him."

"Yes, go on," said the radio shrink.

"But in all the time we've been seeing each other, he's never said he loved me. He's never said anything that would indicate he wants a real future with me."

"And that depresses you," asserted the radio shrink.

"No!" the caller exclaimed. "Because this morning he finally did. He finally did say that he loved me. He asked me to marry him."

"And let me guess," the shrink postulated. "Now you don't know how you feel."

"Right. Exactly. When he finally told me what I've wanted to hear all these years, I turned into a block of ice. I don't even know if I want to see him anymore." The caller sobbed. "None of it makes any sense."

"Your dilemma is a common one, believe it or not," the response drifted frailly through static. "It's much more than the contrived case of cyclic desire, that when we get what we want, we don't want it anymore. In your instance, though I don't know you, I'd say that you've been hurt, misled, or deceived so thoroughly in the past that your psychological makeup has erected a subconscious defense mechanism. Your psyche sets off an alarm—technically it's called a 'biogenic-amine fulfillment shift'—when a romantic situation approaches a commitment phase. Consciously you want love, you want marriage. Unconsciously, however, your psyche throws in a mental monkey wrench, so to speak, to ruin a situation which could lead to further heartbreak and turmoil..."

Kathleen stared limply at the radio.

(II)

"...but I was able to get a rundown on the suture material," Kohls was saying as the sun went down. Spence drove. Kohls rode shotgun. "PMMA it's called, synthetic micronic twine. Brand name's Vicryl, or I should say the stock name. Took me all day to find that out."

Spence looked at him. "Did you call the manufacturer, find out which—"

"To find out which hospitals buy that brand?" Kohls finished. "Of course I did. And you know what? You know how many hospitals buy that brand?"

Spence frowned. "Every—"

"That's right," Kohls laughed. "Every fucking hospital in the country. Bummer, ain't it?"

Spence rounded St. Thomas Circle in the unmarked. Two 3rd District plainclothes followed him in another unmarked, and behind them came a TSD van full of bad boys. "You may have busted the whole case," Spence informed his companion. "How long it take you to find the print on Weston's body?"

"About a minute and a half. Tell me about our girl."

Spence slipped him the girl's booking photo: fiery perfectly straight red hair, deep green eyes, and a pretty face were it not for a tiny harelip. "Willet, Heather, B., four busts for soliciting. High school dropout. She's an orphan. Worked the Starlight Inn, Good Guys, Dawn Rose, and some of the other P.G. County strip clubs before she decided to peddle her ass."

"Sounds like she got a monkey on her back in the clubs," Kohls hypothesized. "You get the r.i.a. back yet on the hair?"

"Yeah, but just PCP and pot. No crack, no skag, nothing pharmaceutical. Simmons was right. Nutritionally depleted, typical pross. Probably eats one Big Mac and fries a day at the 14th and K Micky D's."

"Place of residence on the rap sheet says College Park," Kohls observed. "How come we're heading lower Northwest?"

"That address is phony. We're going to go have a little chat with her pimp."

"There's something, though..." Kohls hesitated. He lit a cigarette off the one he'd just smoked down. All evidence techs chained-smoked one their way to a possible workup scene. Once they got there, smoking was forbidden. "Something..."

"I know," Spence agreed. "The medical angle. What's a streetwalker doing with acute medical knowledge, and access to hospital supplies?"

"Maybe she's got funny friends. Maybe her pimp's a kink."

"Maybe," Spence said. He eyed the big gothic church just off the circle, and the great steepled cross. *The Cross*, he recalled from the killer's passages. It seemed to be a point of reference, an obsessional one. Simmons had said she had monomanic symbol obsessions. The Cross. What did it mean?

Is it this cross? Spence wondered. *This cross right here, on this church?*

"Who's her pimp by the way?"

"Tyrone Chaplin," Spence said.

"Ah, 'Rome," Kohls recognized, snorting smoke. "The guys at POU say he's a pretty nice guy as far as pimps go. Say he kicks girls out who rip-off johns."

Spence didn't care. "I don't care if he's the nicest guy in the world," he said. "One of his hookers might be a serial killer. I want her."

Nightfall came like a slow bleed. Dented and stripped cars lined the sodium-lit street. The rowhouses looked like abandoned fortresses: boarded up, bricks streaked by age and decay. The few that were occupied had barred doors and windows. That mystical entity known as "The Mob" owned all these blocks and domiciles. There really was still a mob. Phony real estate companies hidden by financial "pyramids" worked integrally with the prostitution networks and the fading heroin trade. Soon crack cocaine and crystal meth would push everything out, but until then...

"There's his wheels," Spence said. A white BMW, four door. Pink Cadillacs and cheetah-fur-lined seats were a thing of the past. "You got a piece?"

"I'm a forensics tech," Kohls countered, "not Wyatt Earp. What I need a piece for?"

"In case somebody tries to kill you." Spence unlocked his glove box and gave Kohls his department-issued Glock 17.

"Where's the safety on this thing?"

"Don't ask me," Spence laughed. "Why do you think I carry a revolver? Just stick it in your pants and hope you can figure it out if someone starts popping caps."

"Great. That's just great."

Vehicle doors chunked behind them when they got out. "You two," Spence directed the plainclothes. "Get your tin in plain sight and go around back in case things get hairy. Grab anyone who comes out." Then he addressed the TSD men; they weren't technicians like Kohls, they were what parlance referred to as Goons, big guys for moving bodies, busting doors, taking parts off cars. "Follow us up," Spence said.

"Nice neighborhood," Kohls remarked. Trash littered scrub front yards, broken glass glittered in dry grass. The street wafted a familiar coalescence of scents: fried food, cooling sun-cooked garbage, and, strangely, paint. Tyrone Chaplin's rowhouse stood dilapidated in the yellow street light. Red paint had blistered on its bricks.

Spence and Kohls walked up the steps. When Spence knocked, the door opened against three burglar chains almost at once. Spence stuck his badge and ID in the gap. "I'm Lieutenant Jeffrey Spence, D.C. Police. I'd like to talk to you."

"Talk to who?" asked a defiant black face.

"You," Spence said. "Tyrone Chaplin."

"He's not in."

"Open up, Mr. Chaplin. I have a dated warrant from the D.C. Magistrate to search this premise. Either open the door, or I'll knock it down."

"You and whose army?"

Spence was glad he'd said that, for at the same time his three bulldogs congregated at the bottom of the steps. They all wore bright-red utility shirts emblazoned with METROPOLITAN POLICE TECHNICAL SERVICES DIVISION. Two carried aluminum field kits in fists the size of croquet balls. The third calmly sported a handled steel bar with a big square steel block at one end—a portable door-ram.

"Like I said," Chaplin changed his tune. "Come on in. This door cost 1,500 bucks." He took off the chains. Spence and his crew walked into a nice foyer which led to a well-furnitured living room. Nice throw rugs, nice half-paneled walls, nice framed prints. Outside looked like a typical tenement. Inside looked like typical middle-class home.

Chaplin turned off the stereo; Spence recognized Beethoven's Piano Concerto #2. *Alfred Brendel,* he noted. Chaplin himself was more proof that the average conception of a pimp was largely stereotype. No gold chains, gold rings, no flamboyant clothes. Chaplin wore Gucci's, quality Italian gray slacks, and a hand-made shirt, which left Spence a little disillusioned. *This pimp wears better clothes than me,* Spence realized. *I should ask him where he shops.*

"You want a beer, Lieutenant?"

"No thank you," Spence said. "Let's be nice about this, all right? I have a warrant, which means my men search your place whether you like it or not."

Chaplin sat down in a plush, buttoned armchair. He opened a can of St. Ide's Malt Liquor. "Go ahead. I keep the machine guns and cocaine in a warehouse on New York Avenue."

At least he's got a sense of humor, Spence thought but did not allow himself to laugh. Kohls and his three goons branched off.

Spence went on, standing, "I want to ask you some specific questions, and I need you to give me specific answers. If you bullshit me, I'll take you to headquarters for more intensive questioning."

Chaplin blinked and rapidly shook his head. "Did I wake up in Iran? Did someone rescind the Constitution?"

"I want to know about one of your prostitutes. Heather B. Willet, Caucasian, red hair, 26 years old."

"She dead? Creamy?"

"Who?"

"We call her Creamy. She'd got gorgeous, creamy-white skin, Lieutenant. White as snow and not a pock on her. She's quite beautiful. All my girls are. Would you like to see some of them? I can arrange it."

"Why did you ask if Creamy was dead?"

"Why else would some bad-news-lookin' white cop like you be here?"

"Just answer the question."

Chaplin had bright, intelligent eyes and an intense face like an activist or something. "First of all, I don't want you to think of me as a pimp. I'm a service manager. I provide a service."

"But the service you provide, Mr. Chaplin, is against the law."

"So is letting your dog poop on the sidewalk. So is jaywalking. You ever jaywalked, Lieutenant?"

"No," Spence said. He probably hadn't.

Chaplin made gestures with his hands. "I got an attrition rate here like about 25%, like most any business. Creamy was typical top drawer. You see it a lot."

Top drawer, oddly, meant a prostitute of low seniority or performance status. A bottom-drawer girl, on the other hand, was the best a pimp had to offer.

"I'm not a slaver, Lieutenant. Some guys out there, sure, but not me.

All my girls are clean; they're good girls. If a girl wants to work for me, and she meets my criteria, then I let her work for me. When one of my girls decides she doesn't want to work for me, then I let her go. Like any businessman, I don't want disgruntled employees. You got a girl who's unhappy, she fucks up. Bad for business. A girl wants to fly, I let her fly. A girl thinks she can do better with someone else, I let her work for someone else."

"What's this got to do with Heather B.— With Creamy?"

"Really top drawer. Beautiful, sure, like I said. She was really beautiful bodywise." Chaplin shrugged. "But she wasn't very good. Didn't turn much business, not aggressive, not too good at selling her attributes. Lot of girls think they'll rake big money working the street, but the truth is it's hard work. Lot of girls can't cut the trade once they're out there."

"I still don't see what this has to do with—"

"She booked," Chaplin said. "Flew the coop about two weeks ago or so. You walk in here with your storm troopers so I figure she got into some trouble, got herself killed."

"Did she discuss it with you?"

"Discuss what?"

"Her decision to leave."

"No, no. She just up and left. Disappeared. Didn't even come back for her things. What, you expect a working girl to put two-weeks' notice?"

Throughout Chaplin's monologue, Spence was careful to watch his face, as Simmons had taught him. Tarsal plate fluctuation—the muscles beneath the top eyelids—usually indicated a negative impulse, or a lie. Chaplin held the beer can in his right hand; statistically his eyeline would drift left when lying. Yet Chaplin exhibited none of these characteristics. It was almost a disappointment. *He's not bullshitting,* Spence concluded.

"Did she live here?"

Chaplin smirked broadly. "None of my girls crib here. Most of them have their own apartments, Greenbelt, College Park, Bladensburg. They make livings, Lieutenant. They have cars. They drive to and from work every day just like you. New girls, or slow learners, I crib myself 'til they can get on their feet in the trade. I gotta a rowhouse two blocks down. That's where Creamy lived, with three other girls." Chaplin scribbled the address down on the back of a lawyer's business card. "You want to send your motley crew down there, fine. All my girls are clean. You find any drugs, let me know. I'll give them their walking papers."

Spence found it hard not to like Chaplin. It was hard to exhibit himself as an authority figure. "So your girls don't do drugs?"

"Hell, no. I mean maybe a little crank or pot when you can get it. But none of the tough stuff. You don't believe me, why should I give a shit? I don't want none of that crack shit in my stable. And any girls who fire up, they're out the door. Needle marks on a girl are bad for business, and they don't exactly make for a positive public sensibility these days." Chaplin lounged back, complacent, articulate. "A guy like you, prim, proper, John Law, you probably got me nailed as a bad guy because I happen to provide a mutually agreeable service that's against the law. Crack, skag, ice—that's against the law too, but there's a big difference between that and sexual services rendered between two consenting adults. You ask me, you ought to take all these drug people, line them up along a brick wall, and kill them. I believe that hard drugs are evil; that's why I won't touch a girl who's into them. If I worked girls who were strung out or cokeheads, I'd be just as bad as the assholes who sell the shit to 9-year-olds on the playground." Chaplin shrugged, sipped his St. Ide's. "That's how I feel. You don't believe me, you think I'm feeding you a line? That's too bad."

A pimp with ethics? Spence wondered.

"What the fuck?" Chaplin, frowning, got up and walked back to the kitchen, glaring out. "Hey, your men Shemp and Larry just set off the motion-detector lights in my back yard. Come on, Lieutenant. This is my home, not a southeast hardhouse."

Spence rolled his eyes. He could see the two 3D plainclothes standing astonished in the floodlit back yard. "Just a precaution," he said, thinking *Keystone Cops*. Kohls and the three TSD re-emerged with their field kits. "Place is clean," Kohls told him. "It's just a house." Spence gave him the card with the address for Heather B. Willet's "crib," along with the warrant. "I'll be down in a few minutes," he said.

"Later, boys," Chaplin said as they were leaving. "You want to party with some pretty ladies, you ask for 'Rome."

"Back to Creamy," Spence said.

"Oh, right. Like I said, she booked. Happens all the time."

"She a kink?"

"No. None of my girls are. If a guy gets off on being tied up and walked on by high heels, I tell him to go to Miss Wanda's Massage Parlor. My girls don't do kinks. It's too dangerous."

"Did Creamy ever work in a hospital or a hospital supplier?"

Chaplin set the beer down, making a face. "How should I know? All I know is she worked some tittie bars before she hooked up with me."

This was going nowhere. "What about her father? You know anything about her father? Her mother?"

"Hey, man, a girl's family life is her own business. She didn't tell me nothing about that, and I didn't ask."

"She have any wild friends? Weirdos? Like that?"

"As far as I know, she didn't have any friends. Pretty much a loner. Quiet. And like I said she was top drawer, never really knew what she was doing. All I can tell you about her is that she got four busts, two

PBJ's, two suspended sentences, which I'm sure you already know. And she was beautiful. She had a little harelip you could barely see, but a body like angelfood cake. That girl looked *good* on the street, I can tell you. She could put wood on a monk."

"You know if she was religious? You know of any reason why crosses would have any special meaning to her?"

"She ain't a vampire, if that's what you mean." Chaplin laughed. "These are some freaky questions. You gonna tell me what's going on?"

"No," Spence said. "I can't." He left his card. "Please call me if you see her. And let me ask you one more thing... Who's your clothier?"

(III)

"So where are we going?" Maxwell asked.

Kathleen pulled the T-Bird out onto P Street, and nearly got hit by a cab whipping into the Omni Hotel. "Inconsiderate dick!" she yelled.

"Who? Me?" Maxwell asked.

"No," she droned.

"So you're in one of your better moods tonight, I see."

"Don't give me a load of shit, Maxwell," she said very coolly. She felt tempered, ticking. Her hands were clammy on the wheel. Her emotions felt like thread unwinding, each fiber flying in a different direction.

"So what's new?" he said once they got going.

"Nothing. Not really."

Not really? She couldn't get Spence off her mind; he was one of the threads. *Something must be happening,* she concluded. Had he found any more victims? If not, then why did he persist strong-arming her? *There must be a reason,* she thought. Spence knew more than he was telling.

Maxwell crooked his arm out the window. His fine blond hair blew around, and he was smiling. Georgetown pedestrians milled happily in their droves. Kathleen caught herself examining girls who waited at each crosswalk, and she dismally concluded that almost every single one was better-looking than her. Most were trim young Washingtonians in traditional summer yuppie garb. Sandals, shorts, loose, pretty blouses. *I'm a dinosaur,* she thought. *Why can't I look like those girls?*

Last night, before what she could now only describe as a breakdown, Maxwell had told her she was beautiful. And today he'd left a note that said he loved her. These were nice things to hear. *Maybe I'm just not a nice person,* she reflected. Maybe that's why she didn't feel good.

She parked in a back pay lot on Wisconsin Avenue. Maxwell went to pay the attendant. "I'll pay," Kathleen said. "No," he countered. "It's only fair that I pay for parking, since you're paying for dinner." He laughed, his hair sifting. "I'm broke."

Walking down the street, he reached to hold her hand but she bogusly diddled with her purse.

"So where did you say we were going?"

"Sushi," she said.

"Sushi. Yes."

"You like sushi, Maxwell."

"Do I? I mean, I'm not complaining. I'll try anything once."

"You'll like it. Trust me," she said.

A few minutes later they were sitting up at the bar before a long glass case of multi-colored slabs of fish. A white-socked waitress in a kimono asked for their drink orders. "Two Asahi Drys," Kathleen said. "The big bottles." Behind the bar, the sushi man looked like a punk rock Tojo. Kathleen ordered expertly: "Two orders maguro, two orders toro, two orders amaebi, two orders ika, two orders ikura with quail eggs, two orders uni." The sushi man nodded and went to work.

"Wow, you really know your way around sushi," Maxwell commented.

"I come here all the time."

"Special first." The sushi man leaned over the bar and placed a plate of fried shrimp heads between them. Maxwell leered. The waitress returned with their beers and set a little green tray beside each of them. "I don't smoke," Maxwell said. The sushi man guttered laughter.

"That's not an ashtray, Maxwell," Kathleen told him. "You mix your soy sauce and wasabi in it."

"I knew that," Maxwell said. He attempted to pick up a shrimp head with his chopsticks. The shrimp head flicked to the floor. "Can't take me anywhere, huh?" he said.

She showed him how to use the sticks, not to much avail.

"I read somewhere that certain amino acids in raw fish increase the sex drive," Maxwell pointed out.

"True," the sushi man agreed and set an order between them. "Make you *amorous*." He guttered more laughter, a keen light in his eyes.

"Maxwell," Kathleen groaned. "You don't pour the soy sauce on the fish, you put it in the little dish, and dip the fish."

"I knew that," Maxwell said. "Weren't we going to talk about something tonight?"

"Yeah." Kathleen dipped the end of her piece of maguro into the soy sauce and ate it whole. Maxwell followed suit. "Hey, this is pretty good," he said. "What was it we were going to talk about?"

"Maxwell, I—"

"Look, look!" he enthused. He'd actually managed to needle a shrimp head in the sticks. Before he got it into his mouth, though, it flicked to the floor.

"Maxwell, you're wasting perfectly good shrimp heads," Kathleen complained.

The sushi man guttered laughter.

"Yes, admittedly I am," Maxwell agreed. "But that does not dissuade the irrevocable fact that I love you."

Here it is. Kathleen couldn't think of a response just then. She stared at her sushi, at her beer. She stared at her life.

"Yet you seem to be very bothered by that," Maxwell went on. "If we don't talk about it, we'll never get anywhere."

"Maxwell—" She sighed, looked up, looked down. She looked everywhere but at him. "We haven't even known each other a week." The sushi man busily prepared their orders of ikura, cracking the quail eggs over them, but she could tell he was eavesdropping. She lowered her voice to a whisper. "You can't know that. You can't know you love someone you haven't even known a week."

"Did a burning bush tell you that?" Maxwell asked. "What, did Charlton Heston come down off a mountain with that in his arms? Thou can't lovest if thou only knowest each other a week?"

"Don't be a smartass, Maxwell."

Maxwell shrugged. "Why not? I'm being honest. I don't think what we're talking about should be judged by some socially preordained set of proximal standards."

Preordained proximal standards? "Love at first sight isn't a reality, Maxwell," she said to the shrimp heads. "It only works in the movies."

"This isn't love at first sight," Maxwell corrected. "It's love at second sight. You want to know what's not a reality, Kathleen? Categorizing human emotions."

Was that what she was doing? Before she could form another reply, the sushi man, laying split raw shrimp atop rice lumps, nodded in gruff agreement. "Human love," he said in his elliptical accent. "Never bound. Is like lightning on summer night."

Kathleen was outraged. *Just make the goddamn sushi and mind your own business!* She lowered her voice further. "Maxwell, this isn't the place to—"

"I see. Charlton Heston came down off a mountain with that in his arms too, right? Thou shalt not talk about how we feel in sushi bars."

Kathleen took a sip of her beer from the bottle. "You're being such an asshole," she muttered.

"Oh?" Maxwell glanced up. "Excuse me, sir?" he inquired of the sushi man. "In your opinion, am I being an asshole?"

Kathleen's teeth were grinding. The sushi man placed another order between them. "No," he said and shook his head. "No."

"We're leaving after this order," she said.

Maxwell dipped his raw shrimp—amaebi—into the little dish of soy sauce. "Why are you mad? There's no reason for you to be mad. We're communicating, aren't we? Most relationships fail simply because the people involved fail to communicate—"

"Just because we had sex a couple of times doesn't mean we're in a relationship!" came the fiercest whisper of her life. The sushi man turned away, raising a thin black brow. Kathleen sputtered, disgusted. *I don't care,* she thought. *I don't care if the whole world hears. So what?*

"Maybe it doesn't, you're right. So why don't we try to determine that? At the very least, I have a right to know how you feel, don't I?" Maxwell concentrated, again wielding his chopsticks toward the pile of fried shrimp heads. "Don't I?"

Yeah, you do, she thought, but what did that really mean? Anything? Each response that assembled in her mind fell apart before she could get it out of her mouth. She saw cars crashing, seats flying off Ferris wheels, bridges collapsing. She saw children waving at her but they were too far away to hear what they were saying. She saw skeletons dressed in wedding gowns, and old withered women dying alone. In the glass sushi cabinet she stared at the reflection of her own face and saw a stranger staring back...

"What are you afraid of?" Maxwell said.

Chapter 15

(I)

She remembers what he looks like.

That's good.

She remembers the night she picked up the prostitute.

"Yeah, all right. Whatever you want."

"I have $300. Is that enough?"

The prostitute looked momentarily old in the queer street light. She looked tired. Her red hair looked glossy, wet. "I usually don't do girls," she said. "But, yeah, that should be enough." Her smile looked brittle somehow, like she was very sad underneath. "There's a place up from Vermont. You have a car? If not we'll have to get a cab."

"I have a car," she said.

She'd put on plates she stole from the parking lot at Landover Mall. They were driving up L Street. The prostitute smelled nice. Suddenly she put her head down in the seat. "What's wrong?" "That guy over there," the prostitute replied. "I don't want him to see me."

"Why?"

"Never mind."

She looks across the intersection.

She sees the sharp, handsome black man getting into a BMW. She realizes that he's the prostitute's pimp, and that the prostitute is holding out on him. That's why she doesn't want the black man to see her. That's good, she thinks. That makes it even easier.

"What's his name?" she asked later.

Back at the house.
In Daddy's Room.
Don't hurt her, her mother says. *It's not her fault.*
"What's his name, the black man's? If you don't tell me, I'll have to hurt you. I don't want to hurt you."
The prostitute told her.
Perfect, she thought.
Then she Amytaled the prostitute and sewed her lips shut.

• • • • •

L Street, between 13th and 16th, looks like a black hall of mirrors from all the plate glass on the office buildings.
It's a beautiful, warm night.
She feels happy, sexy.
Beautiful.
I'm a prostitute tonight, she thinks. I'm a whore!
Cars rove by.
Men whistle at her.
Her high heels tick along the dark cement. The sound of traffic, the whistles, the overall sounds of a city night, make her feel free in a great open space. One prostitute passes her on the left. Silly tight gold hot pants like foil. Big brunette curls shiny with hairspray. Little breasts swaying braless beneath a red fishnet top. She frowns over her shoulder as if to say Invader! Two more prostitutes pass in the opposite direction. They're dressed like twins, arm in arm, in short leather miniskirts and pink halters. They, too, frown at her. Of course, she thinks. Territorialism. It shouldn't be long. "No one works this block solo, honey," a fourth prostitute says to her at the dark crosswalk. "You better be careful." High heels tick away on the asphalt. She remains on the corner.
She's staring at the dark church on the corner.
It looks desolate, doomed.
The cross on the steeple catches her eye.
But it's not *her* cross, it's not The Cross.
This cross is meaningless.
There is no power in it.
It does not make her strong against the past.
"You and me, we gotta have a little talk."
The BMW idles at the corner next to a wire wastebasket that reads PITCH IN! KEEP WASHINGTON CLEAN!
The black man is looking up at her from the open driver's window. He's wearing a gray pinstripe suit jacket, crisp white dress shirt, a dark silk tie with a diamond stickpin.
"Get in. I won't bite," he says.
No, she thinks. But I will.
Be careful, her mother says. *Wait 'til he's off the crowded blocks.*

I know, she thinks.

"Are you 'Rome?" she asks. "I'm looking for a guy named 'Rome."

"Hmm," he says. He's driving down M Street now. "What we need to talk about concerns a little matter of professional protocol, not to mention professional etiquette and known doctrines of professional boundaries, not to mention the way things fucking are."

"I know," she says. Signs on buildings pass. THOMAS CLOCK JEWELRY, LATT'S COUNTRY SQUIRE, C & P TELEPHONE COMPANY. "I can't work the street without a pimp."

The black man seems to wince. "You're on the right track, in spite of a slight misapplication of terms. I'm 'Rome."

"Can I work for you?" She keeps her voice quiet, cool. "I need work."

"Um-hmm. Well. That depends." He turns right back onto L, passing the huge pickup spot called Rumors, a Thai restaurant called Star of Siam, and then a city cop parked facing out in an alley. "Only the classiest, the cleanest, and the best girls work for me. I have criteria, which we'll get into later. Before I can fairly even think about taking you on, I want to take you back to my place and rap, find a little bit out about you. Does that sound all right?"

"Sure," she says. "You don't buy a car without taking it for a test drive first."

"Something like that," 'Rome says.

He's looking at her now, at the stoplight.

Do something, her mother says.

Her mother is in the back seat.

Act normal!

She removes a compact from her purse, examines her face in it. She knows he's looking at her, she knows his eyes are roving her the same way Daddy's hands pushed her legs back on the couch while she looked at The Cross.

She's dressed much better than the other girls she's seen. A short black halter dress with a wrap front, a spare gold-buckled belt, pearl earrings, a pearl bracelet around her wrist. The wig gives her shimmering shoulder-length white-blond hair…

"Before you can test drive the car, of course," the black man metaphors, "you have to start the ignition." He calmly places her left hand between his legs, urging her to prod him. She is able to do this without hesitation because when she closes her eyes she can see The Cross, and The Cross gives her the power to fantasize. 'Rome makes a sound like "Mmmmm" as her hand deftly caresses the satchel of flesh at his groin. She thinks of prejudiced jokes, of bigotry and stereotypes, and she wants to say something whory like, "So it's true what they say about black men." She's delighted by what she's feeling in her hand, this burgeoning parcel of sexual meat, and it doesn't bother her at all to be made to feel him like this because for the whole time she fantasizes carefully about cutting it all off with Bruns serrated plaster shears.

"How far away do you live?"

"Four, five blocks up."

Now, her mother says, before you get back on the crowded blocks.

He slides his big black hand up her left thigh.

She shivers a moment.

She doesn't like to be touched.

His fingers slide under her high hem, touch her panties, and suddenly she's disgusted.

It's Daddy's hand.

It's Daddy's hand, she thinks.

It's the hand of every man who ever touched her mother.

Her right hand slips into the purse.

Now! her mother says. Hurry! His girls will see you from the street.

She feels so bad, so small.

She feels like if she died right now, she'd feel better.

She can see his skull beneath his face, like glowing bone.

Skulls mean death, she remembers.

She pulls Daddy's big revolver out of her purse.

She cocks it and quickly presses the barrel into his crotch.

"Wh—" 'Rome big white eyes bulge. "Jesus…"

"Drive where I tell you to drive," she says, "or I'll blow your cock off."

(II)

"It's probably not a good idea for you to stay with me tonight," Kathleen said to the dashboard.

"Nonsense. I think it's a great idea."

They passed long lines of warehouses on New York Avenue. Most had windows broken out of lattices of steel frames. They appeared abandoned, bombed out. In a rubbled lot, several rats the size of puppies glanced up with red eyes.

If you don't want him to stay with you, Kathleen, how come you're heading back to your apartment instead of his? She didn't even want to contemplate what the radio shrink would say about that.

"I'd really like to stay with you tonight," Maxwell said.

Kathleen didn't say anything in response.

When they passed the police station, she thought sourly of Spence, and of his sour face and attitude. She didn't mind being disliked but only as long as she knew the reason. That's what bothered her foremost.

What's the reason?

She needed to distract herself. A large sign on an office building read: IT'S THE CRIMINALS, STUPID. "I don't get it," she said, pointing errantly. "What does it mean?"

"That's the NRA building," Maxwell replied. "I think what they're trying to say is that guns shouldn't be blamed for the crimes people commit with them."

"Oh."

Maxwell didn't say anything more when she pulled into her own parking lot. Kathleen supposed one thing she liked about him was his sense of tact. *He knows when to not say anything.* She thought about what he'd said at the sushi bar. *Am I afraid of communicating?* she wondered. Apartment buildings passed like rows of gravestones. *Am I afraid of my own emotions?*

I'm afraid of a lot of things, she realized.

"How, uh, how come we're driving around in the parking lot?" Maxwell piped up.

Again, she didn't reply. She scanned the rows of cars, idling past in the big T-Bird. When she drove the full loop, she parked in front of her own building. A breeze moved down the lot, but it was hot, humid. The sound of slow traffic came like surf.

"What are you looking for?" Maxwell asked when they were out of the car. She was looking behind her, scanning the parked cars. *Sentinels,* she wanted to say. Spence had told her he was putting a plainclothes officer in the lot round the clock. She didn't know how she felt about that. She didn't know if it made her feel safe, or scrutinized. Knowing that there was a cop out front all night might make her feel peeped on through a hole in the wall.

No, she didn't know at all how she felt about that.

She walked briskly ahead of him, so he couldn't put his arm around her, or hold her hand. Trotting up the apartment steps, an image pounced on her: falling into darkness, an abyss.

Inside Maxwell made himself right at home. Kathleen didn't know how she felt about that, either. He opened the refrigerator for a soda. Then he turned and said, "Do you want anyth—Kathleen? What the hell are you looking for?"

She held the curtain back at the slider, peeking down into the lot. *You're out there somewhere,* she thought, squinting. *Where are you?*

"Sentinels," she eventually answered Maxwell.

"You know something?" He sat down casually on the couch, turned on the TV with the remote. "You have some really bizarre things going on in your life."

"Really bizarre," she murmured. Earlier she'd Express Mailed next month's column to the magazine. She couldn't believe she'd almost forgotten.

"And I'm trying to figure out why you don't want to tell me about them," he went on. He kicked off his shoes, put his feet up on a coffee table full of women's magazines. "Don't you trust me?"

"I trust you," she said. All at once she felt wound down, exhausted. When she looked over, she smirked. Maxwell had turned on a baseball game.

"Goddamn Yankees," he griped, shaking his head. "The second I turn the set on the first thing I see is Ripkin knocking one out of the park. Wells should try pitching with his feet."

"You're a poet, Maxwell," she ventured. "Poets don't watch *baseball*. It's primordial. It's stupid."

"Especially when the Yankees are playing," he added. He turned off the set. "Thanks for the sushi. It was good. It was unique. I never thought I'd be able to say I ate fried shrimp heads..." He leaned up on the couch. "Are you all right? You look exhausted all of a sudden."

"I am," she said. "I don't know why. Can we go to bed now? You know, just to sleep?"

"Okay."

She had the notion that he understood immediately: she didn't want to have sex, she just wanted to sleep. Halfway to the bedroom she turned and saw him peering mystified out the front window. He shook his head then came back.

"...simple human spontaneity," came a voice like mist from the clock radio. It was the radio shrink's show. Was she on all night? "This needn't be confused with abnormal behavioral thought patterns." "But it was just...so wild, so unlike me," a caller said. The radio shrink continued: "It's your spirit, your innermost self, telling you that it's all right to be happy again. Spontaneity is often how we celebrate our joys, our happiness..."

Kathleen turned the radio off before Maxwell could hear. The radio shrink's show often depressed her in her fascination for it, for listening to strangers open themselves. She took off her shoes, unbuckled her jeans, and sat on the bed.

"I'm sorry," she said when Maxwell came in.

"Sorry about what?"

"I don't know." Her desire to sleep made her feel narcotized. Her eyelids fluttered as she slid off her jeans and began to unbutton her blouse.

Maxwell was bending over, clumsily taking off his pants. Something joggled her as she watched him. He had slim legs. His jockey shorts looked tight on his slim buttocks.

Was it spontaneity? She thought it must be something even less complex—her own unassurance of herself, or of her desires. "Maxwell," she said. "You have a great ass."

"Oh, yeah?" He looked over his shoulder, still bent, as he slipped off his underpants. "Women tell me that all the time." Then he stripped off his shirt and cast it to the floor. Kathleen's toes dawdled in the carpet. She was staring at him.

"I thought you just wanted to sleep," he said.

"Well, I guess I changed my mind," she said.

The next procession of minutes didn't seem like time at all. She leaned up to look, she liked to look at him. It made her happy to see his mouth burrowed in the fur of her sex, and happier still to feel him. The wet sensation bloomed, sending antsy shivers up her stomach. She cradled the back of his head and sighed.

Next he stood up right in front her, brazenly naked, his penis erect before her face. "I want you to put it on me," he whispered. He placed a condom packet in her hands.

When she opened it and began to slide it down, she thought what silly things they were. Rubbers. Even the name was silly. She could smell the gritty scent of the lubricant.

"Okay, now," he said. He sat down on the edge of the bed. "This is a special technique I read about. You're supposed to sit on me, like this."

His hands guided her hips. She sat down in his lap, facing him. She put her arms around his neck, wrapped her legs around his back.

His penis slipped right into her, to the base.

"Maxwell, this is kind of—"

"It's called the Vertical Pelvic Alignment Technique. It's supposed to ensure female orgasm."

"Yeah, really?" It felt weird just...sitting on him. "Are you making this up?"

"No. I read about it in a magazine. You'll never guess which one."

"What, *Penthouse*?"

"*'90s Woman.*"

God knew, he probably had. *Maybe one day I'll start to read the magazine I write for,* she thought. But this "technique..."

"Aren't we supposed to, like, you know..."

"No," he said, "not according to the article. We're just supposed to hold each other and rock back and forth a little."

She felt like a monkey wrapped around a tree. Maxwell gently rocked her, running his hands up and down her back, kissing her shoulder and up under her throat.

At first it seemed awkward just sitting on him like this. A moment later, though, it began to feel...nice.

He wasn't thrusting at all. He was just in her. As they rocked, her pubis rubbed against his. *Oh, God,* she thought. Soon she was feeling things she'd never felt before—soft lovely waves diced by knifelike flashes of heat.

"Doesn't this feel good?"

"Yes," she nearly gulped into his ear. She clung to his neck, wrapped her legs tighter. Her breasts pressed flat against his chest, the nipples prickling. Maxwell lowered his arms to gird her waist, and the slow, deep gyrations of their hips intensified. The combination of feelings—his penis all the way up in her, and her pubis steadily rubbing against his—induced a delicious hot churning sensation, spreading upward. Moments later she was mad for the contact, driven for it; she held him tighter and gyrated her buttocks more quickly in his lap.

"Kathleen…"

"Maxwell," she panted, "I'm going to—"

"I want you to."

Her orgasm seemed to implode. It knocked the wind out of her and filled her with dense, earthy heat. Fervid contractions went off like bombs as Maxwell continued rocking her, her pubis rubbing, rubbing, her breasts hot and squashed to his chest. Each time she thought it would end, another contraction seized her, every nerve alight. In spite of the condom, she felt Maxwell come too; his breath raged into her bosom as his arms went rigid about her waist. They fell back onto the bed, spent, cocooned in one another.

"I really do love you," he whispered.

Kathleen couldn't move, she could only lie there splayed on him. She couldn't have said a word even if she'd wanted to.

• • • • •

Asleep, she dreamed. The darkness dripped or ticked. The faceless figure, the abbess of the nightmare, leaned over. The pictures glared, the snake coursing toward her open sex as she lay in naked paresis on the bed.

"Embrace your hatred," the figure said.

In the first picture, the snake's big angled head was just nudging into the opening of her sex.

And in each succeeding picture the snake burrowed deeper, deeper—

She awoke shrieking. Maxwell quickly turned on the light and held her, stroking her hair. "It's all right," he whispered. "It was just a dream, just a dream."

Her eyes felt lidless. She shivered in the heat.

"Kathleen, you have to tell me what's wrong. You can't keep it in anymore. It's tearing you up… Tell me."

Minutes ticked by in his embrace. Her coat of sweat felt like paste. Eventually she said, "A serial killer has been in contact with me for about a week."

(III)

Skulls mean death, her mother whispers.

The heavy revolver feels light in her hand.

It was Daddy's gun, big, awkward.

She found it in the closet a long time ago, the same week—
Skulls mean death, her mother repeats, interrupting.
The Cross shines in The Window.
His face looks like a skull.
"What are you do—"
She can sense her mother's smile behind her at The Window.
The black man is shackled to the bed.

Daddy's Room used to be a den. Where Daddy's friends would do things to her and her mother. It's a mock bedroom now. It's where Daddy fucked her all those times. It's the room with The Window. This is where she sleeps now. Often on blood-crusted sheets. Sometimes she even sleeps with the corpses the night before she gets rid of them. She has to sleep here. So she can see The Cross in The Window.

"You are one crazy psycho bit—"
"Shut up," she says to the black man.
Then: "Creamy," the black man says vaguely. "You have something to do with Creamy, don't you? The cops are looking for her."
"Of course they are. When did the police talk to you?"
"Last night."
"Who?"
She puts the big gun to his head.
"Who talked to you?"
"A guy named Spence."
Spence, she thinks.
She'll have to remember that.
"What are you—" The black man tenses up against his restraints.
She Amytals him with a 3cc Luer-Lok disposable syringe.
Then she gets ready for the rest.

Chapter 16

(I)

Maxwell saved the rampage 'til next morning. Kathleen smirked at him as he stomped circles around the living room. "You're moving," he said. "You'll move in with me."

"Maxwell, I'm not ready for that. I—"

"Don't argue with me!" he suddenly yelled. "A killer knows where you live, for God's sake!"

She crinkled her nose, sipping tea. He shouldn't yell. "I'm not moving," she proclaimed. "It isn't necessary. I refuse to be run out of my home. Besides, there's an undercover policeman in the parking lot day and night."

Maxwell peered skeptically out the slider. "I don't see any fucking undercover policeman."

It was the first real cuss word she'd heard him say, and it immediately disappointed her. "Don't cuss, Maxwell. It's so inarticulate. And there is an undercover policeman out there. Spence said he's in a surveillance car or something."

"Who the hell's Spence!" Maxwell yelled.

Kathleen flinched. "He's the detective running the case. You saw him—the guy at the writers' lecture."

"And—what?" He leaned over, to stare at her. "This killer wants you to write a book about her?"

Kathleen slumped on the couch. "Yes, Maxwell. She's sending me accounts of her murders. I'm going to intersperse the accounts with commentary, psychiatric and sociological analysis. If the police catch her, hopefully I'll be able to interview her. It'll be a good book."

Maxwell was rubbing his chin, looking sourly contemplative. "Accounts? She's sent you accounts of her murders?"

"Yes, Maxwell. That's what I said."

"Let me see them."

This request—or demand—locked her up. No, she could never show him the chapters the killer had sent. He'd be disgusted, horrified...

"No," she said.

"No? What do you mean no?"

Kathleen faintly smiled. "The word denotes a negation, denial, or disagreement. It's an adverb."

"Don't be funny," Maxwell said. "Where are the accounts? In your desk?"

"No," she said.

"They're in your desk, aren't they?" He trod to the desk, began rummaging through the drawers. "I'll find 'em."

"Get out of there!" Kathleen shouted.

"Make me."

"You're so juvenile! You have no right to go through my desk!"

"I have every right," he muttered. "You have no idea what you may be getting yourself into." He paused, his mouth turning down. He held up a sheaf of papers. "Is this them? 'Initiatory Rites? Childhood Memories?'"

"No."

"This is them." He sat down and began to read.

"Don't read it!" she yelled. "It's—"

"Be quiet so I can concentrate, huh?"

She lurched up. "Don't tell me to be quiet! This is my house! You can't tell me to be quiet in my house!"

"It's not a house, it's an apartment," Maxwell said.

"You're outrageous, Maxwell! I'll throw your skinny ass right out of here!"

"Last night I had a great ass," he mentioned, reading. "Now I've got a skinny ass. Women are so ambiguous."

"Maxwell! You better—"

"Look," he said, jerking his gaze. "I'm going to read this stuff, with or without your approval. So just pipe down, all right? Have some more tea. Watch Donahue or something, soap operas."

Kathleen fumed. Her lips sealed to the tightest closure, like a scar. She sat back down and watched him. His long hair hung down as he pored over the pages.

She watched him go pale in increments, just as Spence had. With the turn of each page, his face seemed to transform into a mask of incredulous dread, of slow, creeping, quiet horror.

"Good Christ Almighty," he whispered.

"I told you so," Kathleen said.

He argued with her all the way back to his apartment. "You shouldn't be by yourself," he said. "It's crazy. If you won't stay with me, at least let me stay with you."

"No," she said. She gunned the T-Bird past Blackie's House of Beef on 21st Street. VISIT THE RUSH ROOM a sign invited. MEET RUSH. Kathleen thought Rush Limbaugh was an arrogant dolt. *It's his fault the traffic's like this,* she reasoned. Lunch hour traffic in this city was almost as bad as rush hour. Cars sat backed up at each little intersection, ablaze in relentless glare. "I have my work to do, you have your work to do. We'd get in each other's way; it'd be very inconvenient."

"Inconvenient?" Maxwell's eyes rolled. "We've got something pretty dangerous here and you talking about *convenience?*"

"It's nothing for you to worry about, Maxwell. Jesus Christ."

"Nothing for me to worry about? I thought relationships were supposed to involve mutuality."

There he went again about relationships. "What good does it do to argue, Maxwell?" she suggested. "Psycho killer or not, I told you I'm not ready to even think about living with anyone."

This time he refrained from comment. *Thank God,* Kathleen thought. Conversely, though, she found something inspiring in the argument. Nothing in its context—just the fact: They were lovers and they were arguing. She hadn't had an argument with a lover in years. *Or maybe not at all,* she supposed. *Never.* She felt something vaguely vital about it, something meaningful even though she couldn't guess what the meaning could be.

"Do you think," Maxwell began. He looked ahead through the windshield either stifled or dazed. His eyes slowly went wide. "Do you think all those things are true? Do you think all those things really happened to her?"

"Yes," Kathleen said. As with her, it would no doubt take a while for the killer's writings to wear off of Maxwell's mind. "I'm sure of it. And I'm also sure there's more to come. She's delusional and obsessive. She's killing men based on the motivations of her delusion. What she's doing is the most important thing in her life, and it becomes even more important to her when she relates it all to me. To the killer, I'm the angel of truth who will communicate her testament to the world."

"Yeah, but why?" Maxwell said. "Why you?"

Kathleen shrugged. "Spence says it's my column in the magazine, something about my writing that the killer relates to. It might even just be the *way* I write, my style or something, or the tone of my responses to readers. Some bizarre subconscious attraction, something that only the killer fully understands."

"That doesn't make much sense, does it?"

"Of course not. We're talking about someone who's clinically insane."

When she pulled over in front of his apartment building, he had the most forlorn look in his eyes. She knew what he was going to ask.

"Can I see you tonight?"

She watched traffic crawl up P Street. "Let's not move too fast, Maxwell. Okay? I'll call you later."

He nodded, still diffuse. "I'm sorry I yelled at you."

"I know."

"It's just that this whole thing really scares me."

What, though? Did he mean their prospective relationship? Kathleen felt sure he referred to her contact with the killer. Of course it scared him. But— *I wonder why I'm not scared,* she thought. It was true. She wasn't scared at all.

He leaned over and quickly kissed her.

"'Bye," he said.

"'Bye."

Maxwell got out. Heading toward his apartment entrance, he seemed to drift rather than walk, a attenuated ghost. His long blonde hair blew back when he opened the door. Then he disappeared.

I guess I love you, too, Kathleen thought. She pulled out. A Yellow cab and a Porsche cut her off on the circle but she didn't get mad as she normally would. She felt strangely sated, weird, as she drove on. It took her a while to realize what it was.

I'm happy, she realized.

For the first time in a long time, Kathleen Shade was genuinely happy.

For the first time in a long time, she felt good.

She felt good all the way back home. Until she opened her mailbox and found the envelope.

Moments later she was back in her apartment. She donned Spence's evidence gloves, slit open the envelope, and read the next chapter of the killer's chronicle, entitled "Needle-Work."

Then she didn't feel good any more.

Chapter 17

(I)

Broad daylight. Traffic sounds. Venders selling hot dogs, half-smokes. Pedestrians proceeding to and fro with their lives. Normalcy.

Madness, Spence thought.

"Call the M.E.'s office," he said. "Then call TSD and tell them to send Kohls down here with his crew."

The Traffic Branch cop wore his hat cocked back on his head. He nodded, wiping sweat off his brow, where dovetails of dark hair lay shellacked. The details of his job—a routine one—disheveled him, along with the city's heat. But beyond that he looked ravaged. This was a guy who'd been working Traffic Branch probably 15 years. He'd no doubt seen his share of rough things. *But...this?* Spence thought. He abstracted: If he could look into this cop's eyes, he'd see a spirit mauled by utter incomprehension.

And madness.

"Snap out of it. This is tough, sure, but we're cops. I can't have you folding on me. Make those calls, okay?"

The cop nodded again, shuffled through heat and confusion back to his car.

The cop would have to debriefed. So far they'd kept it all out of the papers; a district reg allowed them to exclude any MCS homicide from the blotters, but there were always leaks, and it was only a matter of time before the *Post* people nosed their way in. They'd probably have to run a wanted soon anyway; at least they had a name and a face now.

The BMW's finish shined like sleek, white ice. Spence noted that it was a 635CSi. *Fifty grand,* he thought. *Must be nice.* The vehicle's trunk lid stood open; Spence thought of a great maw frozen open on a petrified beast.

He'd never seen anything so strange in his life.

A mummy, he thought.

Furrows drew into his brow as he gazed down. Common silver duct tape, two-inch wide, had been used to wrap Tyrone "'Rome" Chaplin into a tight, oblong bundle. He'd been completely cocooned. Only the nostrils had been left exposed. The killer had left the eloquent pimp's district driver's license adhered to the taped chest, but Spence didn't need to see the face to know that the contents of this bizarre bundle was Chaplin. *The first murder with a motive,* he realized. *Psychotic prostitute gets revenge against her pimp, her oppressor.*

But why had she wrapped him up?

What in God's name did she do to him? Spence thought.

"Death by asphyxia," Kohls said a few hours later in the workup room. He could tell first by simple visual examination of the inside of 'Rome's lips, a dark blue/blackish color known as acyanosis. Further microscopy verified this.

"She smothered him," Spence said at the entrance.

"Probably very slowly, over an extended period."

Spence stepped closer to the shiny guttered, height-adjustable autopsy slab. "What else?"

"Won't know 'til I do the Y-section." Kohls looked up from the great dual-eyepieced Zeiss microscope, turning down the lampfield. "Got something...asperous, a scarlet color lining the insides of the nostrils."

"Blood?"

"No, no, it's colloidal. I'll nail it down. Just gimme some time."

"There's not much to give." Spence deliberately stood well away from the corpse, at an off angle. Kohls, after doing a print scan with the laser, had removed all of the duct tape, extricating Tyrone Chaplin from his cocoon of death. This removal left the dark skin strangely dry in appearance, tacky.

"It's funny," Kohls observed. "You ever skinned an animal? Like a deer, a rabbit?"

"No," Spence said.

"The sound is identical, when you pull the skin off."

"Identical to what?"

"When I was pulling the tape off your partner, 'Rome. It made the same exact sound as skinning an animal. Gave me the jeebies, you know? Like I was skinning 'Rome."

Spence found the observation useless. "Did she cut off his..."

"Yep," Kohls said, pointing toward the corpse's hips. "Take a gander."

"No thanks. I gotta drive."

Kohl's brow flitted. "Only found one print, on the guy's driver's license. What's her name? Helen? Heather?"

"Creamy," Spence corrected. "Hairfall?"

"One pube. Fusiformal match. This gal's a piece of work. I can't wait to find out exactly what she did to him. You want to stick around for the Y-section, Lieutenant?"

"No thanks," Spence repeated. "I gotta drive."

"And there's one other thing." Kohls offered the faintest of grins. "You'd see it yourself if you weren't standing so far away from the table. You squeamish?"

"No, but I don't particularly enjoy close visual inspections of corpses whose full genitalia have been cut off."

"Gotcha."

"What's the other thing?"

"She also cut off his right hand. She didn't do that to any of the others. Kind of screwy... Say, you ever get a line on the hospital angle?"

Spence tried to answer with confidence. "We're doing a full background run, the bureau's helping. We've also got—" Then he stopped, as if he'd run into a stone wall. "Who the hell am I kidding?" he admitted. "I haven't got a line on shit."

"Oh well," Kohls commiserated. As Spence left the workup section, Kohls' 12,500-rpm Stryker autopsy saw began to rev like a dentist's drill.

(II)

Kathleen went rigid at her desk when she heard the rapping at the door. Her hands froze over the typewriter. The raps were delicate yet insistent, five, evenly spaced, a pause, then five more. She tried, ludicrously, to make a presumption. How would a killer, a psychotic murderess, knock on a door?

rap-rap-rap-rap-rap

Like that? she wondered.

She doubted it. Then she smirked when she looked in the brass peephole. It was Spence.

"Hello," he said when she opened up.

"Damn. I was hoping it was the Fuller Brush Man."

"The Fuller Brush Man isn't your ticket to literary acclaim."

"Oh, but you are?" she said. "A poker-faced cop in a bargain basement suit?"

Spence's gaze distended. "This suit cost $850. It's made from some of the finest—"

"Relax, Kafka. I was only kidding. Are you here for anything in particular, or just the typical police harassment?"

"May I come in? I'd like to talk to you."

"Well, I don't know," she hedged. "I'm a little busy right now. You see, I'm a militant feminist opportunist. Via my own self-interests, rapaciousness, and overall inflated ego, and in addition to a reactive lack of writing talent, I'm exploiting a tragic circumstance for my own gain. I'm writing a bogus, sensationalist book based on the ghastly crimes of a—"

Spence stepped past her and entered the apartment. "What a hovel," he commented of her living room. "You're not much of a housekeeper, are you? This dump looks like it got the once over by our tactical riot squad. What's that smell?"

"Fresh pig," Kathleen said.

Spence smiled. He perused the room with his hands behind his back. "Aren't you going to offer me some coffee?"

"All I have is beer and wine," Kathleen responded. "You see, I'm a clinical alcoholic, preformed by a genetic-addition propensity that you read about in some magazine."

"Speaking of magazines, when's the next issue of your rag come out? I especially enjoy the column called 'Verdict.' It's funnier than *National Lampoon.*" Spence turned to her like a chess piece. "All jokes aside—"

"Oh, we were joking?"

"—have you received anything more from—"

She slapped him in the chest with a manila envelope.

"Originals, right?" he asked.

"Of course. I rented a copier from Shields today."

"Industrious. I trust you didn't handle the originals until you put on the gloves?"

"I wore the damn gloves, Lieutenant. Now why don't you be like a hockey player and—"

Spence sat down at her desk before the slider. He picked up a sheaf of papers. "These are the photocopies?"

"Yes."

"Good material for the book?"

Kathleen didn't say anything. She opened the slider and lit a Now 100. Spence began to read her photocopies, so not to touch the originals.

"Hmm. 'Needle-Work.' By the way, how's the blazing love affair with Maxwell Platt?"

"Mind your own business."

"It's strange. I read some of his work today in some literary magazines that our research department dug up. Did you know he's had poetry published in *Esquire, The New York Times Literary Review,* even *Cosmopolitan?*"

"What's strange about that?"

"Well, they're formidable magazines, highly competitive markets, I should think—"

"Oh, you think?"

"—and his work is quite well done. Insightful, honest, highly creative. That's the strange part, that a person with such respectable artistic talents should find anything at all in common with you."

"He only comes around for the blatant, indulgent sex."

"Like last night? He was here last night, wasn't he?"

"I know you have your watchdogs on me. You get a kick out of that, don't you? Intruding on real people's lives?"

"It's only for your protection. Personally I'd much prefer to see district tax dollars spent elsewhere." Spence flipped a page of the manuscript. "But Maxwell Platt is innocent."

Cigarette smoke dangled before Kathleen's eyes. "What's that supposed to mean?"

"You know full well that a psychopathic killer is aware of your exact place of residence, yet you're pursuing a romantic involvement with Platt. You're inviting him over here. You don't care about anyone, do you? Platt could wind up dead due to your reckless selfishness."

"That's ridiculous," Kathleen spat. But actually she hadn't thought of that at all. *No, no,* she tried to rationalize. *It's too far-fetched...*

"And it's therefore my professional obligation to see that he's protected when he's over here. That's why I've got the undercover vehicle in your parking lot."

"Why don't you just leave?" Kathleen suggested, but, still, what he'd implied bothered her. "Or maybe it's just that you've got nothing better to do. Big bad muscle-bound existential hot-shot police investigator. What a laugh. It's not my fault that a killer is sending me accounts of her murders. It's not my fault that you've gotten nowhere on this case."

"Quite the contrary," Spence offered. He was reading and talking simultaneously. "We know who the killer is."

Kathleen bent forward. "You... What?"

"She's a prostitute known as Creamy. Her real name is Heather B. Willet. Twenty-six years old, red hair, Caucasian. You know her?"

"How would I know a prostitute, for God's sake?" Kathleen stubbed out her cigarette, thinking. This revelation sat in her gut like a bad meal. Was Spence lying? He'd lied before, she felt sure of it. "A prostitute? That doesn't sound very logical."

"People who are pathological seldom behave logically. And by the way, I'm not an existentialist. I conform to a spiritual philosophy known as solipsisty—the theory that the self is the only thing that can be known and therefore verified."

This comment seemed to stretch her face against her skull, like thin elastic. "The last time I talked to you, you lied to me."

"I didn't lie, I prevaricated—"

Kathleen laughed out loud.

"We've found two more bodies."

Her laughter dissolved. Suddenly, though backed by the blaze of sun, she felt frigid.

"This passage here—" He held up the manuscript she'd received today. "'Needle-Work.' It describes in verifiable detail the murder of a young man named Brad Weston. Traffic Branch found his body in his car about 36 hours ago. He was a barhound, like Calabrice."

"But you said two bodies."

Spence nodded, never looking up. "Early this morning. A black man named Tyrone Chaplin. I talked to him hours before his death. He was Heather B. Willet's pimp. The physical evidence is incontestable. She killed them all. And her behavior patterns are evolving exactly as our forensic psychiatrist predicted. With each murder, her delusion is becoming more and more real to her. I won't bother telling you the details regarding Chaplin's death. I'm quite sure that you'll be informed, posthaste."

Posthaste, Kathleen thought. *Only a dolt would use a word like that.*

When Spence rose, his shadow submerged the kitchen. He buttoned his jacket, made an adjustment to his tie. "Call me when you get the next manuscript," he said.

"What's the magic word?"

"Pretty please with misprision of a felony and obstruction of justice on top."

"Kiss my ass, Spence," Kathleen answered his levity.

Spence retrieved the manuscript, unafflicted. He headed toward the door, then stopped and returned his gaze to her. "I was checking some things," he mentioned. "Public record."

She cast the one-per-hour rule to the wayside, and lit another cigarette. "So?"

"Who is Samuel Curtis Shade?"

Kathleen felt something inside her shrivel, like slug skin when sprinkled with salt. "He's my uncle. He's the—"

"The man who sexually abused you as a child?"

"Yes," she said dryly. "And goddamn you for prying into my personal life. And goddamn you double for even bringing it up."

"I apologize," Spence said. His sober face and attire almost lent sincerity to his apology.

The cat clock ticked.

Almost, almost. Alm— Here.

She heard the words now as clearly as Uncle Sammy had whispered them so long ago. The little bed was creaking; her dolls lined up along the dresser bore witness; the plastic eyes of the cat clock ticked back and forth. From behind, Uncle Sammy's hands molded her nine-year-old body like fresh white dough...

She spoke on, retracted from her own will. A puppet master directed her mouth to configure the words and leak them from her throat. "He sexually abused me from the time I was nine 'til my late teens. My mother was dead. My father was always away on business. Uncle Sammy...looked after me." She gulped jagged stones. "He made porno movies for the mob, and transported them here for development and distribution. In 1988 he got caught in a Justice Department sting, or something like that. He was sentenced to 13 years in prison."

Spence looked away, discomfited. "Well, something happened to him yesterday."

Bright flowers seemed to open in her vision, before a raving light. *He's dead,* she thought. *Uncle Sammy's dead. He hanged himself in prison. Someone murdered him. He died of cancer...something. Please tell me that Uncle Sammy's dead.*

"He's dead?" she asked, her voice like a tiny scratch.

"No, no he's not," Spence answered her. "Yesterday at noon your uncle was paroled."

Chapter 18

(I)

Is she right? Maxwell Platt paused to wonder over his Brother typewriter. *Am I deluded? Has love deluded me?*

If so, it wasn't really love.

Then he tossed his head back and laughed.

She was wrong. He was not deluded.

I'm in love, he thought.

He knew it was true. Since when was truth bound to criteria, to structure? Since when was love bound to rules? There were no rules, there was only the truth.

These seemed appropriate reflections for a poet. *I don't give a damn that I've known her less than a week. I love her. I know I love her. I'm going to marry her. I'm going to spend the rest of my life with her. I'm going to be the father of her children, and I'm going to grow old and die with her.*

He didn't need to know anything beyond that.

From the window, P Street traffic sounded like a river at high spate. Maxwell's deliberating happiness made him feel like the world revolved around him, he its axis.

Now, he thought. He felt risen. The poems of his past were done; it was time to begin the poems of his future. *Good-bye, Exit,* he thought. Now it was time to write a poem for her.

The typewriter regurgitated loud clicking sounds within its steady hum; it was old. The keys tapped sluggishly and often jammed, and you could grow old waiting for the carriage to return. But Maxwell wouldn't dream of replacing it. It was like an old friend, a companion that never let him down. The typewriter provided the tool for his muse. One day, when it broke down completely, he would bury it. *Like a dead loved one,* he thought.

Kathleen's first poem, he knew, would take time, a lot of reworking, rewriting. He felt this would be the most important poem he'd ever write. He typed out the title:

A KEATSIAN INQUIRY by Maxwell Platt

He typed for the rest of the day.
Then he went to his nightstand and got the gun.

(II)

"Your friend, your killer," Simmons said, "is now fully established in the Totem Phase of her delusion. She feels invincible, wholly and completely protected. Her crimes—which she of course doesn't see as crimes, but acts of truth—have risen in her perceptions to a stratum of absolute meaning."

"Wait," Spence said. "Back up." He felt as fuddled as he must look. "Totem Phase?"

Simmons' goatee looked like spun steel. He unconsciously turned a large blue Stelazine paperweight on his desk. A pencil cup faced Spence, which read MELLARIL-S SUSPENSION, Buttermint Flavor! Spence recalled from his one psychopharmacology course that Mellaril was a heavy-duty anti-psychotic drug which often turned patients into pensive zombies. But...buttermint? *At least they've made it taste good,* he thought. Simmons continued, his head atilt. "Pattern serial-killer behavior exists in a total of seven phases. The first few are developmental; we already know about them in this case. The sexual abuse from an early age, the doubtless genetic and environmental ramifications, etc. Your friend has now progressed to the most serious later phase, the Totem Phase, where all of her feelings amass to a single point of reference, through which she executes her crimes. Totem, in this case, means symbol. She feels energized now by the symbol."

"What symbol?" Spence inquired. "You mean the cross?"

"Exactly." Simmons patted the manuscripts. "It's relative to something in her past that she feels protected by. And in this protection she realizes the truth of her delusion."

"But I can't nail it down. I don't even know how to begin."

"You may never nail it down," Simmons enlightened him. "The totem of the typical serial killer is usually a gross abstraction. Something that makes sense only to the afflicted. Psychopathic totems are generally related to the prominent parental figure—the killer's mother, in this instance—and always carries back to early childhood. Strong initial religious assertions, perhaps. Perhaps her mother took her to church as a child, and she remembers seeing the cross above the altar, or maybe she recalls the priest making the sign of the cross. It could've been something her mother gave her, or something her mother wore, a cross on a necklace perhaps. It could be anything."

"In the manuscript she referred to the cross as being illuminated," Spence said. "She writes that it 'glows' like a 'beautiful white fire.' I've got some people checking out all the area churches, to get a geographic list of the ones with illuminated crosses—"

"You're wasting your time," Simmons cut him off. "Psychopaths regularly see the critical symbols of their lives enshrouded by some kind of light—a protective aura, so to speak. These symbols, in other words, aren't really illuminated. The light is a hallucination. The psychopath believes that the light emanating from the totem will protect them. Forget about the cross, Jeffrey. It's a dead end."

It occurred to Spence just that moment: Simmons was the only person who addressed him by his first name. He didn't know anybody else well enough. *Poor me,* he thought. *I don't have any friends.* But what did it matter? "I feel useless," he admitted.

"Don't. You're a very perceptive person. You're driven, Jeffrey, by your sense of duty." Simmons paused to smile. "But for the life of me I can't figure out what that is."

Neither could Spence. *This is all I have,* he thought, and suddenly it was a dreadful thought, fertile with despair. Idealisms didn't work now; the world was a scape of rain and failure. Of inhumanity and lies. Catching one killer would not amend that status. Nor would catching a 1,000. The world would remain as it was. Disinterested. Unflinching in its evil.

Spence felt crushed in the fine clothes. "I don't know what to do," he said. "I don't know how to proceed from here."

"There's never an easy way out, Jeffrey. You know that." Simmons' eyes, in spite of their accrual of years, shined crisply and bright as an infant's. "But you can take heart in some rather indisputable statistics. The Totem Phase always burns itself out, leaving in its wake a catastrophic amine-related depression. It's called the Capture Phase. Very quickly the falsehood of the delusion is unveiled; the bipolar mental state reverses poles, so to speak, locking the killer in an inescapable feeling of capture. The psychopath's self-image is reduced to total meaninglessness... Suicide is the most frequent result."

Spence found no solace in this possibility. He wanted the killer caught, not dead by her own hand. He wanted to see her; he wanted to look into her living face and see that same face looking back in all its reality. Without that evidence, and without the hope of it, he wouldn't feel real himself. He'd feel as though he'd been cheated by a myth, or a ghost.

"She's objectifying the delusion now," Simmons went on.

"How do you know?"

"She killed her pimp—an objective gesture of revenge. Expect her to identify even more closely now with what I told you about the other day. With the nascent."

"Kathleen Shade," Spence said.

"Yes. Kathleen Shade is the link between the murders and the killer's sense of purpose. Throughout the Totem Phase this perception will amplify. The psychotic delusion will build Shade as a trust-figure. The killer will believe that Shade approves of the murders. This can be easily exploited if you handle it right. The killer, as I've said, identifies with Shade for whatever reason. If you can trust Shade, you're at a great advantage. But, of course, if you can't—"

"I'm screwed," Spence said.

"Yes, and so is Shade. She could easily wind up dead." Simmons seemed relaxed as he spoke of this. "Shade, after all, is using the killer's delusion for her own advantage; she has a vested interest."

"The book."

"Precisely. Can you trust Shade to cooperate?"

"I think so."

"Are you still maintaining an acrimonious relationship with her?"

Spence laughed lightly. "She can't stand me, and she thinks I can't stand her."

"Then you're convinced she's unduly independent?"

"Yes, otherwise the Bad Guy routine wouldn't work."

"Good. You remember well. Just be careful. The person you must trust the most, in this case, is not Shade. It's yourself. And I think you know what I'm talking about."

Spence nodded. The easiest way to catch the killer would be to use Kathleen Shade as bait. Spence wondered if he was too ethical for that, and felt slightly shamed when he came to no solid conclusion. As if to pardon the thought, he said, "I tried to get her to move out of her apartment, but she refused."

Simmons smiled. "Did you try very hard?"

"I guess it's pretty stupid for me to lie to you," Spence admitted. "No, I guess I didn't. But I've got a tactical guy in her parking lot, and I'm on her phones under the table."

"Good. Better safe than sorry, civil rights notwithstanding."

Spence didn't much care. "Thanks for your time," he said, and got up. "Did you hear the one about the guy who joined Paranoiacs Anonymous?"

"They never told him where the meetings were held," Simmons said. "How many psychiatrists does it take to change a lightbulb?"

"How many?"

"One, but only if the lightbulb wants to change."

Spence shook his head. "One question before I go. Not only did she cut off her pimp's genitals, she cut off his right hand. Any idea why?"

"Her totem, after all, is more than likely religious. Perhaps it's biblical."

"Biblical?"

"If thine right hand offends thee," Simmons theorized, "cut if off."

Spence contemplated this when he left the office. *Objects of abuse serve as objects of power to be envied—hence the missing penises,* he recalled Simmons telling him a few days ago. In a monstrous way, it made sense. *But...the hand?* he wondered now. What purpose did she have in cutting off Tyrone Chaplin's hand?

(III)

Earlier she finished typing "The Mummy."

Then she Express Mailed it to Kathleen Shade in the special Express Mail box so she wouldn't have to go into the post office.

She drove past The Cross on the way home.

It reminds her of something but she never knows what.

In the basement she feeds the prostitute.

She's getting so skinny, her mother says.

"I know."

You forgot to feed her yesterday.

She blinks. "I forgot?"

Yes, honey.

Suddenly she wants to scream.

How could she forget...

You also forgot to go to work last night.

Her teeth clacked shut.

She goes to the shelves, to the toolbox.

She takes the scratch awl.

She lays her hand on the bench, palm up.

"I will not forget," she says and sticks the awl into the center of her palm.

"I will not forget."

"I will not forget."

"I will not forget."

"I will not forget."

When she's done there's a cross in her hand formed of punctures.

• • • • •

"I'm sorry I forgot to feed you," she says to the prostitute.

Sego Strawberry today.

The prostitute's ribs show like crevices along her side, or like gills.

She's dirty and pale bound to the bench.

Lacerations crust her wrists and ankles.

She inserts the plastic tube between the stitches in the prostitute's lips.

The lean throat wobbles as the liquid meal is quickly gulped down through the tube.

"Isn't that good?" she says to the prostitute. "For dinner we'll have Dutch Chocolate."

Then she goes upstairs to masturbate in Daddy's Room.

The feelings build.

Beautiful, hot flashes of feelings.

She thinks of blood pouring out of incisions.

Men's blood.

As the feelings build she thinks of little birds crowded in a cage, their wings flapping in chaos to get out.

She always waits weeks and weeks to masturbate.

She likes the way the feelings build up.

She likes to masturbate in Daddy's Room because she can see the fiery white light of The Cross in The Window.

Her mother is standing by The Window now, looking out as her beautiful daughter's sleek, strong body writhes in pleasure on the bed, the perfect legs spread, the perfect stitches bared, the clitoris radiating at the intent manipulation, and the intricate, maladapted brain dreaming of all the men she will kill.

The stitches hum.

Her orgasm bursts...

Like the little birds released from the crowded cage all at once.

She's been masturbating not with her own hand but with the hand of Tyrone Chaplin.

Chapter 19

(I)

Maxwell worked on the new poem all day. Often times arose for artists when the creative élan tapped itself out. Maxwell followed William Faulkner's advice: he quit writing in the middle of his peak rather than drain himself dry. There was nothing worse for a poet than an aesthetic hangover due to overwork. Maxwell kept a reserve for the next day—at all costs—or the next day proved useless.

I know you're home, he thought, his ear to the phone. He called Kathleen repeatedly, but she wasn't answering. This did not surprise him. It was a woman's way of articulating the need for distance. *Distance, hogwash,* he thought. He would just go to her apartment, uninvited. You did things like that when you were in love. Love had its privileges.

She loves me, came the thought with a shining certainty. *She just doesn't realize it yet.*

In faded jeans, then, and a powder-orange T-shirt that read *Hanson's Magazine of Literary and Social Interest,* Maxwell locked up, went out onto P Street, and hailed a cab. Twenty-five minutes later he was striding up Kathleen's echoic apartment steps. A white plastic Blockbuster Video bag dangled from one hand.

The bag contained a loaded .38 Colt revolver.

Maxwell's gape lengthened as he glimpsed her through the opened door. Dark smudges underscored bloodshot eyes like soot. She'd been crying. Her hair reminded him of a clump of tentacles.

"I must look like shit," she said and let him in.

"Well..."

Inside was hotter even than outside; it was like stepping into clay oven. "Kathleen," he tried not to complain too pointedly. He turned on the air-conditioning and began closing the windows. "You're going to cook in this heat."

"I like it when it's hot," she said, meandering to the couch. "Heat absolves me."

Maxwell made a frown like sucking lemons. "Absolves you of what?"

"Lots of things," Kathleen muttered.

Maxwell refrained from further comment. It saddened him—and made him mad—to see her like this: doleful, saturnine. *What the hell is wrong now?* he wondered. He left her to close the bedroom window, and found the radio on. Some talk show psychiatrist was counseling a caller in a voice like an alien radio transmission: "—history of mankind is more proof than we'll ever need. Sexual harassment is culturally and historically all-inclusive. We as women must never forget that it is not a privilege but a basic human right to live free of all manner of sexual harassment. And I don't just mean in the workplace—I mean at home, on the street, in the bedroom. When we watch television, when we read, when we go to the movie theater or listen to music. Through centuries of subjugation, the male sexual hierarchy has evolved into a monster of diabolical proportions." The counselor lapsed into a heated pause. "When we succumb to the monster, we fail in all that we are. We must never succumb to the monster of male exploitation."

"What good is that?" a caller retorted. Her voice, as distant as the psychiatrist's, mixed rage with sobs. "I have two kids and a dead husband. I gotta car that breaks down every week and I can barely even afford the lot rental for my trailer. I have to feed my children tuna fish and crackers every night for God's sake. If I don't have sex with my boss, he'll give that raise to someone else."

"Don't succumb," the counselor insisted. "Report the bastard."

"Oh, come on! I'm so sick of hearing that. I can't prove it; it's my word against his. Who are they going to believe?"

The counselor had no answer.

"God." The caller broke into quiet sobs. "It isn't fair."

"No, no it's not."

Maxwell silenced the radio. *No answers for anything,* he mused. He was tired of hearing sad things, of people taken advantage of, of souls in turmoil. Despair, it seemed, flourished without surcease, even in the airwaves, and in the dead space of the ether.

He slammed closed the window, sealing out the heat. It would take all night for the apartment to get cool, hot as it was. Unnamed distresses plucked at his nerves like pizzicato. When he went back out to the living room, and asked Kathleen what was wrong, she told him that her uncle was out of prison.

He sat with her on the couch, all the lights off but one. He held her hand as he listened. Her hand felt dry, cool. "At first I thought Spence might be lying," she said. "It's almost like I'm his enemy; for some reason he goes out of his way to keep me on edge, to keep me in pieces."

"The asshole," Maxwell articulated. "But maybe he *is* lying. Isn't that possible?"

"No." She craned her head back on the couch, looking up at the ceiling. "I called the prison. There's some new early-release program they're doing, to save money. They're cycling people in and out of there like it's a goddamn voting booth. Uncle Sammy was paroled yesterday afternoon. They said he was a model prisoner." She gave a faint, dark chuckle. "Good behavior, they said."

Maxwell cringed for something to say to console her. But nothing came—nothing, at least, that wasn't a lie. What could he say? Don't worry, Kathleen, it's all right? It wasn't all right. You'll forget all about him? She'd never forget, never. How could she?

He wondered what he'd done to her—some obsidian inquisitor in him, with no heart. She'd only implied thus far, never exacting upon details. He thought of dredgers. He thought of rocks turned over to reveal slug slime and nests of worms. *No,* he realized. *I don't want to know. I never want to know.*

But then she told him anyway, as though fate—or premonition—had posted challenge to his negation. It all poured out of her—the blackest ichor tapped through the wounds her uncle had lain into her spirit.

"He'd always call it Sleepytime—that was his cue. He always spoke very quietly and repetitively. He said that there were special secret things that uncles and little girls were supposed to do together. That's why God made uncles, he said. To show little girls the special Secret Things. It was a special secret from God and if I ever told anyone, bad things would happen to me, but little girls who kept the secret would always be happy, and good things would always happen to them and their loved ones." Kathleen's eyes remained riveted upward, to the ceiling. She seemed to never blink at all. "He'd always be talking to me while he was doing it, it was always the same quiet voice. He'd be asking me about school, and about my friends. He'd always repeat key words at particular times. He bought me one of those cat clocks, where the tail and the eyes move back and forth, and he'd always position me so that I'd be looking at the clock while he was doing it. It was always from behind, and he'd always move with the rhythm of the clock. The therapist told me years later that he was actually using some fairly advanced hypnotic techniques, an integral system of vocal and kinesthetic reinforcements combined with subliminal persuasion methods."

Monster, Maxwell thought. Pure, unadulterated evil. He was going to tell her not to say anymore, that she didn't have to, but then he quickly realized how essential it was for her to go on. If she didn't get these things out of her, they'd turn to rot in her soul. She'd been left to sit alone with her past now. The savior therapists were long gone—there was only Maxwell, who sat immobile as she continued in a voice like crust, like gravel.

"Sammy never had a fixed place of residence. Evidently he was always going back and forth to New Jersey. He told my father he was involved in some commercial real estate investments; what he was really doing was running kiddie porn masters from Jersey to some duplication facility here. But whenever my father was away on business—at least a half dozen times a year, sometimes for weeks at a time—Sammy would live at the house, take me to and from school, take care of the bills, etc. He was always very gentle, he was always very careful with my body. He used contraceptive jelly and a variety of lubricants. He'd always rub up against me at first—he never let me see him. That's another thing the therapists said was typical among expert pedophiles. He'd always insert himself in me from behind. He didn't begin to sodomize me 'til I was older, like 13, 14, but it was always from behind so I'd have to see the clock, the eyes and the tail ticking back and forth. He never came in me—I think he was really afraid that I might get pregnant, especially when I got older."

Maxwell morosely remembered what she'd told him a few nights ago: that though her uncle's abuse of her had started when she was nine, it had continued into her late teens. *How many times?* the morbid inquiry occurred to him. How many times had her uncle raped her? *Hundreds, probably,* he realized. *Over all those years? Yes, it had to be. Hundreds of times.*

"He never came in me," Kathleen repeated. Either tears or perspiration sparkled on her cheek. Her hand tightened in Maxwell's; her gaze remained upward. "It was always the same, the clock eyes switching back and forth with the thrusts, the soft ticking sound and his soft voice behind me in the dark." Now she closed her eyes, squeezing something back. "His voice was so light, so gentle. He'd always say the same thing. 'Almost, almost— Here,' he'd say and then he'd pull out of me and he'd grab my hand and gently guide it behind me and he'd wrap my hand around his penis, he'd jerk himself off with my hand."

Maxwell exerted himself to try and decipher how she felt and what she was thinking whenever her uncle did this to her, but a void swelled in his mind, a wasteland.

"'Almost, almost— Here,'" she whispered. Then she leaned against him, her head on his shoulder, and she fell silent.

Whatever a spirit really was—Maxwell's plummeted, a stone dropped into a bottomless fissure. Was it the world that had created her uncle? Was it sociology, environment, and chemical brain defects? Or was it simply evil? If the latter, then what had created Maxwell, and the thoughts that now surged in him? In a fantasy, or a vision, he could easily picture himself killing Uncle Sammy, sticking his .38 right into the guy's ear and dropping the hammer. It would be easy. *You're a poet, not a hitman,* he reminded himself when the image faded. But how was he supposed to feel, after hearing this? Was it evil to want to exterminate someone like Kathleen's uncle?

He waited a long time before he spoke. He sat with his arm around her, thinking and giving her time to calm down. She may even have dozed off for a few minutes.

When she stirred, he reached for the Blockbuster bag.

"What did you bring?" she said. "Videos?"

"Not quite." The bag sat in his lap like something stillborn. "I don't know how you feel about this, but this killer thing has me really worried—the fact that she's writing to you, that she knows your address. And now, with your uncle out of prison, I guess that's one more thing to worry about. That's why I brought this."

"What is it?"

"A gun," Maxwell said. "I mean, you need some kind of protection, don't you? More than some cop in the parking lot who's probably asleep if he's there at all."

"I don't know anything about guns," Kathleen replied, leaning up to look at the bag. "And the killer will never come here. She's deliberately leaving the bodies where the police can find them. She knows the police are well aware of her, and she's smart enough to suspect that they're staking out my apartment. She'll never come here, Maxwell."

"Okay, maybe she won't. But what if your Uncle Sammy does?"

Her refusal to answer was answer enough. She was looking at the bag, at the strange edges formed by its contents.

"I don't think it's a good idea," she eventually said.

"I want you to have it," he persisted. "Just to be safe."

"It's not a good idea. I—" Her voice wandered. "Because if my uncle actually did come here, I'd probably kill him."

So would I, Maxwell thought. *I'd fucking kill him.*

Chapter 20

(I)

She wonders what it would be like to pull out his eyes with Duplay 3-prong cervical forceps.

Or exsanguinate him with an arterial catheter.

Or do a torso job on him.

These are good ideas.

You'll have to remember them, she thinks.

"So why'd you miss your shift last night?"

The night physical plant manager is fat and bald.

He's scribbling on papers at his desk.

"I forgot I was on the schedule," she says.

"Forgot?"

He has a dark mustache like a caterpillar.

His nose is full of tiny broken veins.

She could cut his nose off with the Stille-Liston bone-cutters.

Are you going to fire me? she wonders. *Suspend me?*

"Don't worry about it," he huffs, never looking up. "Just don't let it happen again."

"I won't."

"I'll mark it off as a vacation day."

"Thank you."

This is very nice of him.

But she still would like to pull his eyes out with the Duplay 3-prong cervical forceps.

Later she's downstairs with her cleaning cart.

The ER is empty.

People must not be killing each other tonight, she thinks.

Sometimes she gets depressed.

She wishes she could just sleep and maybe never wake up.

Why are you sad? her mother asks.

"I don't know."

"What?" asks an x-ray tech coming out of the staff elevator.

"I was just thinking out loud," she says.

I was just thinking about maybe doing a torso job on you. I'd put S,K,&F tourniquets on your arms and legs and then saw them off. I did that once. I'd like to do it to you.

The technician is gone.

She feels better when some EMTs wheel in a bleeding black man on a gurney.

The man is screaming in gusts.

There's a bandage taped to his head, and he's screaming.

A crash nurse takes the bandage off to change it.

There's a small bullet hole in the man's head.

Blood is jumping out of the hole.

In moments several masked doctors are surrounding the man.

"Heart rate's saying bye-bye," one doctor says.

"Code Blue!" another yells.

They converge on the man to revive him.

Prod paddles slide briskly over Redux conductant paste.

"Charge up!"

"Clear!"

The LIFEPAK 4 defibrillator buzzes, then thunks.

After five attempts someone says, "School's out."

"Been a veggie anyway. Christ, they execute each other in the street these days."

"So what? Saves tax dollars. These gunshot players we see every night? They're all on welfare, they're all knocking each other off in drug deals."

"Come on," one of the doctors objects. "How do you know this guy's on welfare? What, just because he's black means he's on welfare? Just because he's black means he got shot in a drug deal?"

"He got popped in the head with an SNS, for Christ's sake. And 10-to-one when you read about it in the Metro section tomorrow, it won't even say he's black. If you say he's black, then that's considered racist."

"You're the racist, Mike. Jesus—"

"And you ever notice in the Crime Beat, whenever someone gets charged or convicted, they never say if they're black."

"Maybe it's because they aren't."

"Come on—"

"You should start wearing a white sheet into the ER, Mike."

"Yeah, well, I'll still bet my Porsche that the papers don't say this guy's black..."

"Give it a rest, will ya, fellas? What is this, the 'Geraldo Show?' Every night we gotta listen to the ACLU versus the Grand Wizard."

They all laugh.

"But how about those Skins beating Buffalo?"

"Big deal, it's only exhibition. And what are the Bills anyway, 'cept a bunch of busted assholes who lose four Super Bowls in a row. Just wait 'til the real season starts. Watch the Eagles use the Skins for toidy paper. And Mike can bet his Porsche that Dallas'll roll right over them."

"Dallas? Those milquetoast Texas queers? They trade undies with the cheerleaders, probably blow each other in their pickup trucks. Emmit, Emmit! Pay me four mil a year and I'll rush for a 150 yards a game, too. Just wait'll the Redskins' defensive line gets their hands on that earring-wearing creamcake. The guy puts a potato in his pants before each game, and so do the rest of them. Bunch of cowboy faggots is what they are. Spend the off-season swapping spit and holding hands. If Dallas beats the Skins, I'll move."

"Hey, and let me tell you guys something about football. Look close at the stats. You ever notice how the teams with the most blacks on the first string have the best records?"

"Give it a rest, will ya!"

"Hey, anybody got an ID on this guy?"

"Yeah. John something. Doe."

They all laugh and disband.

She begins to mop up, wishing the man had lived longer.

She liked the way the blood squirted out of his head.

Skulls mean death, her mother says.

She watches her mother carefully injecting heroin into a vein in her foot.

Earlier, she'd seen the resident walking down the empty hall toward the phlebotomy lab. WALLACE, M. PHLEBOTOMY his name tag read. He is the one who fucks the charge nurse up in the new ICU at night. He'd smiled at her and nodded as he'd passed in the hall.

He'd like to fuck us, her mother says.

"I know."

He's just like Daddy, they all are.

I'd love to sew his lips shut and cut off his cock with the Bruns shears, she thinks.

When he'd passed her in the antiseptic hall, his skull glowed beneath his face like a Halloween mask.

Skulls mean death, she thinks.

Now she's up in the new ICU wing which still isn't open yet because of the refurbishments.

The privacy curtains are a nice pastel slate blue color.

It's very dark.

She's peeking around the corner.

She's watching the resident fuck the heavy charge nurse whose white skirt is pushed up over her buttocks.

The nurse's hand reaches under her to play with his testicles.

The resident is standing up pumping her on the edge of the convalescent bed.

He slaps her buttocks every so often.

Look at them, her mother says.

I know, she thinks back.

In her left hand she holds an Arista #12 scalpel.

The blade is like a little hook.

She knows she could kill them both probably before either of them had time to scream.

She'd come up behind him, slide the blade across his subclavian artery, then get the nurse right across the throat.

Then she'd dissect them both on the bed.

She looks at the little sharp hook-blade on the scalpel in her hand.

Honestly! her mother says. *Don't you ever think anymore?*

Her mother isn't in a very good mood today.

No, of course she can't kill them.

She can't kill anyone at the hospital.

She can't kill anyone tonight.

She'll have to wait 'til tomorrow night.

She puts the cover back on the scalpel and slips it back into her pocket.

Tomorrow night, her mother says.

(II)

Spence couldn't sleep. He'd waked repeatedly from an eerie, subterranean dream. A faraway red light was throbbing, like a heart. Spence was being chased through narrow stone corridor whose walls seemed to shed sweat or blood. He could only see by the pulsing light around each corner. Rapid footfalls pursued him, and panting. Running, he drew his Smith snub, but when he checked the five-shot cylinder he found each chamber empty.

Wait a minute, he thought in the dream. *What the hell am I running from?*

He'd never found out, for next he lay awake in his bed. The clock ticked, though, in time with the dream's throbbing light. It was 2:30 in the morning; moonlight hung like a pale film on the window.

It wasn't really a nightmare. Spence didn't have them—he hadn't had a genuine nightmare in years. In the dream, he hadn't even been scared—he was just running.

He rose and padded naked to the bathroom. The fluorescent tube buzzed in snatches, then blinked on. Bleaching light made him look ghastly in the mirror: a muscular cadaver with hole-punch eyes.

He shook a can of shave cream—Edge Gel—and squirted a cross onto the mirror. Squinting, he tried to visualize it as the killer did, through Simmons' hallucinotic aura of light. But no revelatory totem occurred to him. Just a cross of Edge Gel, lime green.

Next he wrote the word—NASCENT—into the glass. Exposed to the air, the gel fizzed and grew larger, limpening.

Simmons had told him to find the nascent.

Nascent, he contemplated. It was an awkward word, stifled. It seemed cryptic. Was it in Kathleen Shade's work? Tomorrow Spence would read every back issue of *'90s Woman* since Shade had been writing for them. He would read every "Verdict" column. Perhaps the killer had written in once, and been responded to by Shade. Or perhaps the killer identified with Shade's response to some other reader's problem.

Or maybe there's no nascent at all, he weighed.

He didn't feel like going back to sleep. Instead, he showered and dressed and brushed his teeth. He checked his gun—timid from the dream—and found the cylinder full of Q-loads. Then he left his apartment and drove to Kathleen Shade's.

Spence's own mother haunted him during he ride. Diced thoughts irritating as pollen in the eye. He could only blame himself that his mother had died never really knowing him. He could still hear her voice from his senior year in high school. *How come you don't go out with friends, Jeffrey?* What could he ever say? He never liked anybody. *I'm so proud of you,* she'd said when they'd beat the shit out of Parkdale High at homecoming. Spence had played middle guard; he'd tackled Parkdale's star RB so hard in the first quarter, the guy had been out cold for the rest of the game. Cracked his fuckin' lights out. Spence was a hero. *But how come you never go out with girls? You have your pick of the cheerleaders!* Then his mother had laughed. *You don't want people thinking you're one of those queer boys.*

No, Mom, I am *one of those queer boys,* he came very close to telling her.

She'd have died right then and there, Spence thought now.

The tac van read RANDOLPH CARTER CONTRACTORS along the sides, with a district phone number. S.O.D. even had a special line; if someone they were staking found the van suspicious and called the number, the S.O.D. operator had a phony spiel all ready.

Intermittent lights in the parking lot seemed to prop the night's hot weight up over the complex; most of the three-story apartment buildings appeared abandoned—lightless, drab, their windows dead. Spence parked and got out. The parking lot swallowed him in its utter silence. He'd radioed ahead through the S.O.D. switchboard to announce himself, rather than risk being drawn down on by whoever their tac cowboy was in the van. A black guy, even more muscular than Spence, stood waiting in a utility shirt which bore the name of the phony contractor.

"Lieutenant Spence?"

Spence showed his badge and ID. "How's it going?"

"Dead night," he was answered. "But the overtime's great. I'm Larkins. Come on into the war wagon."

The van had been parked in the second row, facing Kathleen Shade's building entrance. *War wagon is right,* Spence thought once inside. A locked gunrack on the left shackled a variety of weapons: an AR-15A2 with a Starlight, an automatic shotgun, a Heckler & Koch MP5 submachine gun, and an obscure bolt-action sniper rifle with an ART IV 1.5-6x scope. Another rack was hung with several pistols, a Glock with an extended mag, and some pocket pieces. Larkins closed the van's back doors, sealing them into a cubby tinted by red night-vision lights.

"Anybody made you yet?" Spence asked.

"Naw. We move the van every day. This place is pretty quiet, nine-to-fivers. No punks and not many kids." Larkins offered Spence a fold-down seat hinged to the van wall. The right side, before which Larkins lounged in a swing chair, sported all the van's electronics: three low-light video screens, a triangulator made by General Electric, hash scanners for U.S. Park Police, EPS Uniform Branch, and some of the closer county departments in Maryland and Virginia. There was a lot of microwave equipment too, which tapped into cordless phones, and recording hardware. Mugshots of Heather B. Willet had been posted between the video screens. One screen showed the apartment entrance, another Kathleen Shade's balcony, from concealed cameras mounted behind the seats up front. A blackout curtain prevented anyone from viewing them through the windshield.

"She up there now?" Spence asked.

"Yep. Hasn't come out all day. A cab dropped the blond guy off about 7:30. Lights went out around midnight."

"Love in the evening," Spence remarked. He thumbed through the operating log, noticing different colored ink for each shift. Then he looked at the balcony screen. *They're up there now, in bed,* he thought. *Has she told him everything? Anything? What do they talk about? What do they do?*

It was hard to picture her sexually. He wondered how traumatized her uncle's sexual abuse had left her. How much of that seeped into her sex life now, with Platt? She'd never seemed traumatized at all, nor had she ever displayed the least bit of fear about the killer.

What are you really like? Spence wondered.

"She's got a piece," Larkins said.

Spence's ponderings snapped. "What's that?"

"Looks like a .38, four-inch, kind of old. I think the blond guy brought it over for her. Somebody should tell them handguns are illegal in D.C."

This interested Spence. Had Platt brought the gun by his own insistence, or had Kathleen Shade asked for it? And, in either case, why? As protection from the killer, or from her uncle? "I think we'll let her keep it," he decided. "It'll give me something to bust her chops about."

"I'm sitting here all night waiting for something to go down," Larkins observed, "but I got this feeling nothing will."

"You're probably right. The killer has to know we're on to her. But she's psychopathic. Lotta times psychopaths get fuzzy on the dividing line between fantasy and reality. And they make mistakes. That's what we're counting on. She might come here in a fugue state, or when she's deep in one of her delusions. Then we've got her."

Larkins inclined back, his lat muscles expanding massively as he laced his fingers behind his head. "It's almost like we're using Shade for bait," he said.

Spence's face ticked in the red light. Simmons had implied the same thing, but directly toward Spence. *Am I that desperate?* he asked himself. "Whatever the fascination the killer has for Shade," he said, "that's what we're using for bait. Might all be for nothing now, though."

"What do you mean?"

"Bad timing. Shade seemed very enthused about being contacted by the killer—I hoped to be able to use that, too. But now I'm not so sure. When she was a kid, she was sexually abused by her uncle. She got over it pretty good in therapy... But yesterday her uncle got out of the joint on early release. So now—" Beside the mugshot of Heather B. Willet, Spence posted an 8x10 of Samuel Curtis Shade. "—you've got two people to be on watch for."

"A pedo, huh? Goddamn short eyes." Larkins scrutinized the photograph. "It's funny how you can tell a person's skell just by how they look."

"Yeah," Spence agreed. Kathleen Shade's Uncle Sammy looked like a big angular head on a long neck, beady eyes too close together, bald on top. The face was all cheekbones and hollows, and he had a tight little twist for a mouth. His Adam's apple jutted like a walnut in his throat. "Real sick fuck material here. You think he might cruise by to peep on her?"

Spence shrugged. "I doubt it, not while he's on parole. But just because the corrections board let him out doesn't mean he's not still fucked up. I got a big problem with any guy who diddles with kids. He made a lot of kiddie porn for the mob."

"I hope he's got the balls to come by here," Larkins said. "I'll make sure to read him his rights before I kick his ass up and down the street. Yeah, he and I would party... Kind of sucks for Shade, though. Like she hasn't got enough problems with some killer buzzing her. Now she's got to worry about this scumbucket."

Larkins was right. Sometimes the past could be very haunting. The last thing Kathleen Shade needed right now was a revisitation of her past. It wasn't fair. Any released felon had an automatic restraining order; they were free to walk the streets as long as they didn't go near their victims. Any reasonable intent whatsoever, and they were back in the slam. But Spence also knew that was hardly a protection.

"I'm out of here," Spence said. "Don't die of boredom."

"I'll try not to, Lieutenant." Larkins let him out the back of the van. He looked like a black ghost in the blood-red light. Then the doors pulled shut, leaving Larkins to his monitors and his cache of guns.

Spence walked back to the unmarked. The heat cloyed him, even this late; the only breeze felt like a furnace draft. The world was abed, but did monsters dream? It was a frightening thought. How many people were dying right now, at the hands of killers? How many innocents, this instant as Spence's shoes carried him across a parking lot, expired to torture, to atrocity? And what of other monsters—pedophiles like Kathleen Shade's uncle? Did such a monster's lust rage now with each beat of Spence's heart? Was the spirit of some child—somewhere, right now as Spence drew another breath—being crushed to irrevocability? Spence felt sure of it.

Some world, he thought. He'd been thinking of the world a lot of late. The world made little sense on nights like these.

He stopped before getting into the car. He recalled his dream: being chased by something. But what? His ambitions? His failures? His success?

No, there didn't seem to be much point in anything. The world didn't care. It left people with nothing beyond their dreams.

He looked up at Kathleen Shade's windows, and wondered about her dreams.

(III)

The dream congealed, the darkness reformed into flesh by her horror. Kathleen's legs lay spread, paralytic. The sephulchral figure knelt beside her, its features not hidden by shadows but composed of them. Once again the hands of ink-black bones displayed the morbid Polaroids one after another: the cigar box with the snake in it, the snake dumped out onto the bed, the snake uncoiling, then inching photo by photo toward Kathleen's sex.

"The pictures, look," the figure whispered.

It wasn't a malicious whisper; it seemed instead consoling, compassionate, despite what Kathleen was being shown.

"They're still the same," the figure whispered. "The pictures are still the same. Look what's being done to you. Look, and see what you're letting someone do..."

Kathleen grit her teeth, straining against the manacles of her terror. The darkness churned before the moonlight. Her sweat ran cold.

"Such sad pictures..."

The gun! Kathleen instantly thought. She remembered the gun Maxwell had given her. If she could only break out of this paralysis, if she could only get the gun...

But...

"What would you do then?" the figure bid. "What would you do with the gun?"

Kathleen wasn't sure.

"Would you kill me?"

"I—"

The figure's black, grave-dirt smile broadened. "You need to look harder at the pictures."

"I've already seen the goddamn pictures!" Kathleen shrieked. Her muscles cramped as she jerked against the force which pinned her down. Tendons seemed to pop, cartilage seemed to tear. But, still, she couldn't move. "This is only a dream!" she shrieked on. "It's not real!"

"But the dream comes from you, and you're real. So the dream must be real too."

"No!"

"And what about these pictures?"

Flecks of spit shot off Kathleen's lips. "They're just a bunch of Freudian representations, symbols of my fears, and my—"

"Your past?"

"Yes! They're symbols, just symbols! They're not real!"

"But you haven't looked at the last one yet."

In her struggles, Kathleen bit through her tongue. The figure's hands displayed more pictures of the fat, black snake crawling forward and, eventually, burrowing itself into Kathleen's sex. The third to last photo showed only an inch of the snake's tail dangling out, and in the second to last, the snake was gone.

"You're sure that the snake is just a symbol?"

"Yes!" Kathleen shrieked with blood in her mouth.

"But a symbol of what?"

"My uncle! My Uncle Sammy!"

The second to last photograph drifted: Kathleen's bare legs splayed open. No snake.

It's inside me now, she thought.

"Look at the last one."

Her eyes could not move away, her gaze paralyzed as surely as her arms and legs. In that last photograph, a second figure—a male figure—stood at the front of the bed. A black, boney silhouette-shape against the moonlight. A caliginous, featureless face. Red-lit pits for eyes. In its black hands it held a cigar box.

Kathleen screamed blood.

"Embrace your hatred," oozed the words.

Chapter 21

(I)

When the phone on his desk rang, Spence stared at it. A muse made him go rigid—an aural image. It was inexplicable.

Spence's mother had died of a massive myocardial infarction back when he was still in college. They'd never understood each other very well; they were never really close. When they buried her, he remembered standing blank-faced at the graveside. The service concluded, and Spence walked away. It was only an hour later, in his car backed up on the Woodrow Wilson Bridge, that Spence suddenly burst into tears.

He hadn't been crying as much for her as for himself—his concreteness, his inability to feel anything for anyone.

The memory returned now, as the phone rang and rang. His face felt cold while the back of his head bristled with heat from the sun in the window. He imagined something chilling. He imagined that if he picked up the phone, it would be his mother on the other end.

"Spence," he said into the phone. "Major Case Section."

Jeffrey, he imagined. *You never loved me, did you?*

Yes I did! he suddenly wanted to scream into the phone.

"Got second-pass chromatography back from the McCrone labs in Chicago."

"Who is this?" Spence whispered.

"It's me, Kohls. I'm down here in workup." Kohls chuckled. "Who'd you think it was? Hillary? Vince Foster?"

I did love my mother, Spence thought. *But I never told her.*

"You there?"

"Yeah, sorry." Spence wiped his brow. Even the killer had loved her mother, to the extent that she saw her ghost. He squeezed his eyes shut, then popped them back open. "What's that about McCrone?"

"Got second-pass source spectrums. Remember the first three victims, the human jigsaw? Plus Calabrice, the lawyer. Source specs on the tox-screen read positive for a solvent compound called dimethylsulfoxide. It's an osmotic agent; they use it in hospitals and morgues to preserve histology samples. It's also a topical analgesic, a penetrating emollient. It makes anti- inflammatory salves work better."

"I don't follow."

"Say you tear ligaments in your knee. This stuff, dimethylsulfoxide—DMSO for short—they rub it on your knee. Then, on top of it, they rub on an anti-inflammatory. The DMSO bonds with the anti-inflammatory and carries it deep into the torn ligaments, to reduce the swelling."

Think, Spence thought. *Why would she...*

"And that might explain my own tox-screens that detected traces of isopropanol—"

"Rubbing alcohol," Spence translated.

"Right. For some reason, she's using DMSO to carry something into their bloodstreams, then she's wiping them down with isopropanol to clear their skin for any prints she might've left. For a psychopath, she's pretty thorough."

Spence would have to think about this. If he pondered it now, too quickly, he might miss it. Why use something like DMSO when she had free access to hypodermic needles?

"Then there's your partner 'Rome, the pimp. Remember the other day you where down in the shop?"

Spence remembered. The tacky black skin freshly stripped of the mysterious duct tape used to cocoon the victim, to completely immobilize him. *A mummy,* he remembered. *It looked like a mummy.*

"And I told you I found something asporous and crimson lining the insides of the nostrils?" Kohls was going on. "Well, the AFM computer matched it to a spectrum-index."

"What was it?"

"Powdered red pepper. She blew the stuff into his nasal passages all the way down to his lower bronchi. Can you imagine that?"

"No," Spence croaked.

"I mean, the guy's wrapped up head to foot in duct tape. He can't move a muscle; the only thing exposed are his fuckin' nostrils and she's burning up his entire respiratory tract with powdered red pepper. Can you imagine the pain?"

Spence didn't want to imagine it. He refused to.

"And that's all before she cuts off the guy's works. Jesus to Pete, Lieutenant. You got yourself a real winner here. This chick knows more about torture than Einstein knew about relativity. Makes Adolf Eichmann look like fuckin' Dick Van Dyke."

Suddenly Spence's head felt like a huge weight against his neck. He didn't want to think now—about anything. He felt wholly incapable of it. He didn't want to deduce. He didn't want to speculate. He didn't want to make a single contemplation about anything in the world...

"But I guess we'll get the blow-by-blow eventually."

"What?" Spence said.

"The exact details on what she did to 'Rome. The killer should be sending her account to Shade any day now, right?"

"Yeah," Spence said, rubbing his eyes. "Any day now."

(II)

CHAPTER THREE
THE MUMMY

You read about it once in *Newsweek*, a fascinating article about the Chilean secret police. They were masters of torture. Political prisoners would be handcuffed to chairs in a room. There was a hole in the wall. One by one, each prisoner would be taken to the wall, and his head would be inserted into the hole, and two soldiers would hold him there. On the other side of the wall were several starved dogs. The dogs would eat off their faces. By the time half the prisoners had been given the treatment, the remaining prisoners would be more than happy to reveal any secrets they might have. Often the service would abduct a prisoner's wife and children. The prisoner would be forced to watch as soldiers raped his family, and then tortured them with power tools. They were big on power tools. They liked to drill through joints. They also liked to perform amputations. A limb would be anesthetized, removed with an electric saw and then shown to the prisoner. Sometimes the limb would be thrown to a starved dog, and the prisoner was forced to watch it be eaten. As for female prisoners, their hands would be cut off. Then they'd be gang-raped, tortured with needles and electric prods, and strangled, while other prisoners were made to watch. Religious radicals were frequently sodomized by soldiers in frocks, and then forced to perform fellatio. These scenes were taped and then sent to the subversive's headquarters. One time a subversive's wife had been abducted. She'd been forced to have sex with animals, which was also taped and sent to the husband. To soften prisoners before an interrogation, they'd be handcuffed to a chair in a brightly lit room for days. All the prisoner had to look at were dead children hung by their necks from the ceiling. Prisoners were categorized into three groups. There were those who were systematically tortured for information on subversive activities. Then there were those who were used for sexual recreation and to train the torture squads. And then there were those who were deemed simply as extreme enemies of the state. It was for this latter group that the very special procedures were reserved. Flensing, exsanguination, live brain probes, non-anesthetic surgery. Blow-torches would be applied to genitals. Spinal taps would be administered, and the drained fluid would be replaced by mild acids. Heads would be slowly crushed in steel presses. But one procedure appeals to you more than any of the others. It is perfect for 'Rome. It involves red pepper extract and heavy-gauge utility tape.

You make him drive you home. Daddy's big pistol in his crotch is quite a persuader. You get him cuffed to the bed. The Amytal puts him out in seconds. First you put a packaged tourniquet on his right wrist and you cut off the defiling hand with a Deavers bonesaw. You'll use the hand later. Then you begin to wrap him up. This takes quite a while. You must do a neat job. You want him to look good when the police find him. You need to roll him along the floor to keep the tape tight and straight. When you're done he is completely wrapped up in the utility tape from head to foot. He looks like a mummy! That's what you'll call this chapter. You'll call it THE MUMMY. It sounds scary. The only thing not covered by the tape is his nose, so he can breathe. You put him back up on the bed in Daddy's Room, where the couch used to be, the couch Daddy fucked you on while The Cross glowed in your eyes. The bundle is moving a little now, and you can hear muffled sounds beneath the tape. You give him a shot of Desoxyn so you don't have to wait. You're fascinated by what he must be thinking, to suddenly wake up as a mummy. Sightless, speechless. He can't hear or move. All he can to is breathe and think and be afraid. You're ready now. You think about all the things he's done to women like your mother, and the things he would do to you if he could, and you're ready. You pinch his nostrils shut. The mummy begins to shake. On his upper lip, you sprinkle a line of McCormick ground red pepper. Then you release his nostrils. The red pepper disappears like magic when he is finally allowed to inhale. Now the mummy shakes and shakes, the smothered scream exploding and going nowhere. It's funny the way the mummy vibrates. You clamp the nostrils shut again, sprinkle on more red pepper, wait a little longer, then release. Pinch, sprinkle, release. Pinch, sprinkle, release. Each time you hold the pinch a little longer, to make him inhale the red pepper more deeply. You do this for almost an hour. Don't die yet, you think. With a pair of Doyen bandage scissors, you carefully cut a small square of tape off of the space between his legs. You see that he has urinated. Through the square you pull out his penis and scrotum.

You caress it. The penis is shrunken in terror. You give him another shot of Desoxyn so he won't pass out. You're caressing, caressing. Then you quickly cut it all off with the Bruns shears and stand back to watch the mummy lurch like a frog on a hot-plate. Then you pinch his nostrils shut again very hard. You wait and wait and wait, squeezing his nose shut until the mummy stops lurching and it dies.

Kathleen let the pages slip from her hands onto the floor.

(III)

Man without a country, he thought. The streets smelled sweet. They'd confiscated all the cash at his motel in Newark. That's where he'd lived most of the time when he was making a run—motel to motel—to keep the feds off his trail. A few of his associates put him up, and he had various other places to stay between his treks to and from Jersey. In the business, a permanent residence eventually marked you if someone stooled. At least the goddamn cops couldn't touch his inheritance, which had been rolling over in the CD year after year. He'd paid his debt, goddamn it. People didn't understand anything. He had rights, too.

Samuel Curtis Shade walked into the First American Bank on Pennsylvania Avenue. He looked slimmer in the rust-brown suit, and older than his 47 years. This was reasonable; you turned to porridge in PC. They only let you out two hours a day, but that was better than general pop. Pedophiles didn't last long on the mainline—the players ground you up. At least in PC they couldn't turn him into a cell-block bitch. "I kin smell yo pussy, honk!" they'd yell on his escort to the showers or the quad. "Hey, kiddie fucker! You be my bitch when they put choo outa PC! We'se gonna *bust* you up!"

At least in protective custody, he could think. He could remember. Especially Kathleen...

"There's a penalty on early withdrawal," the teller, a long-faced but otherwise attractive brunette, informed him.

"I don't care." He closed one certificate and transferred it to savings, then withdrew 15,000 in cash. So what if he lost a little interest? As the teller commenced with the transaction, Sammy spied school snapshots of her children on her cubby wall. *Cute kids,* he thought. *And mama's making another one.* The teller was pregnant. It reminded him of some of the flicks he'd made. *Natal Attraction,* one was called. A couple of log-boys double-fucking some coked-up blonde who was so pregnant she looked like she might break her water before the cumshot. Sammy's circuit produced all kinds of stuff—what the feds called "Underground," the stuff you couldn't get from an ad in *Hustler.* Animal tapes, "wet" S&M, rape loops, a little snuff. But most of the circuit's orders were for kp. A lot of it came from the Netherlands; the rest they made themselves in the Jersey suburbs. None of the point people wanted the shit from Mexico and South America. They wanted white kids. Private mail drops paid as much as a grand for a 15-minute 3/4-inch master if the resolution was good; from there they made mass-duplications at each point. A mob guy named Vinchetti ran the works. His net duped a few hundred masters per month, and each dupe was ordered hundreds of times. Big money. Sammy was a production man and a mule; each month he'd drive up to Jersey with orders from the D.C. region, he'd help make the videos, then he'd transport the masters back to D.C. They paid well, a couple of grand per run, but Sammy wasn't in it just for the money.

He liked to see the shit.

The down and dirty, ball-busting shit...

Many a time he'd held the lights while Vinchetti's crew had done a snuff or a wet S&M job on some Jersey junkie. Many a time he'd been cameraman for such bits of cinematic excellence as *My Lover, My Trunk*; *Lassie's Lucky Day*; *Legless in Seattle*; *Fist Party*; *Suzy Likes Showers*. Sammy got a real charge seeing what adults would do when they were desperate. That was it: he liked to *see*.

And sometimes Vinchetti's men would let him do more than see.

But kp was different—that was Sammy's special thing. He'd never hurt the kids. He'd loved them, that was all. Nobody ever understood that...

The prosecutors had finished him; Sammy didn't stand a chance when they started showing some of the kp flicks to the jury, and Kathleen's decade-old testimony against him had only driven a few more nails in the legal coffin. They even passed his private photos around, and the kiddie mags he was in. Sammy'd ratted out most of the points, the main labs and warehouses on the east coast, and all over Vinchetti's distro drops. PC was part of the deal, plus they'd dropped most of the federal charges. He could spin or he could take 50 years in general pop with no parole. Same as a death sentence...

"Thank you," Sammy said to the teller when she gave him his withdrawal. His gaze flicked to the snapshots of her kids. "You have beautiful children," he said.

Later he was on the road. Sammy's slam allowed convicts to keep their driver's licenses valid as long as you were eligible for parole within five years of beginning your stint. He paid five large for a used Caddie ragtop, bought temp tags and insurance through DCAIF at the dealer's. So what if the cops knew he bought a car? *I'm a citizen now, not a convict,* he affirmed.

It was great to be out on the open road again. He stopped by Big Ben Liquors and bought a cold case. Then he cruised up New York Avenue and booked a room at the Senator.

He wasn't stupid. Sooner or later someone in the net would get wind he was out of stir. Then Vinchetti would put a high-five-figure contract out on him. But Sammy planned to be out of the country long before then.

He just had a few things to do first.

Chapter 22

(I)

Kathleen hated going to Spence's office. The afternoon traffic was bad enough, and finding a close place to park. But what she disliked further was the office itself—the drab little vault where the sun always seemed to glare in her eyes. Its compactness made Spence, a large man, appear larger. Again, she thought of golems, with hearts and faces of riverbed clay. But better she come to him than he to her, to comment on her housekeeping talents.

"Don't you have a fax machine or email or something?" she asked after being invited through the frosted-glass door.

Spence didn't look up. "Of course. Law enforcement agency use only…" He was reading. "Another manuscript?"

"'Rome, the pimp.'" She put the envelope on his desk. "Here are the originals."

"Express Mail," Spence noted. "That's interesting. A different mode of delivery each time."

"Aren't you going to read it?"

"No. I already know what happened to 'Rome. I'll read it later, then send it to our forensic psychiatrist. Right now, however, and as you can see, I'm quite busy with some rather dull periodicals."

The desk was a welter of magazines. Closer study showed her that Spence had procured several dozen back issues of *'90s Woman*. "Read carefully. You might learn something."

"Unlikely. I'm looking for the nascent."

"The what?" Kathleen asked.

"For a writer you don't have much of a vocabulary. Don't you know what nascent means?"

"No, but I know what pedantry means. And specious and pernicious and partitivious. And here's another word I know. Asshole." She quickly raised a finger. "Oh, and one more. Dickbrain."

"Nascent," Spence said with no rebuff. "The focal point by which the killer's identification with you came into development. She feels linked, specifically, to you; otherwise she'd be sending her accounts to someone else. I need to know why. Why you? I need to know the nascent." His large, manicured hands gestured the piles of magazines. "It's got to be here, in your writing. There's no other place it could be. There's no other way that the killer could form a sense of identification with you."

Spence was right, but his point went without saying. Kathleen was about to suggest that perhaps it was her wisdom that appealed to the killer, her aptitude in analyzing problems and rendering credible advice. Spence, however, didn't give her the chance. "But this is all so tawdry," he continued. "Boyfriend problems, infertility and impotence, domestic duress, jealousy. It's all the same. I don't see anything in your column that's even close to being intricate enough to transfix a psychopath. This is all so rudimentary, biased, shallow." Spence shook his head in long, slow movements.

"I'm not going to respond to that," Kathleen said. "Because you want me to."

"I could care less what you respond to."

Kathleen turned for the door—

"Don't leave yet. I want to talk to you about—"

—she opened the door—

"—your uncle."

Kathleen closed the door. *Of course*, she thought. *He always does this*. She turned and looked at him, and didn't say anything.

"Did you know your uncle has almost half a million dollars in the bank?"

"Inheritance," Kathleen explained. "Shortly before Sam got arrested, my grandfather died; he and my father inherited mineral properties. Sam sold my father his shares and invested it all in t-bills or something."

"Graduated CDs," Spence corrected.

"Anyway, I thought I already told you that."

Spence reflected. "All that money, yet no home."

"What did he need a home for?" Kathleen suggested. "When my father was away on business, he stayed at our house—"

"To look after you," Spence augmented.

"—and the rest of the time he was…"

"Making underground pornography, mostly of the child variety. Then he'd transport the masters to a mob lab here in D.C. He was smart, actually, in not maintaining a permanent address. It made it harder for Justice to bag him. Unfortunately it makes it that much harder for us, now, to keep track of him." Spence's eyes met Kathleen's for the first time since she'd arrived. "He's in town. That much we do know."

"Why are you telling me this?" By now Kathleen's hatred—yes, she thought she could call it that—held itself in check, like a steady pulse. "I know, Spence," she said. "You keep bringing up my uncle because you think it upsets me, knocks me off balance. You want me off balance, don't you? You think it gives you power over me."

"That's the most ludicrous drivel I've ever heard in my life," Spence very calmly retorted. "I thought I was doing you a favor—"

Kathleen jiggled with laughter.

"—by keeping you informed of a matter that concerns you, and, hopefully, to make you aware of the probability that your uncle is someone you'll never have to worry about again."

This flummoxed her. What did he mean? "Explain," she said.

Spence shot a cuff out of a fine charcoal-gray suit, to realign a gold cufflink. "I don't expect you to be well-versed in the machineries of child pornography. The reason your uncle skated on the federal charges was due to a plea bargain. So was his parole eligibility. He sang like a canary, in other words. Child pornography is almost entirely mob-operated. Your uncle stepped on a lot of big toes. The information he gave the feds closed down the east coast kiddie porn network for months."

"What's that got to do with my uncle not bothering me anymore."

"He won't have time," Spence said. "Organized crime takes care of its own. Ever heard the term Philly Shooters? It's not a drink. Your uncle knows full well that people will be gunning for him real soon."

"What, you mean like assassins?" The notion was hard to swallow. It was something that happened in Coppola movies. Hit men?

"Sure," Spence said. "He's a marked man. It'll only be a matter of days before he leaves the country. Mexico. Costa Rica. Some place like that. We're watching his account. Today he withdrew $15,000, to get ready. When he withdraws the rest of it, that means he's making his move." This delighted Kathleen on one hand, yet enraged her on another. It didn't seem fair: Uncle Sammy fleeing to a life of luxury with a suitcase full of cash. He was a child-molester, for God's sake. "Can't you stop him?" she insisted. "Freeze his account or something?"

Spence shook his head. "As far as our judicial system is concerned, Samuel Curtis Shade has paid his debt to society. And we can't freeze bank accounts unless they're comprised of ill-gotten gains. Your uncle's money is free and legal." He looked at her a moment, cruxed. "You should be pleased. You'll never see him again. Unless he's very stupid."

"In what way?"

"He's on parole. If he does anything—anything at all—that violates his early-release orders, he's back in the Cement Ramada. That includes going anywhere near you, harassing you in any way, breaking the law in any way."

It still pisses me off, Kathleen thought. Something itched at her, deep in her heart. But at least she could work on the book now without any worries about Sammy.

"And speaking of breaking the law," Spence added, "did you know that citizen handgun possession is illegal in the District of Columbia? Did you know that it's a felony?"

Kathleen's stare ran like putty. "Wha—"

"The weapon that Maxwell Platt gave you last night—the illegal handgun—"

Kathleen winced. "You asshole," she remarked. She wondered how many times she'd called him that. No other insult seemed appropriate. "So your undercover crony in that ridiculous van is spying on me? That's inexcusable."

"So you've made the vehicle. Impressive. And remember, that 'crony' may well save your life." Spence paused, creaking back away from the ramparts of magazines, and smiled. "It's an amusing thought, though."

"What?"

"I could put you in jail right now. Right this instant, I could cuff you, book you, and lock you up. I'll bet that'd break some of your starch. Hmm?"

Kathleen couldn't help but laugh. "You're so insecure, Spence. You're so juvenile. I almost feel sorry for you—" She laughed again. "Almost. You think your police badge gives you power, for Christ's sake. Without that, you have no sense of self at all, do you? You've got nothing in your life but this. What's the matter? Didn't you love your mother?"

The look in Spence's eye seemed to dull, and his visage ticked as though what she'd said off the top of her head had ruptured an aspect of his arrogance. Kathleen was nearly taken aback: it was an expression she'd never witnessed in him before.

"That's right," she drew on. "I've got a gun in my home. And we both know you can't do a goddamn thing about it."

"Is that so?" Spence queried.

"Yeah, right." Kathleen continued to laugh, the edge of her disdain twirling like pinwheels. "You're going to put me in jail? Me? What a joke. You haven't got the balls."

Spence's brow lifted high.

"You're like a jigsaw puzzle for preschool kids," Kathleen nearly spat. "You're easy to figure out. If you put me in jail, I'll be out of the picture. And you can't afford that."

"And why is this?"

"You think you're fooling me? Don't make me laugh. I'm the only bait you've got for this killer, and we both know that. Without me, you're lost."

Spence stared.

Kathleen walked out and slammed the door.

Her thoughts divided, then subdivided, like cellular fission. Traffic poured back and forth at the crossing; the DON'T WALK sign never wanted to change. DON'T THINK, she thought, baking in heat and smog.

"Jesus Christ!" she shrieked when she got back to her car. The arrow on the meter indicated EXPIRED; the parking ticket lay flat against the windshield. She knew she'd cranked in an hour's worth of change—she *knew* it. And she'd been in Spence's office 15 minutes maximum. She knew it. When she started the car—hot as an oven inside—a headache kindled in time with the ignition. It felt like a bristly worm throbbing behind her left eye. She pulled out, flailing curses at traffic, and drove without forethought to Maxwell's.

He'd left this morning, as usual, without waking her. EACH DAY I LOVE YOU MORE, he'd typed on a sheet of paper in her MemoryWriter, and on her desk he'd left a single red rose...

She heard his own typewriter tapping away behind the door. Would she be interrupting him? Poets were finicky about their creative space, but then so was Kathleen. The headache raced as she knocked. She nearly fell on him when he opened the door. "Kathl— What's wrong?"

She straggled in more than walked. "I don't feel good. I need to lie down."

"You look terrible," he said, took her purse, and sat her down on the couch. "You look like you've been yelling or something."

"I guess I have been." She kicked off her shoes, closed her eyes. "At myself. I feel like I'm falling apart." This seemed the most pitiful of things to say, and the least like her. "I got another manuscript from the killer," she added.

Maxwell had his arm around her, delicately pushing her hair off her brow. "Was it...bad?"

"It was disgusting. It was horrible. Then I photocopied it and took it to Spence."

"No wonder you're so bent out of shape," he reasoned.

"He's the most hateful person I've ever met, Maxwell." Her voice was nearly shrill now, in its incomprehension. "He absolutely hates me. For the life of me I can't figure out why." Kathleen gave in to a sluggish, reflective pause. Her eyes slid over to Maxwell's. "I know I'm a bitch sometimes. I know I can be aloof, contradictory, cold. Sometimes I do weird things. But...hateful? I'm not hateful, am I?"

"No," Maxwell said. "You're not."

"Then why is he?" she contested. "Why does he hate me? Why does he treat me like I'm some kind of floozy, phony, self-involved no-account?"

"Some people are like that. There's no explanation—they just are. The only way they can remain in control of their own lives is to take advantage of people, use them, put them down. It's weakness, actually. They're too weak—and too inadequate—to interact with others positively. So they use negativity instead."

Maxwell's words buffed enough of the edge off her turmoil to settle her down. The wormlike headache lost some of its bite. She tried to refocus, to be thoughtful. Coming here without notice, unloading her problems on him—it wasn't fair. Maxwell had problems too, yet she'd shown no sensitivity toward that.

She leaned against him. His arm around her gently rubbed her shoulder. "Thank you for the rose," she said. "And the note. You really are a very sweet person."

"Oh, yeah?" was all he said. He stroked her hair, continued to rub her shoulder and neck.

It felt dreamy. Just a few words, and his merest touch, diluted Spence's denigration to something faraway and innocuous.

"Did you have a good day?" she asked.

"Yes, a great day."

"I heard you typing. Are you working on a new poem?"

"Yep."

"Is it a good poem? Do you like it?"

"Yep."

Her words listed. She felt slipping into sleep. "What's it called?"

His fingers rubbing her neck lulled her further, and so did his voice. "I can't tell you."

"Why?"

"It isn't finished yet."

Deeper, deeper, she slipped. "So? You can at least tell me the title."

"It's creative bad luck," he espoused, "to reveal the title of an unfinished work to the person it's written for."

Sleep beclouded her. Deeper, deeper. "What, Maxwell?"

"It's for you," he said.

For me? She was suddenly so relaxed, she couldn't speak.

"Go to sleep now," he said.

Chapter 23

(I)

Everything's ready.
New ideas.
It makes her feel very creative, and very powerful.
She sees her mother standing behind her in the mirror.
Her mother smiles.
Her mother is so beautiful despite blackened eyes, broken teeth, bruises and cuts from Daddy.
Her mother's hands, elbows, and feet are swollen up like discolored balloons from the heroin needles. Daddy made her into an addict soon after they met, so he could control her. He never married her, he just used her to make money. Daddy had a lot of friends that liked to do awful things to prostitutes. He used her mother like a tidbit.
It makes her so sad she begins to cry.
Don't cry, her mother says.
They did awful things to her.
Daddy would beat her mother senseless, so his friends could fuck her while she was unconscious or in pain.
It was a game to Daddy, a kick. He served her mother like a bowl of pretzels at a card game. Quick thrills for his friends. Frequently, he served his daughter too...
Don't cry, her mother says again.
She can't help it.
She's crying now in front of the mirror, her tears making her mascara run.

Her mother's smiling.
She's beautiful in spite of all the pain she's felt.
All the horrible things men have done to her.
Don't cry.
She washes her face.
She reapplies her makeup.
She must be strong like her mother.
An auburn wig tonight.
Long like a mane of beautiful smoke.
A see-through black-lace blouse.
A black, embroidered linen jacket.
Gray stone-washed Guess jeans.
What a beautiful daughter I have, her mother says. *You're so beautiful.*

"I know," she says into the mirror.
And smiles.

(II)

Jams, Johnny Duff thought. He slipped Slayer's "A Season In The Abyss" into the Nak in-dash CD player and cranked up some watts. *Yeah,* he thought. Music always got him in the mood.

He equated his car to himself. A Nissan 300ZX: fast, sleek, turbocharged. Orange, like fire. He'd put on his phony plates tonight, so whatever bar-cooze he fucked over wouldn't get a line on him. Women were paranoid these days. Roofies, GHB. He remembered some jizzbucket he'd picked up in Annapolis a few years ago, she'd actually written down his tag number before she'd gotten into the car. He wished it hadn't been before he'd gotten the Big H, so he could've given her a dose. Then that other time—*Crystal City?* he thought—he'd woken up in some cooze's bed at about four in the morning to see her going through his wallet with a penlight. She hadn't been robbing him, she was writing down his name and address off his driver's license! Johnny had a fake license now, which he always brought with him when he went out on the town. It had cost him a couple of hundred from some printing place he caught in an ad in *Merc* magazine, but it was worth it. Looked just like the real thing, had his picture, height, weight, eye and hair color, but a phony name and address. He couldn't very well pull any good fuck-overs with his real ID in his wallet, could he?

So tonight, Johnny Duff of Arlington, Virginia, was John Richards of Northeast Washington, D.C.

Johnny was 29. He was sharp, smooth talking. He pulled in a good 40 to 50 grand per, selling high-end Nissans; he could talk the fuckers into anything, and he got his own car on the dealership's tab. Salesman

Of The Month seven months out of twelve in '96, he reminded himself. Forty to 50K was good money for a single guy, and Johnny couldn't imagine being anything but single. Marriage was for twits, he reasoned. They sap your cash, sap your social life, then divorce you and take half. Fuck that. Besides, he couldn't pull fuck-overs if he was hitched.

Being single, with a class set of wheels, a nice pad, and righteous bread in the pocket, was too much fun.

He always hit bars far afield, maybe once every two or three months. He didn't want to be bumping into any old stuff he'd done a job on. *They all got it coming, the shits,* he reasoned. Johnny didn't consider a fuck-over to be rape. *Can I help it they get wet just looking at me?* Bar girls were all the same—taking care of number one. When they saw a guy had looks, a slick ride, and cash, they turned into sharks. *I'll show them a shark*, he thought. It wasn't like he was putting a gun to their heads in an alley and making them bend over. They came on to *him*, then Johnny finished what they started. He'd had a lot of good fuck-overs in his time. Giving them a dose was the mainstay kick. He always insisted on using rubbers, to show them he was sensitive to the times; girls liked that. Johnny's herpes was almost always active; he used non-lubricated condoms so the lubricant wouldn't kill the virus. What he'd do, when they weren't looking, was he'd pop a herpes sore onto his finger before putting the rubber on, then he'd rub the discharge on the outside of the rubber, or he'd finger her snatch before sinking in. *Give the bitches a good dose, yeah boy!* he thought. Something to remember their night with Johnny. By the time they realized they had the Big H, they'd probably been fucked by another dozen guys. Johnny particularly liked to pull this move on chicks who were out cheating on their boyfriends or husbands. Two birds with one sore.

Fuck-overs were part of what he was too, like the car, and his threads, and his lifestyle. It was dog eat dog: you either fucked them over or they fucked you over. No way Johnny Duff was going to wind up on the shit-end of *that* stick.

These nights were important to him—they were a ritual. He liked to gear up. He drove around Georgetown awhile first, to eye snatch. Up and down M Street, the lookers were out. Johnny wished he could do all of them, give it to each and every one of them like they never had it before. *Fuck 'em 'til they bust*, he dreamed, and turned off towards Washington Harbor. But Georgetown wasn't his style. It wasn't sleazy enough.

Gear up, he thought. *Gotta gear up.* He thought about cruising down L, maybe picking up a hooker for some quick head. But the dark avenue, its corridor of black stone and glass, showed him little to choose from tonight. Just a few strays; it was too early. Bored at the succession of stop lights, he picked up his car phone and punched in 1-900-LIVESEX—

local girls, he'd heard. A voice like slow, running honey answered: "Talk to me, baby. Let's get it on."

"Jesus Christ!" Johnny replied, "your pussy stinks so bad I can smell it over the phone! What kind of a loser are you anyway? You too stupid to get a real job?"

"Fuck you!" the girl shot back.

Johnny laughed. "I wouldn't fuck you with an elephant's cock. It'd be too small, big as your stinky pussy is. Get a life." He switched off and dialed another one.

"Pleasure Line," another oozing female voice answered. "You ready to party?"

"Let me start with a joke," Johnny said. "You like jokes?"

"Sure," the woman said. "I'll play with myself while you tell it."

"Fine," Johnny said. "Here goes. What has a little dick and hangs down?"

"What, sugar?"

"A bat," Johnny answered. "And what has a big dick and hangs up?"

"What?"

Johnny hung up, barking laughter.

It was best to hit the pick-up joints late; by then most of the cooze was drunk and showing their true colors. Johnny parked the Nissan in a BMI garage. "The Lot," as he called it, was always a great way to gear up first. A dress code kept out the riff-raff, and the talent was state-of-the-art.

The doorman, spying Johnny class clothes, let him in at once. Lancelot's was D.C.'s best strip joint, strictly high-class, not one of these redneck shithouses with dancers who had more tattoos than teeth. Johnny got a stageside seat upstairs, ordered a Heineken from a waitress with a killer rack. The stage, an elevated half-circle backed by mirrors, glowed before him. Lights flashed to Foo Fighters; Lancelot's was rocking. A dancer who looked just like Heather Locklear moved with the beat, absolutely flawless in her nakedness. Patrons gathered round the stage to tip her; the deal was you stuck a buck in her garter for a good, close look at her bod. And it was none of this g-string shit at The Lot; the girls stripped down to the bare muff. Some of the regulars had made a little local fame. There was one dark-blond chick who'd been on some TV shows including Howard Stern, and a redhead who'd supposedly been gang-banged in an Italian restaurant by two congressmen and a certain senator from up northways. Then there was the black chick who'd been hounded by the illustrious mayor, before the asshole had been thrown in jail for smoking crack in front of a hidden FBI camera at the Vista Hotel. All of them had bodies that could clear out a fucking monastery.

Johnny settled back, nursing his beer. The Lot was just his primer, an appetizer of vision. Applause exploded when the Foo song went off;

after each cut, the dancer had to empty her garter it was so full of cash. *What a can,* he thought as she bent over. Hoots fired like rifle shots. Her tits tossed below her grin, legs like statuesque pillars rising to the trimmed bush. *Yeah, perfect,* Johnny thought. But maybe that was the problem. These girls were too perfect; they didn't seem real to him. They were unreachable. That's why he liked to go on fuck-overs; bar girls he could reach, all right. He could crank off a couple good nuts, and leave good-sized dents in their souls.

Next a strawberry blonde stepped onto the stage. Her big implanted breasts showed off nipples like the tips on cannon rounds. Johnny watched without much interest. *No, not real enough,* he conceded to his beer. He was itching, he was ready to get out of here and hit a bar. *Let's see,* he mused. The all-time best Johnny Duff fuck-over. Which one? He'd had some doozies. The music, Rage Against The Machine now, beat with his thoughts as the dancer twirled. What had been his greatest conquest? There was the blond broad he'd picked up in some Hampton Mall dance dive. Early forties, made no bones about being married. "My husband's at a meeting in Chicago," she'd said and winked. "He won't be home 'til tomorrow night." Johnny followed her back to her nice, quaint little suburban house. Next thing he knew she was buck naked on the bed, begging him to tie her up. Johnny was always one to oblige a woman's wishes. He'd tied her up good and tight. "You have condoms, don't you?" she asked. "I got 'em, but I ain't using them," he was kind enough to inform her. "Doesn't look to me like there's a whole lot you can do about that right now." She fought against the stocking bonds as Johnny stripped. "See?" he said. He showed her his pride and joy, pointing to a nice, open herpes blemish. "Got a present for ya," he said. Once she knew the score, she started screaming, but Johnny put a lid on that and fast. He stuffed her frilly panties in her yap, tied another stocking through her teeth, and climbed aboard. *What'd I fuck her?* he strove to remember now. *Three, four times?* He'd jerked the last one off in her face, and then he'd left, neglecting, of course, to untie her. He wanted her hubby to have something interesting to come home to the next day. *Your wife picks guys up in bars when you're out of town,* he'd written on the wall. Then there was that silly shitfaced brunette who'd put the make on him during the Halloween party at The Network. Dressed up in some dumbass devil costume, so drunk she could barely walk. He'd driven her back to her apartment in Severna Park. She didn't even give him time to hang a piss before she was blowing him on the bed. But every few sucks she kind of paused and wobbled. Then she lurched up, groaned, "Oh, God, I'm gonna—" and then bent over the bed and blew chunks all over the nightstand. Johnny couldn't help but laugh. "I'm really sorry," she slurred, "I guess I drank too much," after which she slumped over and passed out. Johnny saw no reason to neglect the indulgence of a perfectly good erection for the paltry fact that she was passed out. That would be derelict. So he hauled off her silly devil's costume and rolled her over on her belly. Then he spat a loogie in her crack and sodomized her. The girl remained out cold for the whole thing. *Why waste water flushing the toilet?* he reasoned after he gave up his nut. This was a timely concern; Johnny believed in conservation. So before he took his rod out of her, he pulled a good long hot beer-piss into her rectum. *Johnny on the spot,* he thought, and wiped his cock off on the curtains. Before he left, he wrote on the wall: *I butt-fucked you and pissed up your ass. Happy Halloween. And Happy Herpes!*

There were many more. He supposed he cherished them all, and why shouldn't he? The raucous music brought him back; Johnny smiled now in the aura of memory. Memory served him well, his past feeding energy to his future. The blond stripper gyrated like a top of flesh; her silky hair rose like a skirt. Then she slid down on her side and lifted a leg 'til it was perpendicular. Within the trimmed, waxed public hair, the slit of her vagina seemed to smile at him...

Time to stop looking and start doing, he concluded. He tipped the blonde a five, paid his tab, and booked.

Outside, the city night seethed. The lines were too long at Hatter's and Jonah and the Whale. Rhythmic vibrations filled the air; at the corner, black kids were playing pickle can drums like an African war dance. Across the street, Whackie the clown juggled flaming sticks for a passerby audience, and from some distant crevice in the city, a lone trumpet brayed over the night.

Hearsay's looked good; they rarely had a line because the joint was so big. Johnny strode into the crush of patrons. No line, sure, but it was crowded like mad. The bar stretched on, cavernous, dark, yet deafening in laughter and bass-laden music.

Like Hell, he thought. *And tonight I am the Prince of Lies.*

He scouted Hearsay's three great rooms, and squeezed through the dancefloor, taking advantage of the opportunity to rub his upper arm against some top-heavy yuppie brunette's 44Ds. *Enough to make a guy go on a milk diet,* he fantasized. *Baby, I'd suck on those hooters 'til you didn't have enough tit left to fill a training bra. Then maybe I'd do you a big favor and suck on that big pussy of yours 'til your uterus popped into my mouth.* He ordered a Mich at the back bar, eyeballing the T&A. Most of the girls had guys with them—smug overdressed D.C. putzes—or were with friends who chattered away like parrots. Here was ditzy blonde in a shiny silver dress—and with stained teeth—running her hand up her boyfriend's ass-crack, some typical city shithead with dick-stupid eurofag black hair and a goatee, all dressed in black. *Christ, honey,* Johnny thought. *Why don't you just pull his pants down and fist-fuck him right here in the bar?*

Another blonde, with hair so platinum it looked white, and with a racehorse bod, was sticking her tongue so intently down some bald guy's throat it looked like she was trying to make him throw up. A table of couples argued rather heatedly over who was American history's greatest writer, William Faulkner or Kathy Acker. Acker seemed to be winning, but Johnny hadn't heard of either; he didn't know from writers.

Writers were pussies.

A Bonnie Raitt tune rasped from unseen speakers. The husky, sexual voice about made Johnny pull a stiffer, like maybe he could mosey up to Platinum Baby and jerk off a good-sized nut right into that crispy, phony hair of hers, or maybe give Silver Dress some Special Delivery Johnny Duff Pearl Drops to whiten up those pot-dark teeth. *You think maybe you can take your thumb out of Euroboy's ass long enough for me to fuck the dog shit out of you? I gotta friend I'd like you to meet. His name is Mr. H.* Johnny's rampant hormones and social vehemence were going apeshit in his head now. *I need a fuck-over,* he affirmed. *Otherwise I'm gonna bust my pants and rip a gusher of peckersnot across the bar right into some yuppie bimbo's Amstel Light.* Johnny needed a loner, he needed a mark. *I need to sink,* he thought, each word resounding like a hammer to brick. *But every beaver's got a cock tonight.* This frustrated him. Silver Dress bent over for her purse; Johnny wished he could be invisible and maybe take a bite out of her fat ass, then give Euroboy a good kick in the lumps, if he had any. Baby Platinum was still tonsil-eating with Bald Guy. *Christ, why don't you just stick your* head *down his throat?* Johnny wouldn't mind conking her on the bean with her Corona bottle and treating her to a free Dr. Duff Beer-Piss Enema.

He milled around another hour, wandering amid waves of muffled music, dim light, hot bodies. When his trek took him full circle he was back at the bar. "Another Mich?" the keep asked. *Yeah, and how about a nice wet box I can shoot a creamer in?* Johnny thought.

"Yeah," he said, and in a dissociated blink of music and light and mindless chatter and inane laughter, a stark, cock-stiffening voice behind him said, "A man with a mission."

Johnny turned.

A subtle smile. Gray jeans hissed as trophy-winning legs crossed on the stool. "You look like you're on a mission. You look like you're looking for something."

Yeah, you. Johnny went into a cool lean. "Maybe. Everybody's looking for something, somewhere, aren't they?"

Lustrous auburn hair. Perfect, straight ivory-white teeth behind the perfect smile. "It's best, though, when people looking for the same things find each other."

Ho, Mama! It was time to spiel. No rings, he noticed. And no telltale kind of boyfriend jewelry shit. Just her, all woman right there next to him like a gift of flesh dropped into his lap. Johnny got to talking, the usual bar jive. He didn't hear half of what came out of her mouth, but he didn't need too. You could tell, sometimes you just knew. She was looking to get laid. "I like the summer best," she was saying in that soft, soft voice of hers. A faint perfume made Johnny think he might come in his pants. "Like right now," she was saying. "Hot, you know? Real hot."

"Yeah, me too. Brings out the best of things."

Another smile. Her hair, backed by bar light, could've been a halo. She looked at him as she listened. She never seemed to blink. *You lose your brain, Johnny?* he alerted himself, *the last time you took a shit? You forgot to introduce yourself!*

"By the way, I'm Johnny Richards," Johnny Duff said.

She offered her hand, which reminded him of a sleek, perfect little bird. The smile fixed on him.

"So what's your name?" he asked after a long pause.

"What are names, anyway? You don't want to know my name, do you? Knowing my name has nothing to do with what you want. Or with what I want, either."

Johnny about shit his shorts. *Might as well be wearing a FUCK ME sign.* But she was throwing him for a loop; he wasn't used to girls who came right out with what they wanted. "I'm the D.C. scout for the William Morris Agency," he lied. "Screenplays, novels with film potential, that sort of thing." This line always got them going, seemed every cooze in town had some pipedream idea like, "I tried writing a novel a long time ago," or "I've always had this great idea for a movie," after which Johnny would ask about it and act like it was hot stuff, and then he could say something like, "Get it down on paper and I'll send it to our people in New York." *Yeah, always got them going, a great in, a great way to exploit their makeshift dreams for the gain of his Eight-Inch Wonder.*

But this girl didn't seem to care.

All she said in response was, "Sounds like an interesting job. I'm a masseuse."

Masseuse? he thought. *Some job.*

"I give good back rubs," she said.

Johnny had to lean against the bar, not because he was drunk, but because her looks were turning his knees to jelly. *Back rubs,* he thought. *Masseuse. Jesus.* She looked like she'd been poured into her gray designer jeans. Up top she wore a light black jacket over a transparent black blouse. When she reached for her glass of wine, Johnny could see it all in the jacket's sharp V: tits big and firm as grapefruits; dark, erect, robust nipples. *This peach is gonna get the Johnny Duff fuck-over to end all fuck-overs,* he avowed to himself. *Gotta giant jizzer for my baby tonight.*

"I guess we all have some things, you know, little obscure things about ourselves that we're especially proud of."

"Sure," Johnny concurred. Who knew what the fuck she was talking about? *Little things? Johnny's got a big thing that you can take care of just fine,* he thought. *And a couple of rocks that need a bigtime draining. I'm gonna come so hard in your box my spooge'll be shooting out your nose.* "You're right. A lot of times it's the little things we do that mean the most."

She smiled. She sipped her drink. She recrossed her legs and said, "It's getting late, isn't it?"

"Yeah," Johnny drifted more than spoke.

Another smile, another sip.

The perfect teeth gleamed.

The perfect press of her perfect breasts shone darkly through the transparent black blouse.

"Yeah," he repeated.

Her beauty was knocking him out: the call of her flesh, and the heady lust, like a silent litany instilled into his blood by the reckoning of her parts, and the whisper, a spirit, as one perfect thigh slid across the other, and the perfume, an angel's presence, in her angel's hair, all a bright light, a simmering blinding blaze in his face. And then her eyes. Those big blue green gray neverblinking eyes.

Chapter 24

(I)

Spence let the day die behind his back. Past midnight he was still in his office; it never occurred to him to go home. All day, and as headquarters changed shifts at 11 p.m., Spence had remained behind his desk, reading and rereading every word Kathleen Shade had written for *'90s Woman.*

He couldn't say he was engrossed. Shade proved a talented wordsmith and analyst; her "Verdict" column—over 50 entries since she'd been hired—instead cast Spence out in some vague cryptic alienation. It was more than the psychical differences between men and women, but something impartially, and simply, human. Had Spence been a woman, in other words, he felt certain the barren alienation would remain.

That, and the sheer lack of answers to the teeming question. The relative common denominator—the nascent. The word itself seemed cryptified too, more so than his own hollow feelings.

Not one single "Verdict" entry involved sexual abuse, delusional behavior, or psychiatric illness. Almost all, instead, responded to interpersonal relationship problems: infidelity, incompatibility, jealousy, divorce, estrangement, etc. No link whatsoever that might shed light on the killer's solicitation of Kathleen Shade. Impulsively, Spence snatched up the phone, punched in Simmons' home number. He did not apologize for calling so late, nor did he even first identify himself when Simmons answered. Instead Spence merely said: "It's not here."

"What's not?" Simmons inquired.

"The nascent."

"Ah," Simmons replied at once. "The christening of the icon. Your keystone is eluding you, eh? Or are you eluding yourself?"

Spence didn't quite know what he meant, but it sounded like one of the good doctor's discreet implications. Was it Spence's maleness that obscured his perceptions? Or, conversely, was it that he'd never, ever in his life, been close to a woman? *I'm gay,* he casually told himself. Was that it? He knew less about how women thought than he knew of quantum physics, non-Euclidian geometry, the Crimean War. But...

No, he thought a moment later. *It isn't that I'm not seeing something, it's that there's nothing here to see.* "I'm not eluding myself," he spoke. "It's just not here."

"You've read all over Shade's magazine writing?"

"Yes. All of it. And it's not here."

"You're quite sure?"

Spence tried to fully assess the question. "Yes," he said. "And I'm not missing it. It's just...not...here."

"Hmm," Simmons said.

"Maybe you should look at it," Spence ventured.

"Why, Jeffrey? Do you doubt your perceptions?"

"No."

"Then what practical use can there be in redundancy? If the nascent is not in Kathleen Shade's magazine writing—" Simmons lapsed, chuckled like a whisper. "—then it isn't in Kathleen Shade's magazine writing."

"Thanks. That helps me immeasurably."

"This killer," Simmons drifted. "This maniacal, incalculable psychopathic murderess... You want her very much, correct?"

"Yes," Spence said.

"Dead or alive, correct?"

"Correct."

"In fact you want her more than you've ever wanted anything in your life." Simmons' pause seemed like a stone wall. "Correct?"

Spence closed his eyes, suspended himself in the possibility. Eventually he answered, "Yes."

"That's quite sad, Jeffrey." Simmons' lax, easy tone changed at once to something almost scolding, or critical. "It's nearly pathetic: that the apprehension of a purveyor of death should be all that you look forward to."

Spence dwelt on this also. *It's true,* he realized. *It is pathetic.* Then he said, "I don't care."

"Have faith, Jeffrey. There are still investigative avenues for you to plunder."

"Oh, yeah? Where?"

"Tomorrow," Simmons said. "Come and see me tomorrow."

"But I want to know now," Spence dryly pleaded.

"Go home, Jeffrey. Go to sleep."
"But I don't want to go to sleep."
"Good-night, Jeffrey."
CLICK

Ballbreaker, Spence thought. He drummed his fingers on the blotter. His muscled forearm looked like a bad wax carving in the lamp light. Through the window, he could hear sirens shrieking miles and miles away...

He grimaced at the stacks of magazines. *The nascent isn't here. Period. And if it isn't here, then where the fuck is it?*

His eyes, then, tracked to the window, to the frame of black glass beyond which churned the city, the world.

And the primeval night.

(II)

"I sewed your lips shut," were the first words he heard.

His consciousness seeped back into his head like slow, steady drips building to a stain, then a puddle, then a pool.

I'm in hell, were the first words he thought.

Johnny Duff couldn't move. An etching pain radiated about his face. Low to his right, a small fluorescent tube glowed but that was the only light. The rest of the room—if this were a room at all—seemed formed of slabs of dark and half-dark. The pain flared when he tried to speak, his tongue frantic in his mouth against the fresh, tight stitches, and again he thought:

I'm in hell.

The form—blurred, alabaster-white—swept closer.

"Usually I scrape the eardrums, and glue the eyelids shut too. The energy from every sense I shut down goes directly to the only sense that's left. That's the theory, anyway. I like it."

I'm going to die, Johnny Duff thought. But the thought was more like a squirming, hopeless flight.

The soft voice continued from the slablike dark. "In other words, the less Daddy can move, the less he can see, hear, or speak, the more he can feel."

The white blur blended back.

To the left, a window hovered. She seemed to be staring out the window.

He'd been handcuffed to the bed, ankles and wrists. He'd been stripped. He inclined his head against the zipper of pain that was now his mouth, and saw his naked flesh alight on one side. And the other side: pure darkness.

His memory squirmed along with the damped, smothered horror.

Eventually, he remembered what sequence of events had brought him to this little cranny of hell:

Her heels clicked down the cement ramp of the underground parking garage on 19th, her ass sliding deliciously in the gray jeans. "This is your car?" she asked, surprise in her voice.

"Sure," Johnny replied in his no-big-deal tone. He opened her side, let her in. When he was in himself, he gunned the Nissan's OHC V6 Turbo a little, and cruised out of the lot.

Not much of a talker, he assessed. *Good.* She sat back in the leather seat, legs crossed. "I like nice cars," she said a little while later. "Wow, even a car phone."

"Gotta have it, you know. For the job," he lied. "These agents in New York, they don't like to leave messages."

"I love nights like these," she said.

Johnny frowned. It was like she didn't even want to hear his bullshit. Most girls went gaga. *Who cares?* he conceded. *I'll be jamming her silly in a few.* He could feel his herpes itch, and he smiled. *I'll pop a big one for ya, Ditzy.*

He followed clipped directions. Michigan Avenue. Right onto South Dakota. Left onto Bladensburg. Suddenly she leaned over, put her arm around him. "Don't touch me yet, okay?"

Johnny's brow did a jig. "Okay."

"You just drive, and I'll touch you, okay?"

"Whatever you say."

"I mean, just wait 'til we're there before you touch me, okay? You have to promise."

Jesus, what a weirdo. "I promise," he said.

She leaned closer. He could feel her breath on his neck as he took the Nissan through each vacant light. They were heading out of the city. Her perfume baited him; her right hand stroked his legs…

Then she was kneading his groin through the loose, Savane slacks. *Gonna be pitching a tent like Ringling Brothers,* Johnny thought, tensing up a little. Kneading, kneading. It was so delightfully lewd: the perfume, the hot breath a half-inch from his neck, and her hand working him up. *Careful you don't tap that geyser, Ditzy. I'm kind of planning on saving it to shoot up your ass.* Each time he glanced left he could see her gorgeous right breast just sitting there in her jacket V. He could see the triangle of her jeans, so tight a gap formed. Johnny was getting hot around the collar. *You keep this up, and I'm gonna pull into the nearest alley and bust into that pussy right now.*

This was great. Through the next several traffic lights on Bladensburg, she was actually panting. *She's feeling my cock through my pants and she's getting hotter than the lid on a pot-bellied stove.* This would require some special considerations. A chick this good-looking, this hot?

Johnny's gonna have to dream up a special fuck-over for Ditzy here, he resolved. *I'm gonna rock on this all night.* If only he could get her to let him tie her up, then the rest would be cake. She seemed kinky enough; weird girls liked kinky things. He wondered what she was into.

"Next left," she whispered. Her hand came away. *Just in time,* he thought. He turned down a dark street, passed a fire station, and rows of dark little houses. Johnny had expected an apartment. "You live in a house?"

"I inherited it from my mother."

"You got roommates?"

"No. There's only me."

So mama's dead, huh? Well that's too bad, 'cos I'd fuck the stuffing out of her too. Any mama that could give birth to a brick shithouse like you deserves only the best. Johnny feigned interest. "What about your father?" he asked.

She stalled.

Bad move, Johnny thought. Nothing turned a chick's pussy off faster than the wrong question. *Her old man probably died of brain cancer or something, and I just blew the whole ballgame.* But then she said, in a drier voice, "He was never really married to my mother, he just came around a lot. He...left...a long time ago."

Johnny nodded, pretended to be sympathetic. "My dad ran out on my mother too," he lied, "when I was a kid."

Now her voice reverted to something close to a croak. "My father...didn't...run out."

I better get off this subject. "Nice houses," he commented. Actually they were cracker boxes, dumps. "Quaint, cozy."

"End of the street," she said. "On the right."

A yellow sign read DEAD END. A burned out streetlight left little to be seen. Her joint, the best he could tell, looked the same as all the others: brooding, run down a little.

When Johnny pulled the Nissan into the driveway, she took a plastic box out of her purse, an electric garage door opener. "Pull in," she told him as the door groaned to raise. *Oh, I'll pull in, all right,* Johnny avowed. *In and out and in and out*—But the garage was empty, and he hadn't seen a car in front of the house.

"Don't you have a car?" he asked.

"Yeah. I left it in the city."

"What kind do you have?"

"A blue Festiva." Suddenly she seemed impatient. "Don't worry about my car. I thought you wanted to fuck."

That's calling the kettle black. Johnny clammed up. Behind him the garage door shuddered closed.

"Want some wine?"

"Love some," Johnny answered.

Inside looked like something off a David Lynch set. White walls had faded to a dingy yellow in the living room. An old couch and recliner, old green carpet and curtains that looked moth-eaten. In the corner stood a Philco television that must've been 30 years old, and there was an equally old steepled radio with a big circular lighted dial. Some scrappy late-night jazz scratched from the dried monaural speaker.

Everything's so old, he observed. He could see her getting the wine in the cramped kitchen. A big white enameled refrigerator with rounded corners; a white stove with black burners. No dishwasher, just a rubber sucker-mat next to the sink, and a dish rack.

"So what did you say you did?" he asked just to keep some kind of conversation going.

"I work in a hospital," she said, her back to him. "I'm a janitor."

Johnny made a face at the response. Earlier, hadn't she said she was a masseuse? *You little liar, you.* But...a janitor? The job didn't fit with her looks. *Baby, you can mop my floors any time.* He was staring into the kitchen. His eyes felt plastered to her ass, and those long, long legs. Only now did he realize how tall she was, maybe six foot. *Tall girls're fine as long as they're sleek,* he reasoned. He'd fucked over a few who weren't so sleek. Nothing worse than a tall one that's fat. Big ass and thighs, big calves, big size 11 feet. *Fuck that shit, man.* But this peach? Her height only augmented her contours, her trim long lines and curves. Johnny was getting hard again, just looking...

A tacky old card table stood at the other side of the room, with a typewriter, some stacks of papers, and a couple of magazines. *'90s Woman,* he noted. *Tonight, Ditzy, you're gonna meet a '90s man.* She reemerged, having poured red wine into juice glasses. "What are you writing?" he inquired, indicating the typewriter.

"What do you care?" She handed him a glass. "Come on."

He followed her down the drab hall. She closed a door to her right. "Basement," she said. Johnny smelled something minutely funky. Another door to the left stood open; inside he quickly noticed weights, a bench, exercise equipment. "You work out, huh?"

"What do you think?" she said ahead of him.

Johnny was growing a bit weary of this sudden smart-ass tone of hers. He'd be fucking her over soon, sure, but that wasn't the point. *Maybe a good smack on the noggin and a few hours of steady ass-fucking'll tone down some of that sass, huh, Ditzy?*

"Here's my room," she said.

Johnny looked past her as she entered. The room didn't jibe either. He'd seen his share of women's bedrooms; they were all the same in ways. There were always frilly pillows on the bed, vanities, makeup boxes, jewelry boxes, shoe racks on the closet door, framed snapshots, prints on the wall. But not here. *Weird*, Johnny thought very resolutely. *Fuckin' weird.*

Bare wood floors. A brass-rail bed, higher than usual. A single old dresser facing the bed with some sort of wood cabinet on top. A tawdry pole lamp lit the corner with hooded bulbs pointing different directions. The lights looked like cones, or wizards' hats. Weirdest of all was some kind of long varnished nightstand on casters, with a tacky flex-arm fluorescent lamp on top.

All four walls stood bare. No pictures, prints, no decoration of any kind. The room's only adornment, it seemed, was the lone window to the left, with shutterslats instead of curtains, and a closed closet door.

"This used to be my father's den," she said. "Now I sleep here."

She turned off each cone on the pole lamp. All that lit the room now was the meager fluorescent light on the castered stand. She stepped out of her shoes, and went to look out the window.

Pure-ass weird, but who cares? Johnny remembered. He'd never see her again after tonight. She could be as weird as she wanted. He took another sip of the cheap burgundy, then set it down. The room smelled funny. Like (She said she worked in a hospital?) a hospital, a faint yet biting antiseptic scent. At least the brass bed looked promising. He could tie her up good on those big shiny rails and fuck her over in grand style. *Gotta play the game awhile first,* he reminded himself. He didn't want to be scaring the shit out of her yet. *A little later for that, once I've got her tied down.*

"What are you looking at?" he asked.

She was just standing there, her back to him, staring out the little window. She made no response. The fluorescent light tinseled the room's darkness, which she seemed to be a part of now. Half-blended, half-formed. She slipped out of the black jacket, never turning. Then she squirmed out of the tight gray jeans.

Now we're rocking. Johnny stripped down to his BVDs in less time that it took him to flex his cock. "Lie back on the bed," she whispered. Johnny obliged. For a moment he had a strange image as she moved through the dark: that she was just a pair of legs walking around the room. No body. Just legs. That was all he could see 'til his eyes adjusted. Those two bare, beautiful white legs. She opened the closet door to get something; Johnny noticed several wigs hanging inside. Was she wearing a wig? *She can be bald-headed for all I care,* he thought. Then she turned, approached the bed. She still had on the see-through black blouse, and black panties. He could see her smile.

She was holding something in her hand.

"What's that?" he asked, hands behind his head as he lay back.

"Massage oil." She held the plastic bottle up. That's what it said on it: MASSAGE OIL. "Turn over so I can give you a back rub."

I'm easy, he thought and flipped over. The bed creaked a little when she climbed on. She sat on him, her crotch just behind his ass. Next he felt several spurts of the warm oil land on his back. Her hands deftly massaged it into his skin. Then a few more squirts 'til he was slick with it. He could hear the slick sound as her fingers worked over his muscles. Then her hands opened flat and pushed up and down as she leaned forward. *This ain't bad at all,* he thought, closing his eyes.

In moments it was like a dream. It was like he was floating. "Is that good?" she kept inquiring. "Yeah," he kept murmuring back. Her fingers were turning him to putty; he could drift off to sleep. This was the best back rub of his life.

He concentrated on the sensation: the nimble hands sliding up and down in the oil, the nimble fingers plying every muscle. Then they opened around the back of his neck and over his shoulders, rubbing, rubbing...

"Is that good?"

"Yeah."

"Let me get these panties off," she said, and climbed off.

Johnny rolled over. He felt stupidly relaxed. She climbed back on, sitting on his thighs. *Aw, what a bush!* he thought. It splayed between her thrust legs: dark, plush, but not straggly. Her hand tickled over his erection in his shorts, then she leaned forward again, running her hands smoothly over his chest and the tops of his shoulders. Johnny raised his hands—

"No," she nearly snapped. "Not yet. You can't touch me yet. I touch you first. That's the deal."

"Sure, babe. Whatever you say." He lowered his hands. *What's her hang-up?* he wondered. But it was better to let her do what she wanted first, that way she'd be more inclined to trust him. "Anything you want," he droned. "Anyway you like it."

He watched her lean up a moment, and skim off the sheer black blouse. That about did it for Johnny; he doubted he'd ever seen a rack of tits so perfect in his life. No implants, either. Large but no sag, firm. Gorged dark nipples sticking out. Johnny wished women had milk in their hooters all the time, not just after they'd dropped a rug-rat. *Wouldn't that be great?* he thought. *I'd suck this pair bone dry.*

She rubbed his chest a little longer, then sat up. "You can touch me now," she whispered. "Anywhere you want."

The words sounded echoed, hollow. Johnny didn't quite yet realize what was going on. His eyes pasted on her breasts, her pubis, diverting him. She looked like something made of smooth marble, and her smile appeared more Buddahlike even than human: gleefully empty. Then he saw her hands—

What the hell's that on her hands?

The thought beat down.
She was wearing rubber gloves.
Surgical gloves.
And when he went to raise his arms—
God in heaven what the hell is wrong with me?
—his arms didn't move at all.
The wine. She musta put something in the w—
"Look," she whispered.
She knelt up, thrust her hips forward.
"See?" she whispered. "See?"
Johnny's vision sunk in muck—
"See?"
—his eyes closed to slits—
"See?"
—through which—
"See?"
—he could barely—
"See?"
—see.
The madwoman's fingers parted the outer lips of her sex.
"See, Daddy? You can't hurt me anymore."
But he could see enough, before consciousness winked out: the pink minora sewn shut by wide surgical stitches.

And now, awake again, Johnny realized that his own mouth had been similarly sewn shut. Through the chaos, some sliver of his psyche attempted to reassemble order—not an easy task when one awoke to find himself handcuffed to a brass bed in some interstice of hell, with a demon at the bedside.

"Don't worry. You won't die. I have a coagulant salve."

In the half-light, off to the left, he could see her, her sleek back to him as she busied herself in some arcane chore.

"But you won't pass out, either. I've injected you with about 200 milligrams of Desoxyn. It'll keep your heart-rate in high enough numbers to prevent your nervous system from shutting down against the pain."

He heard metal clinking. She seemed to be assembling something, some object with a crank of some sort. Then she was picking something up, which glinted.

"Because that's the important part. What you feel. What I make you feel."

His heart was ticking like a bomb. Each time his arms and legs fought against their fetters, a loud metallic *snap!* resulted.

snap!

"Stop that."
snap!
"It's annoying.
snap!
"Stop it!"

Then she turned. She was still naked. She still wore the hideous, tight rubber surgical gloves, the color of condoms.

Bobby pins held her short, black hair tight to her scalp. She'd been wearing a wig, and he could still see the other wigs hanging on the inside of the closet door.

And what was that thing with the knobbed handle? And she was holding something now, wasn't she? In her gloved hand, against the smooth, flawless-white abdomen, something glinted.

What is that? he thought, squirming. *What's that thing in her hand?*

Perhaps she'd deciphered the question. Perhaps, as she gently and so silently approached the bed—perfect in her naked beauty, and even more perfect in her madness—perhaps she'd seen him ask the question through the sinking, melting, coalescing terror in his wide-open eyes. For, next, she held the implement up in the hellish white light and answered:

"These are Bruns serrated plaster shears."

Chapter 25

(I)

Kathleen's eyes fluttered open to weird dices of light. It was the television—a cable sports channel—with the volume all the way down. She'd fallen asleep on Maxwell's couch, and here was Maxwell himself, asleep in her lap. One arm curled around the back of her waist, the other under her thigh; he was using her stomach for a pillow. The colors from the TV throbbed in and out of the apartment's cool, air-conditioned darkness. She thought back…

Did I dream? she wondered.

She couldn't remember, which was just as well. The recurring nightmare was draining all her energy. Even thinking of it made her grow gooseflesh.

Someone was dreaming, though.

She'd never known Maxwell to snore—thank God—but he did occasionally utter silly noises in his slumber. Sometimes he even talked, nonsensical fragments or errant words. In her lap now, he snuggled her and murmured: "They're coming."

"What? Maxwell? Are you awake?"

He was not awake. His arm tightened about her thigh. "They're coming to get you, Barbara," he mumbled.

Barbara, huh? Kathleen faintly smirked. *So he's dreaming of old girlfriends.* She couldn't very well hold that against him, though it irked her just the same. *You could at least be polite enough to dream about me, Maxwell. That or keep your mouth closed when you're off in slumberland.*

Baseball men were running around the lit TV screen. Kathleen looked around. Highlighted against the slider window, and the moon, the silhouette of Maxwell's typewriter stood out. A sheet of paper wagged from the roller.

The poem, she thought. Earlier he'd said he was writing a poem for her. It would be shitty of her to read it without his permission, but...

She couldn't help it.

Very gently she edged out from under Maxwell, then stood up. When she was sure she hadn't wakened him, she turned and tiptoed toward his desk.

She squinted over the sheet of paper in the machine and began to read: A KEATSIAN—

"Don't you dare," sprang Maxwell's voice.

Kathleen turned guiltily back around. "I thought you were asleep. I—"

He was sitting up in the dark. "You're not supposed to read it yet. It's not finished... Did you read it?"

"No," she said.

"But you were going to, right?"

"Well..."

"How much did you read?"

"'A Keatsian'—and that's all."

Maxwell hesitated. "I don't think I believe you."

"I don't care!" she said. "And you're hardly in a position to be giving me a ration of crap. Who's Barbara?"

Maxwell leaned forward. "Who?"

"Who?" Kathleen haughtily mimicked. "You know who. Barbara, your dream girl."

"Kathleen, I don't know what you're—"

"You said her name in your sleep."

Maxwell fell silent a moment, deliberating. "Barbara? But I don't even know any— Oh, wait a minute. The movie."

"What movie?"

"While you were sleeping I had the USA network on. They were running *Night Of The Living Dead.* One of the characters' names was Barbara."

"Come on, Maxwell," she replied. "Can't you lie better than that?"

"I'm serious," he insisted. "This guy with glasses was saying 'They're coming to get you, Barbara,' and then this zombie started chasing her. I think he wanted to eat her."

Well, I guess he's not lying, Kathleen concluded.

"Aw, can you believe it?" Maxwell complained. Scores flashed on the silent TV. "The Yankees lost again. Looks like I'm going to owe Chizmar another case of beer this year. Highest paid batting staff in baseball and the best of them couldn't hit a beachball with an ironing board. Nobody loses to Baltimore four times in a row. Nobody."

"I have to go now, Maxwell," Kathleen said. She slipped on her shoes and picked up her purse.

"It's almost four in the morning," Maxwell protested.

Was it that late? "I really should go—"

"But I don't want you to go. Stay here with me."

"I need to get up early," she excused. "I'm pretty much done with the outlining. I'm ready to begin the actual text."

"Text? What text?"

"For the book, Maxwell. The book about the killer."

Maxwell let that one sit a while. He seemed to percolate from the couch. "What does the book have to do with you not staying here tonight? Did I forget to use my deodorant?"

"I like your deodorant, Maxwell."

"It's foolish to leave now. You shouldn't be driving home through the city this late."

"I'm a big girl," she said. She knew she must be confusing him now, sending mixed signals. But she wanted to go home. She wanted to be fresh in the morning to begin. Perhaps she'd even begin tonight. Nighttime seemed the best time to start such a book. *The dead of night*, she thought. "I'll call you tomorrow," she insisted. "Besides, you need to work on my poem."

"I never see you long enough to give it to you. I guess I could always give it to Barbara."

"And I guess I could kick you hard in your poetical ass, couldn't I?" She quickly kissed him on the lips.

"Why don't you reconsider and let me make love to you?"

"I wouldn't be very good tonight."

"I would," he said. "Guaranteed. I'll give you boundless orgasms."

Yes, you probably would. The extemporaneous suggestion sparked a crude lust, but it didn't feel real. She felt too distracted for sex right now, too pent-up in other things. Better that she wait, when it could be real, and good for both of them.

"Soon," she promised. "You'll see."

"Is that what you tell all the guys?"

"No, just you. All the other guys I lie to."

"Oh, well, in that case..."

He looked forlorn sitting there in the dark. He seemed to fidget, hands clasped. "I love you," he said.

She kissed him again and left.

Her shoes clapped rapidly down the steps. In the lobby, the desk guard glanced up from a magazine with the bizarre title *Palace Corbie*. He eyed her, pinch-faced, as she pushed through the exit doors. P Street lay before her, abandoned. The warm night air refurbished her anticipations about the book. She hustled across the street, heels scuffing asphalt, and when she was halfway into the parking lot, Maxwell's voice echoed high to her rear.

"I love you," he said.

The words boomed in the street, a swarming concussion. Kathleen turned and looked up to see Maxwell standing on his dark, second-story balcony. A tepid breeze sifted the fine, blond hair.

"I guess that sounds pretty corny," he considered. "Such words, spoken from a balcony, in the middle of the night."

"I doesn't sound corny, Maxwell," she said, and laughed as she unlocked her car door.

His next words echoed louder. "Come back up here so I can make love to you. We can do it all night."

Kathleen's face turned hot red. "Maxwell! The whole neighborhood will hear you!"

Maxwell shrugged. "So? I want them to know; I want everybody to know that I love you."

The empty street amplified the words to something greater than words, it seemed. She and Maxwell could've been the only two people in the world just then. She looked up at him, nearly staring, as if adrift. "I love you too," she said.

"What? Hey!" Maxwell almost fell off the balcony. "What did you say!" he shouted.

Kathleen slid into the T-Bird, closed the door, started the engine. She could still hear him shouting: "What did you say! Did you say what I think you said? Say it again!" *Now I've done it,* she thought. She pulled out of the lot and drove off. Maxwell's booming voice followed the car all the way up to Dupont Circle: "Come back here, Kathleen! Say what you just said a minute ago, damn it!"

She laughed in spite of the consequences; it had seemed so unconscious, and so easy all of a sudden. Kathleen rarely said things she didn't mean to people close to her.

I guess I meant it, she realized.

The city remained empty all the way home, the pallid sodium darkness deepening its alleys, its littered streets and cement. Back in her own parking lot, she stuck her tongue out at the van. *Randolph Carter Contractors my ass,* she thought. They moved the van every afternoon; it wasn't hard to figure. *Solely for my protection, huh, Spence? Just more bullshit.* Spence needed someone close by in case the killer decided to drop in for a visit, that was all. In fact she felt sure Spence hoped that would happen. *He could care less what happens to me, so long as he catches his killer.*

She shouldn't even think of him; the mere sound of his name in her head—Spence, Spence—pummeled her mood.

Up in her apartment, she bolted the door, opened the slider and some windows, and shed the hot tank dress. She lit a Now 100, poured some iced tea, then sat down to appraise the disheveled papers on her desk. *Yeah,* she decided. *I'll start tonight.* The book's first segment should detail the sociological considerations of mental illnesses, and their effect on long-term pattern behavior—things she already knew about from college, and from her experience at the magazine.

But what should I call it? There was a question. What title would she give the book? *How about... Female Serial Killer? Ridiculous. Or... Murderess? No, no, that stank too. Too generic. How about...* She paused on the thought. *How about... Portrait of the Psychopath as a Young Woman?* She paused further, then: *Yes,* she thought.

And at that same moment, as she confirmed the book's title, she looked at the clock, saw that it was 4:12 a.m., and realized that the phone was ringing.

(II)

Spence awoke from a deafening dream of the sound of helicopters, looked at the clock, saw that it was 4:18 a.m., and realized that the phone was ringing.

Helicopters? he queried. *Why dream of those?* The night conspired to confuse him: the phone ringing, his grogginess, and also the sound of his beeper going off. He blinked himself awake, in the cloying dark, tried to shove away the dream's sonic thud.

Then he answered the phone. "Yeah," he said.

"This is Central Commo," a brisk male voice announced. "Lieutenant Spence?"

"Yeah," he said, and suddenly it occurred to him that the heavy whopping sound of the dream—the helicopter—was still in his ears.

"Six minutes ago, the killer made telephone contact with Kathleen Shade," the commo man said.

Spence moved as fast as his heart, jerking up, turning on the lights, clearing his mind. "Trace the call through the public index," he ordered. "Did you trace the call?"

"Trying, sir, but—"

"What the fuck do you mean trying?" Spence profaned. "It only takes two or three seconds to trace a station nowadays. Are the fucking computers down?"

"No sir."

"The MSC flag is locked into the program; the mainframe will lock onto the signal binaries. If the trace isn't coming up on the public station index, then it's got to be cellular. It's either a portable phone or a mobile phone. Do I gotta tell you guys everything? DF the fucking signal."

"That's what I'm doing, sir. A cellular trace takes time."

Spence was pissed. "How long did the phone contact last?"

"That's what I'm trying to tell you, sir. The conversation is still in progress."

Spence yelled "Call S.O.D. right now and—"

"I've got six triangulators on the road already, Lieutenant, and every patrol car in the city on priority standby. I've also got three helicopters up. One of them should be at your address any minute now."

It was no dream at all. The sound of helicopter rotors grew closer, louder. "It's already here," Spence said and hung up. He dashed about the bedroom, hauled on slacks and a shirt, stepped into his shoes without socks. He grabbed his gun, his ID, and, inexplicably, a tie. Then he was out the door and jumping down the stairwell three steps at a time.

The neighbors'll love me, he thought, and then stepped out into what had to be the most ludicrous scenario of his life. He could imagine how he looked: A man in crushed clothes and unbuttoned shirt, hair sticking up, waving his police badge into a one-million-candle-power helicopter spotlight. In the middle of a quiet apartment parking lot. In the middle of the night. The spotlight swelled. The helicopter—a rebuilt white Bell JetRanger—descended amid the chugging cacophony of its props, and a mad wind siphoned about Spence, which nearly sucked his unbuttoned Christian Dior shirt off his back.

A ladder rolled out of the open cabin, and Spence climbed in.

"Lieutenant Spence, I presume," the pilot shouted, in a bulging black PAC helmet that looked like and insect's head.

"Get this thing up," Spence said. He fumbled to button his shirt. "You're going to raise my condo fees."

"Welcome aboard. I'm Geralds, Aviation Section night commander." He thumbed over his shoulder. "The cowboy behind you's Fisher."

A black guy in tac utilities nodded from the seat behind the pilot. Headset under a Kevlar helmet. Ballistic glasses. A long semi-automatic rifle with a mean scope in his lap. *S.O.D. sniper,* Spence realized. *Probably itching to blow something away.*

"Strap in, Lieutenant, unless you want to go through the roof of Constitution Hall." Geralds pulled back on the pedals, jammed throttle, and the helicopter rocketed off and up. Spence saw lights blinking on in his apartment building as he fastened his belt.

"Got Central Commo screaming for you, sir." Geralds handed over a headset. Fisher plugged him in, then gave clipped instructions as to the assignations of the mode selector. "One is Central Commo, sir. Two, Cabin. Three and four Airborne units and All Units, respectively. Five, Auxiliary."

Like I'm supposed to remember that? Spence thought. He felt for the selector switch, clicked it to One. "You've DF'd the signal, right?" he said.

"The triangulation reads positive," Central Communications told him, "but it's not holding long enough to put a tack on the board."

"That means it's definitely a mobile phone; that means she's moving. Keep the fucking DF on the fucking signal."

Spence, not ordinarily a profane man, imagined every profanity. Beyond the windshield there was only blackness, oblivion, yet somewhere in that void, the killer was awake, alive, talking...

"Lieutenant? You there?" the dispatcher asked.

"Yeah, quiet," Spence said, rubbing his eyes. "Let me think a minute. I can't think in a helicopter."

The sound of the turboshaft beat against his skull, and his stomach tossed against Geralds' over-the-top piloting. "Is the connection still in progress?" Spence asked.

"Affirmative," replied the dispatch.

"How long for a positive direction-find?"

"Depends on the lay. Couple of minutes if the weather's clear but she's got to stop or at least slow down. And the second she hangs up, we lose the DF."

"Fuck, piss," Spence said. "Of all the fucking things."

"I'm keeping on it."

Spence thought of a T-bone steak being dangled before a chained dog. *The universe is walking all over me,* he thought.

"We just got something on the DF board," Central Commo announced. "Then we lost it."

"Well then find it again!" Spence yelled. "This is a fucking disgrace!"

Geralds' brow rose. Fisher stared blank-faced.

"There it goes again, Lieutenant," the dispatcher affirmed. "We just got another positive DF, but it winked out before the board could process it."

"Fuck!" Spence yelled.

"And—yeah—there's another one."

"So the killer's still on the line with Shade?"

"Affirmative."

This was infuriating. "There's gotta be some way you can at least grab a general loke."

No reply, just a pause shuddering with the props. Then:

"Got it!" the dispatcher rejoiced. "Upper east Northeast, it looks like, sir."

Spence's heart was racing. The prop chugged like a flak cannon. He knew he must look to Geralds and Fisher like a pansy sweating the schoolyard bully. His stomach wobbled vigorously. He sat back in the hard metal seat, to catch his breath, to try and regain his cool. *I'm running this whole show and I'm almost pissing my pants,* he thought. Geralds frowned as Spence began to put on his tie.

Then the commo dispatcher confirmed: "You're right, sir. The trace came through, Bell Atlantic Cellular, listed subscriber is a Jonathan Richards Duff, address—"

"I don't give a shit where he lives," Spence said. "Give me his car. Give me something we can see."

"Subscriber vehicle listed as a '96 Nissan 2-door, 300ZX, 6-cylinder, orange."

"Put an all-points out on that vehicle—now," Spence commanded. "I want everything that moves heading upper-east Northeast."

"Roger," confirmed the dispatcher.

"You got that, Geralds?" Spence asked.

"Upper-east Northeast, yes sir."

"So start flying this thing like you got a pair. Make me throw up."

Geralds and Fisher smiled. The pilot's hands and feet jerked to opposite positions; suddenly the prop noise revved and Spence's heart was in his intestines. Geralds veered to such an extreme that the helicopter made the turn on its side. "I'm falling—help!" Spence cried. Gravity snapped him against the seat straps. His gun flew out of his lap and began to bounce around the cabin. Geralds and Fisher were laughing aloud.

Then the helicopter evened out, soaring through dark. Spence had been one pulse short of vomiting.

"Here's your weapon, sir." Fisher gave Spence back his snub. "You all right?"

Spence gulped, nodding. In the observation ports, the city's streets looked like an arteriogram, lit blood passages coursing through cluttered darkness. Tiny flashing red and blue lights, dozens of sets, could be seen racing along the veins all in the same direction. *I got three helicopters, six commo vans, God knows how many S.O.D. vehicles, and every patrol car in the city under me,* Spence inventoried. *If I can't catch her with all of that, then I should be pumping gas.*

In another second, Central Commo was back on his headset. "I gotta positive DF, Lieutenant. Shade's still on the line. The signal isn't moving anymore."

Again, Spence bellowed: "Give us a—"

"All units," the dispatcher announced, "Signal 5 to 2500 block South Dakota Avenue, 31st Street and Ames. Orange Nissan 300ZX. Confirm ID and standby."

Spence's free ride through the heavens felt like a trolley on bad tracks. Geralds had one eye on radar and the other on a small terminal roving a D.C. grid map. The city was less than six miles wide. "How long 'til we're there?" he asked.

"Thirty, forty," Gerald's answered.

"You're shitting me! Thirty to forty minutes?"

"No sir. Seconds... Hold on."

The helicopter plummeted. Now they were close to rooftops; below looked like an industrial section. *Come on,* Spence thought, *come on, come on.*

"Will you be unassing, sir?" Fisher asked.

"Huh?"

"Will you be getting off the aircraft?"

"Uh, yeah," Spence said.

"Hook him up with a hand-held and earphone," Geralds advised. "Gonna be louder than the Super Bowl down there. Give him the megaphone too."

Fisher affixed both to Spence's beltloops, then plugged in the earphone. Spence, pointing to Fisher's scoped rifle, said, "I may need you to use that."

"Just tell me which eyeball, sir," Fisher replied. "But try to get me in close, like not past 300 meters."

Jesus, Spence thought. *These guys think in meters.*

Long flat buildings swept past them below, giving way to darkly lit streets. Patrol units were easily seen now flying through turns and around corners. Then Geralds said, "There it is."

Spence pressed his face against the door window. A residential section opened up past the industrial park. Beyond that, through building alleys, he could see South Dakota Avenue. Parked on a main street, by itself, sat the orange Nissan.

"You run the radio show from here," Spence ordered Geralds. "Nobody shoots unless I say so. Got it?"

"Yes sir."

"Now let me out of this thing."

"Sir, it might not be such a hot idea for you to go down there. Let Fisher go, he's gotta vest."

"Let me out," Spence ordered.

"Unbutton," the pilot said to Fisher. "You heard the man. Then take your firing post."

The spotlight grew on the street, and the Nissan. Suddenly it looked like daylight. Another helicopter appeared like magic to their right. Fisher, umbilicaled by canvas straps to metal hooks, slid open the cabin door and threw out the ladder. The helicopter hitched down in jagged increments…

"Commo check," Spence heard Geralds say through the earphone on his handheld. Spence pressed his mike button, said "Test," for lack of anything else. Geralds nodded and Spence climbed out.

Fisher sat out on the edge of the cabin, aiming the rifle. Spence took three or four rungs down the ladder, then dropped the rest of the way to the street. What good were all those years of weight training if he couldn't take an eight-foot drop? He hit the street, stumbled, and fell, tearing the knee out of his slacks. *Come on, Curly!* he thought. Mobile units poured in all around him, tires screeching, cops spilling out of doors to assume defensive positions behind their vehicles. When Spence got up, he was standing in a lake of insane, throbbing light and noise.

He heard Geralds delegating orders in his earphone: "All units hold your fire until you've received the firing command. Acquire target: occupant of orange Nissan, white female, red hair, passenger side..."

Yes, Spence could see her now. He stood twenty feet before the car, and he could see her, the tumult of red hair, the unearthly face staring back at him through the windshield.

"Watch for crossfire and standby," Geralds was saying. "Do not fire until you've received the firing command. If you receive the firing command, do *not* shoot the guy in the white shirt..."

Stepping forward, Spence raised his small revolver. To his rear, waves of guns cocked, and more vehicles screeched to halts, popping with lights. Then the third helicopter appeared above the alley which sided the car, a sniper with a laser sight aiming down from the cabin.

Spence's stare seemed to pour over the pallid face behind the windshield. Something premonitory assured him that if he emptied his Smith snub right now, all five rounds would land in the visage that opposed him. However...

"Get out of the car!" he yelled into the GE megaphone.

The face, like a big pale egg lain in a crimson nest, only stared back in reply. Spence could see her blinking slowly. His gun felt like a component part of his hand. Not at his professional best, he yelled again into the megaphone: "Get out of the car right now goddamn it and put your hands up in plain sight or I'll fucking kill you! Do you hear me? I'll fucking kill you!"

But again the only response was that uncanny and nearly astral blank stare.

"Lieutenant," Geralds radioed. "Fisher's got a perfect bead..."

Spence was thinking of Simmons, and the phase-classifications of this particular insanity. The last phase, the Capture Phase. *Is this it?* he wondered. A reactive depression leaving the killer helpless against a sweeping urge to die? In the windshield, the woman continued to blink. Her discolored mouth seemed to droop.

A moment later, though, Spence thought: *No, no.*

"We gotta bead, Lieutenant. Just give the word."

No, no, no, he went on thinking. He dropped the megaphone and unclipped the handheld. "Hold your fire," he directed.

Then the woman lurched—

"She's moving!" Geralds yelled. "You better let us—"

"Hold your fucking fire!" Spence yelled back. He could've cried. "It's...not...her," he said.

No, he could see that it wasn't her. He could see that it wasn't even a woman...

Spence put his gun in his pocket. As he walked around to the Nissan's passenger side, a half-circle of gun-pointing cops followed him up.

He opened the door. The occupant fell out onto the curb. Not a woman at all but a lean man in red panties and a stuffed, red-lace bra. His skin looked fishbelly-white. The sprawling red wig slid off against the cement.

Despite the scene's din, Spence heard nothing now. He knelt down. Blood was running like an open tap from somewhere. The dying man's cool hands groped up as if to fondle oblivion. Spence noted the severed stitches encircling the lips, bandaged ankles and knees, and eyes so bloodshot they shone full red.

"Help us find her," Spence pleaded. "We need to know where she is, where she took you, anything—any detail."

The man died.

Jesus...

On the dashboard a typed note had been taped. It read:

SORRY I MISSED YOU, MR. SPENCE.
BUT MY MOTHER AND I WILL DEFINITELY KEEP IN TOUCH.

CREAMY

Jesus, Spence thought again.

A frantic voice squawked from inside the car. Spence looked past the blood-filled passenger seat and saw the car phone dangling from the wheel.

"Are you there? Are you still there?" Kathleen Shade was saying on the other end. "Don't hang up. Are you there?"

Spence hung up the phone.

Chapter 26

(I)

No, they never understood. None of them did.

Like Sammy's one and only brother, Jack. Big developer now. Invested half his inheritance into commercial real estate and some construction projects, and kept the shares Sammy sold him on the side. A successful, respected business man. Sammy remembered Big Brother's parting locutions quite well: "If I ever see you again, Sam, I'll kill you—" (cool voice, calm, very in control) "—and if you ever go near my daughter again, on our father's grave I swear I'll kill you. You're a degenerate, a disgrace." These amicable words had been spoken to Sammy at the D.C. Courthouse, the day he'd been sentenced. And what had Kathleen said? "I hope you hang yourself in prison."? Something like that.

Piss on all of them, he thought. *Why should I care what they think about me?* At least he was honest. At least he didn't deny the things he'd done in his life, nor the desires that motivated him. A degenerate? A disgrace? He smiled, taking the Caddie ragtop down Patrick Henry Boulevard. Who could define those terms? And by what criteria? It was bullshit. There was no good and evil. There was only the world and the people in it and the things they thought and they things they did. That was all. Sammy didn't give a shit about people who didn't give a shit about him. Why should he? It was supply and demand—hey, if he didn't make the flicks and mule the masters, then somebody else would. Evil had nothing to do with it, nor criminal intent, nor degeneracy. If people wanted something, then someone would provide it, whether it conformed to the law or not. If people got off watching snuff or wet S&M or rape loops, then they would have it. *And if some people like to watch viddies of adults having sex with kids,* Sammy reasoned, *then what's wrong with that?* At least to Sammy, demand legitimized supply. To hell with society's definition of evil, of criminality, etc. None of it made any sense.

It wasn't Sammy's fault, was it? It wasn't his fault that there were plenty of people out there who liked to watch underground flicks. Some people got off on that, fine. Sammy himself did too, and he freely admitted this. It turned him on—seeing the heavy shit. And if it turned him on—and if it turned hundreds of thousands of other people on—then there must be a reason. The reason was instinct, he felt sure. Not some forced desire to be evil, not some conscious willingness to like things that the majority of society says you're not supposed to like. Christ, in Jersey they had women begging to be in Vinchetti's productions; nobody was forcing the chicks to do that shit—they volunteered. And why? Because the price was right. Quid pro quo. Vinchetti needed fresh inventory, and the women needed their crack. And the fucking clients wanted the tapes, so what was the problem? It didn't matter what it was. It didn't matter if it was a Disney flick or a snuff flick. People wanted it. Christ, the month before he got busted, Sammy helped Vinchetti's crew make one flick called *Barnyard Babes* that got a 2,000-copy order the instant it hit the points: a couple of biker chicks burned out on PCP, doing the works with horses, pigs, sheep. There was even one flick they duped, a bootleg from Amsterdam where some coke addict put a live eel in herself. This wasn't bullshit, it was true. And it was still supply and demand. If clients didn't buy the shit, then Vinchetti'd have no reason to make it. There were 40 million alcoholics in the country but you don't blame the fucking guy behind the counter at the liquor store. Cigarettes killed 400,000 people per year but you don't send the tobacco farmers up on murder charges.

And, all right, maybe it was a little different with the kp and the prepube stuff—Sammy knew that. Most of the time the kids were abducted, or traded along in the regional circuits—but that was Vinchetti, not Sammy. It wasn't Sammy who was snatching the kids from malls and playgrounds. All Sammy did was help make the flicks and transport the masters to the dupe labs in his point, and, yeah, every now and then they'd be short a camera-cock, so Vinchetti's production men would let Sammy step in and do a little of the rodwork. By then most of the kids were deprogrammed anyway, and he'd never been rough with any of them. Hurting the kids would be unthinkable. Nobody understood anything these days. There were societies out there now, organizations where members actually paid dues. The North American Man-Boy Love Association, The West Coast Adult-Child Care Chapter, and even one called Christian Parents For Positive Sexual Enlightenment. It wasn't just Sammy, it was a lot of people, whole communities of them.

Sooner or later, Sammy reasoned, *the world's gonna come around and see the light.*

Back when Sammy'd been making flicks, he'd covered his back. He'd duplicated all of his keys—to everything—and kept them in a safe place in case he ever went down. Also, copies of point lists, mail-drops, various addresses. Private mail boxes and safe-deposit boxes were hard to trace. You could rent a safe-deposit box or you could buy one outright. When you bought one—a couple of grand—there were no questions asked. Sammy headed out to Glen Burnie that morning—if the place had gone under, then his shit would be gone and that would be that, but: *Jesus saves!* he thought. Behind the little strip mall, just off Route 2, the same red-lettered, white sign loomed. E-Z MAIL, POST BOXES, SAFE DEPOSIT, REASONABLE RATES.

It was all still there in the little combo-lock metal box.

The keys—a big clump of them on a silver ring—were what he wanted. Keys to the warehouses, the processing labs, some storage joints; no doubt, all of these places had been closed down years ago. There were also some keys to a few drop-points and hideouts. They'd all probably bitten the dust too, after all this time. But Sammy didn't give a shit about any of that... The ring also contained the keys to his brother's house.

And no doubt, somewhere in his brother's house would be an address book. And somewhere in that address book would be the one address and number Sammy needed to have: Kathleen's.

First, he called the house number— "This is Jack Shade. I'm not available now, so please leave a message after the beep." Sammy hadn't left a message. Then he'd called his brother's office number, identifying himself as Richard Hertz of F.O. Day Construction, Inc. "I'm sorry, Mr. Hertz," the secretary had informed him, "but Mr. Shade is in Los Angeles right now, attending a realty convention. He won't he back in town 'til the weekend."

"Thanks very much," Sammy said. "I'll get in touch with him next week."

It was a leisurely, sedate drive to Northern Virginia. He grabbed a quick bite at a restaurant he remembered called R.T.'s, had Pan-Fired Louisiana Shrimpcakes and a side of Southern Fried Squid. *Yeah, I ate like this every day in the joint, sure,* he joked to himself. On the wall was a signed picture of the President, along with the plate he'd eaten off of, for God's sake. It was funny, though, how when you were in the joint, the outside world became something completely alien. You didn't give a shit who was President. You didn't give shit about wars. *The Gulf?*

Bosnia? Fuck it, kill 'em all. North Korea building nukes? Let 'er rip. Drop one on the Capitol. The deficit? Gimme a break! In stir was like being on another planet.

Back on the road, Sammy let his thoughts sail with the wind over the Caddie's open top. *Good things come in threes,* he remembered the wives' tale. *One, my keys still in the box, two, Jack out of town...* Somehow, Sammy knew that fate would grant him a third kernel of good luck: that his brother had not changed the locks on the house...

He turned quickly off of Duke, and headed down toward the Old Towne waterfront. North of the main drag came the ritzy communities. The subtly pretentious architecture seemed New Englandish somehow, old Colonial styles, fastidiously renovated. He spotted the house and parked around the corner. Manicured lawns and lush trees teemed in the summer sun. Between the houses the water glimmered. Jack Shade's house looked exactly the same, though it seemed larger. Everything seemed a little larger to Sammy now; six years in stir, in a 10x8 box of bricks, had a way of distorting one's sense of proportion. *Just walk up like you own the place,* he thought. He whistled up the driveway, then up the fieldstone walk. He noted no neighbors milling about, no traffic. The same Arrowhead alarm plate blinked red twice a second when Sammy stepped onto the porch. *The system's on, and that means no one's inside.* Sammy raised the tubular alarm key, took a hopeful breath, and turned off the system. *Yeah, good things come in threes,* he thought. He unlocked the front door and walked in.

Fine. Good, you're in. So don't fuck around. No address book in the kitchen. He remembered a basket beneath the phone, containing spare car keys and an old address book. *Fuck,* Sammy calmly thought. The big butcher-block-wood country kitchen remained, but the basket was gone. *Den,* he directed. *Big Brother's office.* The quiet opulence seemed to shout in his face. High, dark genuine paneling. Huge teak desk. Crystal and pure-gold carriage clock on the mantel, ticking slowly. The ticking reminded Sammy of another clock, from his past—the clock he'd bought for Kathleen when she was—what? Nine? Ten? The moment flashed a warm vertigo, and an image: The plastic eyes and tail switching to and fro, tick, tick, tick, as Sammy's hypnotic, gentle whispers lulled her into the trusting trance... He moaned audibly, right there in his brother's den, thinking of his brother's daughter. *All I ever did was love her, Jack. I didn't hurt her.*

What about YOU, Jack? Huh? What did you ever love in your life, I mean besides yourself, and your fucking land deals and condos? Three days after your own fucking wife's funeral you were flying to California to buy up some new waterfront. At least I was with her, Jack. At least I was here when you were too busy to be a father.

And I never hurt her...

Sammy ground the memory away with his teeth.

DIGIDAK ADDRESS LOG read the letters on the bizarre device. It sat on the desk, no bigger than a wallet. *Some newfangled computer thing,* Sammy equated. The world had changed while he'd fermented in prison. *What the fuck happened to the good old fashioned Rodolex?* He blew 10 minutes figuring out how the thing worked. INDEX one button read. Sammy pressed S, for Shade, then SCROLL. No Shades. Then he pressed K, for Kathleen.

And there it was.

He jotted the address and number down on the back of his parole officer's card. Then he made to split.

It was just something he had to do before leaving, an intercession perhaps. He would not ask for forgiveness—love wasn't something he felt the need to apologize for. It was something else, deeper. Just to see her again, to talk to her one last time before he disappeared...

He stood in the foyer. *Get out,* a voice told him. *You can't be getting caught in here. But...*

The memories whispered to him, as gently as he'd whispered to little Kathleen. Immediately, he felt violated, crushed by the vehement misunderstanding of others. They'd stolen from him—they'd stolen six years of his life. They'd stolen his entire past...

Then he remembered.

Next, he was mounting the curved, banistered stairs, up and around, to the long hall. Some of his past was still here, wasn't it? A little piece? After all this time, he'd forgotten.

When Sammy'd stayed to look after Kathleen, he'd had the spare room. Last room on the end, on the left. Here he was again now, after years and years. His fingers touched the knob. The hinges actually grated from disuse when he pushed open the door. *Figures,* he thought. The room had not been touched. That was his brother's style, to write things off as if they'd never existed. Just one glance assured him that the room had not been cleaned—it probably hadn't even been entered—since his arraignment.

Dust lay an inch thick on everything. The entire room was gray. Cobwebs rounded the corners, and hung like tendrils of rotted fabric from the ceiling. The bed was gray. The dresser, the night table, the walls—all gray. Even the once-vibrant plum-colored carpet was gray by years of dust.

Sammy had never had much of a personal supply of pornography; being on the road most of the time prevented that. When he'd been busted, he'd been staying in a motel. The feds had grabbed everything, including the several cigar boxes of Polaroids Sammy kept for personal use. They booked all the masters he'd been carrying as evidence, and they'd also booked the cigar boxes. Sammy could've keeled over when the prosecutor had passed those cigar boxes along to the jury: all those snapshots, all those kids.

Vinchetti's crew didn't mind Sammy snapping a few pix for himself every now and then. There'd been a few mags, too, mostly imports from Amsterdam, and a few vintage domestic jobs. But those cigar boxes—his little treasure chests—were gone forever. Except one.

He knelt in dust. He reached under the bed. He knew it was still there even before his fingers touched it: the one box they never got. Sammy'd kept it secreted in the box spring, beyond a tacked flap in the cheesecloth lining.

Still here, he thought.

He opened the box. He gazed down into it, as if into a holy light. A foreign mag called *Jubilaum!* Dutch kids, or Germans. And one of Vinchetti's mags from the 70's, before he'd graduated to the wonder of video tape. *Come Play With Us,* read the title. A third mag—*Santa's Coming!*—starred Sammy himself, dressed up as Father Christmas. *Sweet kids,* he reflected, thumbing through the glossy pages. *Christ, I had a whole head of hair back then.* But in the bottom of the box was a single envelope. And in the envelope was a single Polaroid...

The snapshot shined in his hand. Yes, his past. One little tiny piece of Sammy's past that had not been taken from him.

It was a snapshot of Kathleen.

Eleven, twelve, he guessed. Whenever he was finished, he always talked her gently into sleep. He'd taken several pictures of her, but this was the only one left.

So beautiful, he thought, staring at it.

It was the only one he needed.

This house, this picture, this room—it all took him back to another time. His memory was a sweet whorl. *Kathleen, Kathleen,* he thought. But there was another room too, wasn't there? Another vault of his past?

Kathleen's bedroom, two doors down, lay in the same state: festooned by cobwebs, bedrabbed in dust. The furniture of her tender years, of course, was gone, replaced—Kathleen had lived in this house through college—but that wasn't the point. This was still her room, *the* room...

No, Kathleen hadn't been like the others at all. Sammy really had loved her—it was just that people didn't understand how complex real love could be. In the joint, they'd had special names for pedophiles: 'Lester, Kiddie Fucker, Short Eyes. Well, they could all fuck themselves now. *'Cos I'm out, motherfuckers, and you're not.* A month from now Sammy would be partying on the beach, with enough cash to set him for life. Lotta guys would've folded, but Sammy had played it right, the plea bargain, the spin on Vinchetti, the whole deal.

But how right am I playing it now? he wondered.

He couldn't help it.

He just…couldn't.

Sleepytime, he thought.

He lay on his side, on the bed and on his memories. He was looking at the picture of her, nearly in tears. He unbuckled his pants…

He couldn't help it.

The cat clock was long gone, but he could still see it… Softly ticking as he whispered. *It's Sleepytime, Kathleen. You know your Uncle Sammy loves you, don't you? This is the special thing that uncles and little girls do. It's a special secret from God. Sleepytime, Sleepytime.* It didn't take long. She was so pretty. He loved her so much. *Almost,* he thought. *Almost. Alm—*

"Here," he whispered.

(II)

"—want to do my story?" asked the voice on the tape.

"Yes."

"You agree, then. It's an important story."

"Yes," Kathleen Shade answered. "I've already begun to work on it."

"Skulls mean death."

Spence pressed the PAUSE button on the tape player. He seemed more rugged today, he hadn't shaved. He twiddled his thumbs behind the big metal desk. "Skulls mean death." he said. "What do you suppose she means by that?"

"I don't know," Kathleen said.

"Is this the first time she's called you?"

Kathleen laughed with little humor. "You've got a lot of nerve asking me that. You've been tapping my phone."

"Well, she could've called you before we put the tap on. Did she?"

"Isn't it against the law for the police to tap somebody's phone without their permission?"

"Under ordinary circumstances, of course. But under exceptional circumstances? Such as these? We don't need permission when such a surveillance is deemed by a judge to be relevant. When a citizen's life is in reasonable danger. And when such a surveillance would provide a positive utility regarding the active investigation of a grievous crime. Check Section XI, paragraph 2a of the District Annotated Code: Telephone Surveillance and Protocol Pursuant to Investigative Operations of Major Crimes."

"This isn't China, Spence. I shouldn't have to worry about your big ears in my apartment every time I pick up the phone."

"And as I've striven to remind you, quite often, our surveillance is also for your protection."

Striven? she wondered. "Uh-huh. And I'll bet you own the deed to the Empire State Building."

Spence set his chin in his palm. "Are you going to answer my initial question? You always evade questions that you don't want to answer."

"Yes," Kathleen stonily stated. "This was the first time the killer has called me."

"But you'd like her to call again, as frequently as possible. Wouldn't you? For the book?"

"Yeah. And maybe if she calls enough times, you nimrods will be able to catch her."

Spence had explained last night's debacle, the traces, the DF, the helicopter ride for nothing. Could the killer really be that much smarter than Spence and all his technology? Someone must have faith in the man, to put all those resources, all those men and all that equipment, at his instant disposal. *But if I was the police chief,* Kathleen fantasized, *Spence would be cleaning the toilets.*

"Jonathan Duff, Arlington, Virginia," Spence noted to her. "He had phony plates on his car. I wonder why... Anyway, he's the seventh victim, at least that we're aware of. She's maintaining a formidable accretion of bodies."

Yes, she was. And Kathleen knew that the account of this latest victim would be in her mail soon. Perhaps tomorrow. Perhaps today.

"Let's listen some more," Spence said. "Shall we?" He pressed the PLAY button:

"You are a great woman," the voice drew on, "to be what you are, to rise above. Like me. We are both great women. You'll see."

"I don't know what you mean," Kathleen said on the tape. In the background, the car engine could be heard, and every so often, a dismal moan.

"You'll see," the voice repeated. It paused—perhaps she was turning. Then: "There it is! I can see it!"

"What? What can you see?"

"The Cross. It's... I can see it. It's beautiful."

"You're religious?" Kathleen asked.

"No."

"Tell me about The Cross."

"No. We all have our crosses. I do. You do... Sometimes, I can look at a man's face and see his bones. I can see his blood in him. My mother shows me their blood."

"Tell me about your mother."

"She..."

"Did you love her?"

"She tells me things. She tells me how to be honest, and smart."

"But your mother's dead. You said so in the first manuscript."

"She's not dead. She'll never be dead, not really. Don't you know what I mean? Like, when you really love somebody?"

Kathleen remembered the pause which followed. She remembered trying to think of some tactic to keep the killer on the line, some way to feign a bond. How complex was the killer intellectually? Would she see through such a ploy? "I'd like to be your friend," Kathleen said. "We should be friends, we should meet."

"Now you're lying. If I agreed to meet with you, you'd lead the police right to me."

"No, I wouldn't," Kathleen bumbled back. "You should trust me—we should trust each other."

"Why?"

"Because then we'll be stronger. Against them."

Another static hesitation. Was it working?

"Against who?"

"All the men out there who would hurt us," Kathleen answered. "There're lots of them. They're all over, everywhere. We have to be careful."

"So...well..." The voice receded again to the faint, grainy drone of the car's engine. "Then I guess I should tell you where I live, or some place to meet me."

She's testing you, Kathleen had realized. "No," she said, "don't do that! The police are probably bugging my phone."

Spence paused the tape player again. "I'm impressed by your intuition," he told her. "At least I think I am. You knew that the killer was baiting your motives."

"Of course," Kathleen replied. As always, the sun glared in her eyes from the window behind Spence, to deform her frown. "The only way I can gain her trust is to act as though her delusion is real. Otherwise she'd never believe a conspiracy proposal. If I'd asked her where she lives, she'd have hung up."

"Good," Spence approved. "Very good." He turned the deck back on and slightly increased the volume.

"But if the police are bugging your phone, then they just heard you say that," the killer's strangely gentle voice continued. "What would they say? What would this... Mr. Spence...say about that?"

This had surprised Kathleen. How did the killer know Spence was involved with the case? "To hell with the police," Kathleen answered, "especially that asshole Spence. They can't touch me. I can do whatever I want, I can talk to anyone I feel like talking to. It's a free country."

She hoped that the pauses after each of her statements meant that the killer was thinking, making considerations of trust; Kathleen needed her to believe she was on her side. This time, though, the killer responded: "The Cross is like a big star that takes the pain away. That's why I look at it. Everybody has a cross to take the pain away we all have pain I can see The Cross even when my eyes are closed I glue their eyes closed taking away the pain is what I'm talking about Mother I know don't be upset I take the pain and give it to someone else I put it somewhere else all the pain that Daddy made my mother feel all the things he did to her when he came over he always made me watch he'd fuck me while he made me watch people do things to my mother but now I know how to take away the pain you should have seen the way this one lurched when I cut it off sometimes they pass out from the pain so I wait 'til they wake up I sew their lips shut so they can't make noise and I think about The Cross while I'm working on them and it puts the pain into them it takes it out of me it takes it out of my mother and puts it into them it's our power, did you know that? No I guess you don't know that yet."

Kathleen's own voice turned dark with the question. "What? What's our power?"

"Pain."

In the next pause, a car horn honked. She seemed to be making a turn, and muttering something inaudible. "It's time for me to go," she said next. "I'll be in touch. You're almost ready."

"Ready for what?" Kathleen asked.

"But first you need to be purged."

"What?"

"You're still corrupted."

"In what way?"

"I will show you away from your corruption," the killer avowed. "I will purge you."

Next came abrupt, nondescript sounds. Thunking. Mumbling. A long, low moan—distinctly male.

"Don't hang up!" Kathleen pleaded. "Are you there? Are you still there?" She made this plea for many minutes more, until she heard the sirens, the helicopters…

Spence punched off the tape. "She's very calculating," he suggested. "She deliberately didn't hang up, even when she left the vehicle. She had a good idea that we were trying to trace the call and DF the mobile phone signal. She was toying with us."

"Where did she disappear to?" Kathleen wondered.

"No doubt she'd previously parked her car somewhere nearby, probably in one of the alleys off the main road, or somewhere in the industrial site. She drove away five minutes before our units arrived."

Kathleen felt uncomfortable in the hot seat, the sun in her face. "How did she know about you?"

"'Rome, the pimp. I'd talked to him the day before we found his body."

"And what was all that stuff… Most of the conversation she sounded very clear-headed, coherent. Then she goes into the bit about the pain, taking her mother's pain away, and all that."

"Psychiatrists call it word salad," Spence enlightened her. "A fairly common trait in bipolar psychosis. One minute she acts and sounds normal, the next minute she's completely dissociated, completely submerged in her delusions, to such an extreme extent that only she can understand herself."

"Like split personality?"

"No, no, nothing like that. It's a conversion of mental dispositions, an exchange from the reality state to the delusory state. That's why we're having such a hard time catching her. In the reality mode she's very sharp, even rational. She's able to keep control over the delusion." Spence took the cassette out of the tape player, appraising it with his gaze. "But it's...chilling, isn't it?"

Kathleen fumbled with an unlit cigarette. "What do you mean?"

"The voice, or I should say the idea. The idea that the voice we just heard belongs to a woman who's tortured and murdered at least seven men."

Chilling? Kathleen thought. Suddenly she was famished, like she could eat a whole box of sugary cereal, or an entire pizza. She could eat a whole jar of peanut butter 'til it lodged in her throat. "I wouldn't say chilling as much as alien. Like something inhuman speaking in the voice of a beautiful woman. I wonder what she looks like. I wonder if she's beautiful."

"More than likely, she's very beautiful," Spence said. Today he wore an unusually wide, striped tie, but it looked crumpled. "Serial killers frequently take the specific element by which they were abused as children and turn it against the people they perceive to be their enemies. Her father sexually abused her, her father was a man, so now she's utilizing her sexuality to put her in a clandestine position of power over men. Every man she kills, to her, is her father."

Daddy, Kathleen thought.

Spence pushed back his rather unkempt hair. "But I wonder what she meant when she said that you were corrupted, and that she would purge you of your corruptions?"

"I wish I knew."

"It's a little scary, isn't it?"

"No," Kathleen said. Somehow, it wasn't scary at all. Again, she thought it more alien than anything else.

"Well, whatever she means, we can use it to our advantage. She's beginning to trust you. She's beginning to believe that you desire to be in league with her, for the sake of her 'story.' It's important that you do everything you can to make her continue to believe that. Keep acting as though the police are not only her enemies, but yours too. Moreover— and obviously—she hates men. If she believes that you, too, hate men, then eventually she'll trust you enough to arrange a meeting, or perhaps to make an unscheduled visit."

More games, Kathleen thought. Spence had actually been tolerable today, until now. *Trying to scare me. Trying to rattle my cage,* she thought. *Next, he'll probably mention Uncle Sammy.*

"Not to change the subject," Spence went on, "but I just want you to know that we're still trying to locate your uncle."

"For my protection, right?"

"Yes."

"And because any outside interference from my uncle could botch your investigation, destabilize your human bait, right?"

"In a sense, yes."

"Thank you at least for not lying to me, like you usually do. We get along much better when you don't lie to me. I might even like you some day."

"Implausible. And it's even more implausible that *I* would ever like *you*," Spence said, back to his stone-cold face. "Condescending, reactionary, unrealistic, feminist—"

"You really are a prick—"

Spence offered a dismayed look. "You just got done saying that you want me to be honest."

"—a humorless, unfriendly, unmitigated *prick*."

"And as I said before, the more she trusts you, the greater the chance that she'll make an effort to meet you. I can't imagine why, but to her you're a 'Great Woman.' You represent something that she absolutely envies. Which leads me to my next point."

Kathleen lit her cigarette, dragged deep, and spewed smoke toward Spence.

"Regarding a certain unregistered, illegal handgun that your boyfriend gave you? Which, in addition, I've been lenient enough not to prosecute you for possessing?"

"What about it, Spence?"

He gave her the oddest look, as if making a consideration against some nameless physical strain. "Keep it close at hand," he advised. "And keep it loaded."

Chapter 27

(I)

Maxwell felt dissipated, like he'd done 12 hours of road work. It was a joyous exhaustion, though. Writing, even to the point of physical stupor, always left him radiant. In joy.

He stood now on his balcony. Mid-afternoon nailed the city down with planks of heat. Below, traffic jerked up and down P Street. All he need do, at any given moment, was glance at the city's slog of traffic to be grateful he didn't own a car.

He didn't need a car. All he needed was his muse, his fingers, and his typewriter.

And Kathleen, he thought. *The missing piece of my life.*

But, no, she wasn't a piece. She was an entity. She was a beautiful, wonderful woman whom he loved. *That must be it,* he postulated. *So unadorned, so simple. Isn't that what everything is all about, from the beginning to the very end of the world? Love?* It sounded so blatantly idealistic, but he knew it was true. It was the meaning of life. It was the meaning of—

Everything...

Okay. Great. But does she love me? She'd said she did, but didn't people often say things they didn't mean? Wasn't human love, in all its import, partly or even fully impossible to define?

Did Kathleen even know what love was?

But these questions were futile. *I can't spend the rest of my life weighing questions,* Maxwell substantiated. *I have to live my life based on the things that I KNOW about myself.*

This made much more sense. He knew that he loved her. Therefore, he must proceed from there.

Maxwell was not a traditionalist, but he'd learned, in his own experiences, that most women were, even when they said they weren't. He'd never, for instance, sent a woman flowers. He'd send poetry instead, because poetry was eternal. Weren't eternal symbols far more meaningful? A dozen long-stemmed roses were withered and ugly in days, and in the garbage, but a poem never lost its petals, a poem never wilted and died. Wasn't it a better display of love to give a piece of himself than something he could buy in a store? Of course it is, his poet's psyche agreed. But, still, there always came times when traditionalism must be acknowledged.

I'll have to buy her an engagement ring, he thought. He'd never done that before; he didn't even know how to make such a purchase. He knew they cost thousands of dollars, though, so at least he knew something. What was the procedure? Should he buy the ring on his own, and give it to her when he proposed? Or should he propose first, and then let her pick out her own ring? *I don't even know her ring size,* he thought. And then he thought: *I don't even know if she'll say yes...*

That didn't matter, though. *Follow your heart,* he thought. In these times, in truth, what else was there to follow? Social trends? Politics? Material? No, none of that was real. There was only love.

Am I being unrealistic? he wondered. *Am I rushing things?* And what of the timing? Was this the optimum time to make his proposal? Haunted afresh now by the memory of her uncle's sexual abuse? Bulldogged and spied upon by police? Harassed by a psychotic killer? No, by all intents, it probably wasn't the optimum time, but that didn't matter, either. What he felt in his heart could only be made true by his own concurrence of self. Time was always now.

The moment...is now. And if it isn't now, then it's false. It's ashes. It's dust.

It's settled, he concluded. His long hair wavered in his eyes as he gazed off the high balcony. *Today I'll price engagement rings.*

The poem was done. He'd written it dozens of times in the past two days. He'd honed it, crafting and recrafting, structuring and restructuring. He'd spent an hour deliberating over the placement of a comma, and another hour removing it. There came a point in the revision process when the work could be embellished no further. Minutes ago, Maxwell had reached that point. The poem was as good as he'd ever be able to make it. The poem was done.

He remained gazing off the balcony a while longer, to clear his brain of the wringing muse. Then he went back in. The platen pawl clicked when he rolled the poem from the typewriter. He read it a final time, then nodded.

He hand-wrote KATHLEEN on an envelope. He put the poem in the envelope.

I'll give it to her tonight.

Maxwell Platt, then, grabbed his wallet and keys, and just as he would embark to survey the local jewelry stores, there was a knock on the door.

(II)

"The femoral artery," Kohls was saying. With an unlit cigarette, he pointed to an anatomical chart. The artery, in red, and its accompanying inferior vein, in blue, ran just forward of the inside of the thigh, at the groin. "Expertly severed, probably a longbladed scalpel. She knew exactly where to make the incision. Exactly."

"I should've scrambled a med-evac chopper the instant I got the call," Spence regretted. "If there'd been an EMT crew there, the guy might've lived."

"No way," Kohls countered. Now the unlit cigarette bobbed in his lips as he technically absolved Spence. "The femoral is deep and big—a major artery. Like I said, she knew exactly what she was doing. It's too high to tourniquet. Once it's severed, you're dead in five minutes. Fucking Dr. Kildare couldn't have saved this guy. You could have had an operating room on the street with you and he would have bled to death before anyone could get in there with a clamp."

Spence felt a venal relief—venal in that it wasn't the victim's life that concerned him as much as what he could've told Spence if he'd survived.

"Latents?" he inquired.

"One. A good tip-ridge on the edge of the tape she used on that note she left you."

"One," Spence considered. Then he articulated, "That's fucked up. It's always one or two prints. Why? She's obviously taking steps to conceal her latents, but there're always one or two. Not dozens, just one or two. And she knows we've ID'd her. She left her name on the goddamn note. It doesn't make sense."

"She's a crazy."

"Yeah, but still... What about hairfall?"

"Same," Kohls said. "Couple of pubes, couple head-strands. Fusiformal match with the others, and the hairs we got out of her hairbrush at her crib. The wig was synthetic."

Spence let a sideglance flit quickly to the bleached corpse on the slatted morgue table. Just once. He was sick of looking at corpses minus genitalia. "Dissimilarities in modus? I noticed the mouth..."

"Sewn shut and then cut back open—right," Kohls agreed. "Can't guess why. And she didn't glue this guy's eyes shut, or pop his ears like the others. For some reason she wanted him to hear her, and see her, and talk."

"But why sew his mouth shut and cut open the stitches later?"

"My guess, as far as the probable sequence," Kohls offered, "she knocks them out with the Amytal first, then she sews their lips shut, then she brings them back to consciousness with the Desoxyn. She wants them conscious while she's working them over, that's why she's sewing their lips shut first, so they don't make a ruckus."

Spence's jaw locked as he considered the magnitude of pain, of being conscious as the genitals were cut off. "But wouldn't they pass out from the pain?"

"Sure. And she keeps bringing them back with the Desoxyn injections. It's hard to pass out when your heart-rate's topping 300."

"What else she do to this guy?" Spence dared to ask. "Why were his knees and ankles bandaged?"

"Drilled, looks like about a long three-eighths-inch bit. Right through the joints."

Again, Spence tried to contemplate the sheer eminence of agony. *Drilled,* he echoed Kohls. *Right through the joints...*

"She also snipped off the ends of his nipples, the very ends, the greatest concentration of nerve-endings. And we got what looks like repeated abdominal punctures—she was sticking a dissection needle or something similar directly into his navel. It wouldn't kill him, but it'd sure have the guy jumping... And when she cut off this guy's cock, she did a real pro job at cessating the bleeding. Johnson & Johnson high-pressure bandage, prothrombin coagulant paste. She doesn't want them dying on her before she's had her fun."

Was that what it was? Fun? *Not fun,* Spence realized. *A catalyst, to keep the delusion real.* He remembered what the killer had said to Kathleen Shade, on the tape. *It's her power,* he thought. Kohls opened one of several refrigerators and retrieved a Coke. While the door was open, Spence noticed evidence bags on the shelves; one bag contained a human foot, another bag contained an ear. Still another contained—at least what seemed to be—someone's forehead, complete with eyebrows. "What the hell's all that?" he asked. "That stuff's not from this case."

Kohls popped his Coke. "No, just various shit. D.C.'s already exceeded last year's murder rate, and it's only August. Each year gets worse. Got druggers machine-gunning each other every day. Last week this 34-year-old woman is driving her three kids to school, and she gets caught in a 9mm crossfire—Uzis, for God's sake, and MP-5s. Her head burst right in front of her kids; most of the triggermen got away. Same day somebody took one rifle shot—a dum-dummed 7.6 deuce—at a Metrobus. Hit a teenaged girl in the neck. She was gonna be in the

Olympics or some shit, now she's quad. Couple of players on dust took down a KFC in Southeast, cleaned out the registers, bagged every wallet in the joint. Before they split one of 'em decided to push a customer's face down in the deep fryer. 7th District Tac picked him up a couple hours later; they asked him why he did that, and you know what he said? He said 'For the hell of it.'"

For the hell of it, Spence thought. *For the hell of it.*

"GW student, theology major," Kohls ambled on, "comes back to her apartment one night about eight, and there's a guy waiting for her. He beats the shit out of her, sodomizes her 'til midnight, then shivs her with a carving knife, nicks her aorta. She's only got a couple minutes before she bleeds out, right? She crawls outside 'cos the rapist trashed the phone before he left, and her neighbor's coming home from work and he sees her crawling out of her apartment, and it just so happens the guy's a paramedic. He does an open-heart cut-down on her right there in the fucking parking lot, with the neighbors holding flashlights so he can see—and she *lives.* That's great, right? That's beautiful. Two days later, the rapist reads about it in the paper; he goes to the hospital where she's recovering, walks right into her ICU, cuts her throat, and walks out. Nobody sees him, no ID, no nothing. Beautiful world, ain't it?"

Fuck the world, Spence thought. He wished the world would crack open and suck everybody down into its magma. *Why bother living? Why bother trying to do anything?* he conjectured. The world wasn't worth it. *Just suck everybody down, good and evil alike. Let God start all over again.*

"Be right back," Kohls said. "Got a photo-mass spec coming out the hopper on this guy." As the technician disappeared to another room, Spence, in order to avoid looking at the prostrate and quite dead Jonathan Duff, flipped through a copy of Washingtonian magazine that lay on Kohls' desk. BEAUTIFUL, ANGELIC ASIAN LADIES, read one classified. Friendship/marriage! Free brochure! Another one read DOMINANCE & SUBMISSION—The Black Mask is a caring support network featuring lectures/workshops focusing on safe, sane & sensual relationships. "What the hell..." Spence muttered. CROSS-DRESSER SERVICE—Confidential, experience total feminine image transformation. "You've got to be shitting me," Spence muttered. Next page: HOLISTIC MASSAGE, GREAT MASSAGE, EUROPEAN MUSCLE MASSAGE, ICHIBAN MASSAGE, DYNAMITE PRO MASSAGE. There were dozens of massage ads. In the worst recession since the late '70s, how good could the massage business be?

"Same old, same old," Kohls said, appearing with a Canon medical-spec-printer readout. "Got DMSO, Amytal, and trace isopropanol in the bloodstream. And isopropanol all over his back. She's wiping their backs off with the iso."

"Why?" Spence asked.

"Prints, I guess—"

"Wait." Spence held up a hand. "The DMSO carries stuff into the bloodstream through the skin, right?"

"Yeah."

"And if the isopropanol is in his bloodstream, and it's also on his back, then that means he had the DMSO on his back first, right?"

Kohls considered this, rolling the unlit cigarette in his fingers. "Yeah, I guess so."

"But he's also got Amytal in his bloodstream, right?"

"A truckload. What are you getting at?"

"What's the physical nature of DMSO?"

"Stock pharm? It's a colorless, oily liquid."

"A colorless, oily liquid," Spence repeated. He was thinking of the massage ads. "Would DMSO carry barbiturates, like Amytal, into the bloodstream too, through the skin?"

"Sure," Kohls affirmed.

Back rubs, Spence thought. The oldest come-on in the book. All of the victims had been young, physically formidable men. The average man in most cases could easily overpower a strong woman, yet these guys were all being tortured to death. How was the killer getting them shackled down against their will? How was she getting them to do that before they got wise and could take physical steps to fend them off? Spence thought again of the ads. *Back rubs,* he thought, and then he thought about what Kohls had just told him.

And then he said, "I think I know how she's knocking them out."

Chapter 28

(I)

CHAPTER FOUR
MANBURGER

The dimethylsulfoxide comes in a caramel-colored 120cc glass bottle. The Amytal is made by a company called Abbot, and the iv version comes in 100-mg vials. You mix four vials with about 2 ounces of the DMSO, and shake it up in a plastic bottle that reads NORD, SWEDISH MASSAGE OIL.

"What's that?" he asks.

"Massage oil," you say. You show him the bottle. "Turn over so I can give you a back rub."

You're rubbing his back now. He didn't see you slip on the surgical gloves. You have to wear the gloves or else the DMSO will carry the Amytal into your own system. "Is that good?" you ask several times, and he always murmurs back "Yeah," as your hands rub the liquid into his back. He goes unconscious in a matter of minutes, and you sew his lips shut with the pretty violet suture. Then you bring him back with an i.m. shot of Desoxyn. You don't glue this one's eyes shut, and you don't rupture his eardrums with the Skeele curette. You need this one to see, and to hear. It's comical how he's moaning and trying to talk with his mouth sewn shut, especially when you show him the Bruns serrated plaster shears. The whites of his eyes instantly hemorrhage to the color of tomato juice when you cut off his—

• • • • •

Kathleen stopped reading. She felt broached, sour. The small, neatly typed words seemed to project something between their lines that threatened to deplete her before she even read them. Was it foreknowledge? Or simply tone? The manuscript had arrived—again, via Express Mail—just minutes ago. Just minutes, she thought, and already the despair was dragging her down. It appeared larger than the previous manuscripts, more pages that promised to be full up with atrocity...

It's the sound they make that particularly excites you, the closed-off scream, the explosion with nowhere to go. And the way their faces lengthen against their stitched-shut lips. When the lovely Bruns shears close, this one's entire body arches up like he's being levitated by a magician, and the only thing that keeps him from sailing away are the stainless-steel Peerless detention cuffs clasped to his ankles and wrists. But you need this one to live. There's still something you want to do. So you quickly apply the coagulant salve to the gushing wound, then strap the white pressure bandage into place. He goes into shock for a few moments but the Desoxyn brings him back. It always does. Usually you don't care if they die at this point. But this one must live. You still have plans for this one. That was beautiful, your mother says. "It was, wasn't it?" you say. When he's fully conscious again, you hold it up for him to see, and you watch his eyes while it dangles from your fingers in the light. Suddenly those tomato juice eyes are so wide you think they could jump right out of his face like a cartoon. He knows what you've done now. He realizes what you've taken away. You smile in the light. "See?" you say, jiggling it at him. "See? It's not yours anymore. It's mine. But if you're a good boy, I might give it back to you. Are you a good boy? Is Johnny a good boy today?" Make him do it, your mother says. She's standing by the window. Behind her you can see The Cross. He won't want to, so you're going to have to make him. "I know," you say. "I know Johnny will do it because he's a good boy. And good boys always do what they're told." He's groaning now. The initial pain has settled down enough for him to think. You're always very interested in what they think once they realize what you've done to them. You're ready now. You're all ready for the rest. "By the way," you say. "Did you like the back rub? I told you I give good back rubs." Then you walk across the room to the dresser where you've set it up. The wood floor feels warm beneath your bare feet. Your whole body feels warm. Your skin is tight and shining. Your breasts feel hot with blood. He continues to groan behind you, the muffled noise like a machine buried deep in his throat. You have a machine too. You hope he likes it. "Yes, I've decided that you're such a good boy that I'm going to give it back to you. Okay?" Wait a minute, honey, your mother says. I— "I know," you say. "It's okay. Daddy made you that way, you can't help it." Just a minute, it'll only take a minute. You don't need to watch her. You've watched her enough times. Most of the veins in her arms have collapsed. Once Daddy had tied her up for a friend, and he'd tied twine around and under one of her breasts 'til a vein had swollen near her nipple and he'd injected the heroin into that and then released the twine. Okay, I'm ready now. First you get the gun out of the dresser, Daddy's big revolver, and you make sure it's loaded. You've read a lot about the famous serial killers like Dahmer and Ed Gein and Henry Lee Lucas and Albert Fish, and you've read about their cannibalism. But this never appealed to you. In fact it disgusts you. You would never want anything from a man to be inside of you. But you have your own idea now, a much better one. You turn on one of the cone lamps so he can see what you're doing. It's very important that he sees what you're doing. He must see everything, exactly. You take out the little plate. You put your hand on the crank. "See?" you say. "Do you see what this is?" He's craning his neck. He's looking. He sees. The machine on the dresser is an old Roto-King meat grinder. Then, "See?" you say, and you hold up the severed cock and balls. "Do you see what this is?" He groans again way down deep in his throat. "Watch," you say. "Watch what I'm doing now." You push it all into the round steel hole looking over your shoulder and you turn the crank. You grind it all up, and after only a few cranks it falls out of the little chute onto the plate. The plop of meat looks pale like the ground chicken and turkey you've seen at the Giant. You bring the plate to the bed. "I hope Johnny's hungry," you say. With a pair of Heath double-curved suture scissors you snip open the stitches in his lips. His mouth falls open to let out the low, gurgling groan. You cock Daddy's big rusty revolver and put the barrel to his head. In your other hand is a spoon. You take up a spoonful of the ground meat and bring it to his mouth. His mouth snaps shut. "Open!" you say. "Open your mouth!" His eyes squeeze shut and you can see that he's actually biting his lips closed and he's shaking his head no no no no and you nudge his temple with the gun, saying "Open your mouth and eat it! If you don't eat it I'll blow your head off!" but he keeps shaking his head, his entire face squeezed shut. "I'll blow your brains out! Open your mouth!" No no no no, he keeps shaking his head. Make him! your mother yells. Make him eat it! But you can see that he isn't going to. You've got a gun to his head and he doesn't care. For a moment this intrigues you. He doesn't care anymore. He wants to die. He's not going to eat it and he wants to die. He wants you to kill him. Make him! your mother keeps yelling. You put the gun down and plug in the Black & Decker. "Okay, if Johnny's going to be a bad boy, he'll have to be punished." The drill screams but then he's screaming even louder when the carbon-steel bit grinds smoothly through his left ankle and then his right. "More?" you ask. "Does Johnny want more?" You give him more. His scream doesn't even sound human this time, when you drill through his knees. Weird smelling smoke drifts up, his blood and cartilage cooking in the holes you've made in his joints. "Has Johnny had enough? Is Johnny going to be a good boy now?" He's fading out, tremoring. "Don't you die yet!" you yell and throw ice water in his face. You give him another shot of Desoxyn and start slapping him hard in the face over and over again 'til your hand begins to hurt and you grab him by the hair and shake his head around 'til he revives. You press your palm against his forehead. You hold the spoonful of meat before his lips. "Are you going to eat it now?" you ask. "Are you going to be a good boy now or do I have to give you more?" He's barely sensible now but he looks at you with those shiny red eyes and he croaks, "Fuck you." "Okay, okay," you say. "If Johnny wants more, then Johnny gets more." In the castered stand you keep all of your things. You rummage around until you find the Gracey periodontal curette, a long pin-sharp needle set in an aluminum handle, and you stick it right into his navel. Once, twice, three times. Each needle-stick makes him make a sound like a big dog barking. A few more times, stick, stick, stick, right into the navel, and his chest is heaving and he's still making that barking noise and his breath is grating and mucus is pouring out of his nose, stick stick, stick, a few more times, and then he's finally nodding like his head is on a paint-shaking machine, nodding yes yes yes yes, and you stop. You poise the first spoonful over his lips and say, "Open," and his mouth opens. "There," you say, "keep it open," and he does, his eyes squeezed shut as spoonful after spoonful you put the pale ground meat into his mouth. "Close," you say next. His mouth closes. "Swallow," you say. His face freezes, his mouth frozen full of the strange meat, but his throat doesn't move. Make him do it! your mother yells. "Swallow it! Be a good boy and swallow it!" His throat doesn't move. "Okay, okay," you say. You plant your palm against his chin, push back hard so he can't spit the meat out, and you straddle him, and you keep pushing back on his chin, jamming his jaw shut, and then he lurches twice when you snip off the tips of his nipples with the Heath scissors. "Swallow it!" you yell, pushing, pushing back and eventually you see the single throb of his throat as he swallows the meat. You climb off him, smiling. "That's a good, good boy," you say, patting his stomach. You turn to your mother and say, "See, I told you Johnny was a good boy. He ate his manburger all up."

Kathleen put the manuscript down, stood up shakily, and trudged to the bathroom. She hadn't eaten anything today (and it was unlikely that she'd eat for some time) but she slid down to her knees before the toilet and threw up regardless, just a few strings of liquid. Her face felt pasty, not from the vomiting but from what she'd just read: the imagery, the words, and the contemplations that lay beyond all that. Had the killer really done these things? Could anyone? According to Spence, the killer's deeds had thus far been authenticated by medical examination of the bodies. *What am I getting myself into?* she finally asked herself. *I'm collaborating on a book with a psycho-killer.* This was the first time that the impact of that fact hit her. *A murderer. A crazy person...*

When she meandered back to her desk, she noticed that still more remained of the manuscript; the killer had sent two chapters this time, the second entitled CHAPTER FIVE, MORE CHILDHOOD MEMORIES. *Impossible,* Kathleen thought. There was no way she could read anymore now. She was simply not up to it.

Maxwell, she thought. Did the thought arrive merely as a diversion? She hated that about herself: never knowing the true reason that things occurred to her. Perhaps the thought arrived because she loved him. *I wish I knew,* she thought.

She photocopied the entire manuscript on the copier she rented from Shields. Then she slipped off the absurd "evidence" gloves, and called Spence. "Lieutenant Spence," she was told by a man with a voice like gravel falling out of a dump truck, "is having a meeting with Dr. Simmons." *I'm supposed to know who Dr. Simmons is?* she thought. "Tell him the militant feminist columnist Kathleen Shade called, will you?" she said and hung up. *Good,* she thought. *Now I have an excuse to go to Maxwell's.* But why would she need an excuse? Why couldn't she call up Maxwell right now and say I'm coming over. I want to see you?

I'm insecure, I'm emotionally unstable, she rendered to herself. *I'll make up an excuse like, Maxwell, I just got another manuscript and Spence wasn't in, so I thought I'd drop by.* It was easier. It was easier to make excuses than to reveal her true self. At least for now. She hoped the day came when she'd feel uncomfortable making excuses.

The traffic didn't fray her nerves like it usually did when she drove to Maxwell's. A Pakistani grinned when she pulled into the pay lot and doled out seven dollars. When she crossed P Street and stepped into Maxwell's lobby she stopped cold. A man with a ponytail and a woman with hair cut short as a Marine's jabbered before the elevator. A dim corridor behind the empty guard's desk was barred by a proverbial yellow ribbon which read POLICE LINE, DO NOT CROSS. "What happened?" she asked. The man with the ponytail answered, "The security guard got shot to death about an hour ago. They found his body in the alley out back." "That's terrible!" Kathleen exclaimed. *Death so close,* she thought. Was it the same guard she'd seen last night reading the magazine? Had Maxwell heard the gunfire? *My God,* Kathleen thought. *Death is so close all the time and nobody ever realizes it.*

She took the stairs up, leaving the couple to wait for the elevator. More images questioned her. *Diversions?* she wondered. Suddenly her head felt stuffed with visual sensations—of sex. She wanted to feel Maxwell's mouth between her legs. She wanted to feel his penis in her. She wanted to come. But were these her true feelings, or just more pleas to distract her from the killer's newest account of atrocity? Somehow, it didn't seem to matter. To hell with reasons. Her lewdness, or her love, wrapped about her. She wanted to be in bed with him. *Now,* she thought. *Right now.*

She knocked on Maxwell's door. She decided she would kiss him before saying a word. *That's right,* she thought. *I'll put my tongue in his mouth and reach around and squeeze his ass before I say anything.*

But when the door opened, she could've screamed. It was not Maxwell who'd answered her knocks.

It was Spence.

Chapter 29

(I)

"Hi," she says. "I'm a friend of Kathleen's. I have a message she wants me to give you."

The blond man looks back.

He's slim, almost svelte.

He's reasonably attractive, but she thinks, *What does she see in him?*

"Oh, I'm sorry. Come on in."

She accepts the invitation. "So how do you know Kathleen?" he asks once he lets you inside.

"We both work for the magazine."

"You said she has a message for me?"

"Yes," she says. "This."

"What the—"

From her purse, she's pulled the big revolver.

She's pointing it right in his face.

"This," she repeated.

"Wait a minute. I—"

"Don't say another word," she instructs. "Lie down on your stomach and don't make a sound," and at the same time she grabs him by the hair, keeping the gun to his head, and throws him to the floor, and she's straddling him, her knees pressed into the backs of his shoulders.

He's pinned, his face in the floor.

"Not a sound," she says.

He doesn't struggle.

She presses the barrel against the back of his skull with her right hand and with her left hand she removes the implement from her purse, a spring-operated device called a Busch Automatic Injector, also known as a "chicken-stick," mainly for diabetics who don't like to give themselves their insulin injections with a conventional hypodermic. She presses the injector into the side of his neck and it goes snap! and in a fraction of a second automatically expels 200mgs. of sodium amobarbital into his bloodstream.

"You're...," he mumbles.

She flips him over. "What?"

"You're the woman...who's been writing to Kathleen."

"Yes."

"You're...the killer."

"I'm The Purifier," she corrects. "Kathleen is a great woman, but she needs to be purified. She needs to be purged."

He's out.

She leaves a brief message, slings her purse, then puts him over her shoulder. He's not that heavy. She should have no trouble getting him downstairs.

She's going down the stairs.

"Help me!" she pleads in the lobby.

The security guard at the desk looks up from a magazine called *Cemetery Dance*.

"What—"

"My friend's in epileptic shock, I need to get him to the hospital!"

The guard picks up the phone. "I'll call an amb—"

"There's no time! My car's right out back. Help me!"

The guard takes the blond man off her shoulder.

She frantically leads him down the hall behind the desk to the fire exit and bangs through the door.

"Quickly!" she says and opens her car door.

The guard puts the blond man in the front seat.

"Thank you!" she exclaims.

"I hope he'll be all right."

"Don't worry."

"Holy sh—" the guard says when he turns to find the gun pointing at the bridge of his nose.

The big revolver jumps and emits a huge sound.

The guard's head ruptures.

She gets into the little blue Festiva and drives down the vacant alley. Away.

(II)

"What the hell are you—"

Spence showed her in. "Maxwell Platt has been abducted—"

"No!" Kathleen shrieked.

"—by the killer. About an hour ago. She took him out the back of the building. She killed the security guard with a large-caliber weapon."

"It's not possible," Kathleen stammered. "It's got to be a mistake."

"There's no doubt," Spence said. He pointed to the wall.

Very slowly, Kathleen's gaze crawled up the white sheetrock. Behind Maxwell's desk, and the pillar of magazines in which he'd been published, were the following words, written in lipstick:

YOU MUST BE PURGED OF YOUR CORRUPTION.
YOU ARE TOO GREAT A WOMAN.
EVENTUALLY YOU WILL UNDERSTAND.

"So now we know," Spence said, "exactly what she meant when she called you. Somehow she found out about your relationship with Platt. Platt's a man. She considers any man to be a blight, an element of corruption. Before she can trust you completely, she feels that she must purge you of your corruption." He turned to the slider, erect as a handsome men's wear mannequin in the finely cut dark suit. "I hope you're happy," he said.

Kathleen glared. "What do you mean?"

"You knew how dangerous the situation was. I warned you. I even told you it was grossly irresponsible to pursue a relationship with Platt while the killer was at large. I told you you were jeopardizing his life, and all you did was scoff. Are you scoffing now? Platt's gone, and it's all your fault."

"Go to hell, Spence!" she spat back. "And where were your people? You could've prevented this! You should've been staking out Maxwell's apartment too!"

"Oh, sure. In fact, we should be staking out every apartment building in the city. We should have a cop in every bar, every alley, every staircase and street corner. Every shopping center and convenience store. Every bathroom. Every closet." He looked at her in genuine disgust. "I barely have the authorization to procure funds for one stake-out assignment much less two. You had to persist, didn't you? You had to egg this guy on when you knew full well what could happen. What the hell do you care? Now your book will be even more exciting, won't it? The biographer's lover actually kidnapped by the psychopath…"

"I hate you," Kathleen whispered. She sat down on the couch. She felt mummified, dried out by shock. But Spence was right. *It is,* she thought. *It is my fault. It's all my fault. Somehow she found out about Maxwell, she saw him leaving one morning, followed the cab home. He's…with her now.*

Beyond that fact, she could think no more. She began to cry, gritting her teeth, clenching her fists 'til her nails dug into her palms. Her tightened face was a rock from which tears were wrung.

"No witnesses," Spence related. "Except for the guard, but she took care of him. Third District Homicide got the gunshot call. Then they called me. I got a TSD crew coming out now, for all the good it'll do. She obviously parked out back in the service alley, to reduce the possibility of a passerby seeing the vehicle."

But as hard as she tried to resist it, the question bloomed as a steady pressure in her head, like an artery swelling to burst. Kathleen quelled the silent sobs, her throat shriveling. "What," she asked, and gulped, biting off each word, "do you think—she'll do to him?"

Spence's brow crooked. A bald reluctance flushed his face. "Who knows?" he responded.

"Is she—going to—kill him?"

"He's lost. There's nothing anyone can do about it."

"Is she going to kill him!" she shouted.

Spence seemed to chew the inside of his cheek. "You're going to have to come to grips with the reality of this entire scenario. In the killer's delusion, you are a great woman whose only flaw is allowing yourself to be corrupted by inviting a man into your life—Platt. She exterminates anything she deems as corruptive. It's all part of the delusion. Compassion is an alien trait to killers of this type. They've been shown no real compassion in their own lives; therefore, they can't demonstrate compassion themselves. People aren't people to them. They're objectified *things,* either to be envied, or despised. She despises men because they symbolize the objects of her trauma."

The question, defeated now, famished, etched out of her mouth. "Is she going to kill him?"

"Yes," Spence said.

Every bone in Kathleen's body seemed to fuse. Her jaw fused. Her teeth fused. Her eyes melted.

"In all likelihood," Spence continued, "she will kill him after a protracted period of torture. The extent of her torture will probably surpass that of any of her victims thus far, which is compliant with her psychological profile. For whatever reason, she envies you; you are something she sees as being greater than herself, and anything that dares to corrupt you, or interfere with her fantasy of being allied with you, will call for a particularly ferocious extermination. With each murder so far, she has out-done herself. With Platt she will no doubt out-do herself ten-fold. I'm not saying this to upset you, I'm not saying this to amplify your grief. I'm only telling you this because it's important for you to accept and therefore adapt to the gravity of this situation."

All she could do was look up at him, her teeth ground shut, her throat sealed.

"Furthermore," Spence went on, "you must prepare yourself for the rest."

"The rest—of what?"

"After she dispatches Platt, she will undoubtedly send you her written account. Down to every last detail."

Needle-Work, she thought.

The Mummy, she thought.

Manburger, she thought.

Her face fell into her knees.

All...my...fault...

Spence was walking away from her, then back. His voice sounded a 100 feet above her as she stared between her knees into the carpet. "I know how you feel about privacy, and I know that you feel I have invaded yours to reckless abandon," he said. "I contest that I have—I'm only doing my job. Nevertheless, I read this only because it happened to be in the perimeter of the crime scene. If I had known what it was, I wouldn't have read it."

"What are you talking about?" came Kathleen's parched whisper.

"This is obviously for you."

"What?"

"It's obviously something he wrote for you. It's unfortunate that he never had the opportunity to give it to you."

Kathleen raised her head. Spence was holding an envelope.

"I found it on his desk," he said.

The envelope read KATHLEEN. It hadn't been sealed. *The poem,* she realized when she slipped the piece of paper from the envelope. She blinked hard, to clear her vision, and read:

A KEATSIAN INQUIRY by Maxwell Platt

Quickened to this heaven, and so enspelled,
the poet looked at her asleep in bed.
He heard her breathe, and beyond befelled
the myriad verities he never said.
Dare he wake her beauty in the moon?
For what he spied—such love!—and in
that precious moment didst nearly swoon.
Yet on she slept a lovely sleep;
here is the image his love doth reap.
Oh, where is she now, and what are her dreams?
And he remembers how the moonlight gleams,
a resplendent angel in fine light dressed.
And the poet thinks: Yes, I am blessed.
Only a moment in the quiet of the night,
an angel—yes!—in linens of light.
And now, my love, my Kathleen, awake.

> Open thine eyes for providence' sake,
> and for my joy now adrift in nether.
> My love for you goes on forever.
> All passion's night, and Muses' day,
> and to his heart he then did pray
> for the power to speak!
> So shall he say it now, so the truth shall be:
> Kathleen, will you marry me?

Kathleen reread the last line through fisheye tears. Then she looked up at Spence. He was standing away from her, facing her. His suit jacket hung unbuttoned, and inside of his waistband she could see the small clip-on holster and his gun. She wasn't sure how long the moment lasted, or the desire, but she wanted to reach inside his jacket, take the gun, put it to her head, and pull the trigger.

(III)

When Maxwell's consciousness bled back into his brain, there seemed to be blobs of light hanging frozen before his vision. A clack resounded. He heard someone breathing. Then one of the light-blobs approached, its details turning crisp, and he remembered. *Her,* he thought.

Clad just in black panties and a bra, the beautiful body stood to his left. He could see the trim, alabaster abdomen, the bellybutton, the twin bottoms of breasts satcheled in the black bra.

The beautiful face stared down.

I've got to get out of here, came the stark, moronic thought.

Then she raised her left hand.

Oh, my—

She was holding a power drill.

—God.

"Are you ready, Daddy?"

Her finger squeezed the plastic trigger. The drill's motor engaged, filling the confines of this place—and the confines of Maxwell's soul—with the scream of its hellish, unending shrill.

When Maxwell tried to move his legs, he couldn't. When he tried to move his arms, he couldn't.

When he tried to open his mouth to scream...he couldn't.

So he screamed in his mind. His body tremored. His muscles cramped. His eyes pushed forth in their sockets.

The drill screamed on.

Chapter 30

(I)

The feds called them "Short Points," out-of-the-way bars or porno places where requests for certain desires could be made. Sammy felt secure that Vinchetti's people didn't know he was out of stir, but he didn't want to take a chance by going to a place where he might be recognized. A short point was safer. It cost more but it was worth the piece of mind. Short points were hard for the cops to get a handle on because transactions were never made on the premises. You paid for a middleman.

Sammy still remembered a few.

New Carrolton, in P.G. County. A few blocks off the main drag. NEWSSTAND vibrated the sign in tacky red neon. Local laws made them cover their windows. The insides of these places always smelled the same, like pine cleaner and grunge. Sammy walked in to find the joint empty, save for an oriental guy behind a high counter. Adult video tapes lined the walls from floor to ceiling. *Pap,* Sammy thought. The legal, licensed shit. The current trend seemed to be flicks with names that mocked Hollywood productions. *Rambone. Sperminator II. Backside To The Future. Edward Penishands.* Sammy chuckled aloud. Even the gay section sported such titles: *All Hands On Dick, Sleeping With The Enema, Rear Admiral.* A mag rack stretched through the center, 10% of which was, also via local ordinance, devoted to regular magazines like *Newsweek, Sports Illustrated,* and the like. Sammy even noticed a copy of *'90s Woman* staring him in the face. Hardcore porn mags weighed down the rest of the rack. *Cumshot Revue, Pizza Slut, The Hot, Wet Best of Selena Steele!*

Sammy picked up one called *Cum Bath* and set it down on the counter along with a crisp $100 bill. The lingo was like a password. If you didn't get the lingo right, you didn't get shit.

"Anything short these days?" Sammy asked.

The counterman didn't look at him. "You a cop?" That was the first thing they always asked, to beat a bust with entrapment.

"No," Sammy said. "Are you?"

"No. Live stuff or something to eye?"

"Live. Of the double-x variety. Can you help me out?"

The counter guy made a quick call, murmuring only, "You open? Gotta double x." Then he hung up, pocketed the 100, and told Sammy, "Here're some slugs. Last stall. Fifteen minutes. Okay?"

Sammy nodded and went to the back, after picking up some box slugs the proprietor had slid across the counter. Through a curtain, on either side, were video stalls. Sammy slipped into the last one next to an EXIT sign. The lights went out when he dropped some slugs into the box, on which had been affixed a label: WARNING! THIS COIN BOX IS PROTECTED BY A MOISTURE-SENSITIVE ALARM! Sammy, bored, punched through the eight-feature selector and looked at the screen. It was all conventional fare: generic porn queens with silicon-embellished breasts and electrolysized pubic regions doing it every which way with equally generic nine-inch California golden boys. They all looked the same, and even sounded the same in their waves of fake-orgasmic groans. The hard underground Sammy used to make made this stuff look more tame than Barney the Purple Dinosaur. *The average chump who rents this shit probably doesn't even know hard underground exists,* he thought. *No way in hell you'd ever catch any kp or prepubes here.*

A few minutes later there was a knock. *Finally,* Sammy thought. He opened the stall to face a tall white guy in painter's pants and a buzz-cut. "You a cop?" he asked.

"No," Sammy said. "Are you?"

"No. Right out back. Five-minute ride. That square with you?"

"Sure."

He followed the guy out the back exit door and got into a primer-patched old Chevy Nova. The car pulled out of the lot onto a road lined by subsidized apartment buildings. "You want a girl, right?"

"Yeah," Sammy said. "Prepube. Doesn't matter."

"Okay, two bills for black, three for white, four for a blondie."

Sammy thought back to his Polaroid of Kathleen. "I'll pay five for something slim, short light-brown hair."

"I think we can do that. Gotta see your green first."

Sammy had already rolled the bills up with a paper towel. He slipped the wad out of his pocket, touching it only by the edges. He didn't want his prints on the paper. Then he passed it to the guy. "How far's the den?" Sammy asked.

"Right around the corner."

Here was more Justice Department slang. A "den" was a private residence, almost always an apartment, and was presided over by a "den mother." Den mothers were female drug addicts who rented out their children to people like this mover in the painter's pants, in exchange for crack money. If a den was connected, as were many of Vinchetti's, it was known as a "safehouse," where middlemen on the move could stay between jobs or hideout when the heat was on. It was not uncommon for den mothers to actually sell their children for lump sums (between 5,000 and 10,000) to mob connected porn outfits. According to recent Justice Department statistics, over 30,000 children disappeared per year in the United States. Of that, approximately 10,000 were never seen again, and a majority of this latter third were suspected to be den children sold to support chronic drug habits. Back when Sammy had been in the business, Vinchetti's people paid bonuses to den mothers who kept themselves perpetually pregnant and promised to sell their children to The Circuit once they were four or five.

Broad daylight receded behind them; Sammy followed his mark up an odoriferous stairwell to the apartment. Inside sat a malnourished white woman with stringy brown hair stuffing envelopes in front of a soap opera. She was probably 30 but looked 50; her lined face glowed beneath its waxen pallor when the guy asked: "Katie in her room?"

The woman's head wagged.

Sammy's escort took him down a dark hall that smelled like urine, emesis, and cooked onions.

"I'll wait out there with the broad. An hour, okay?"

"An hour's fine," Sammy consented.

"She's a little hyperactive, and a little fucked up in the head. You know. Her mother was drinking like a fish and smoking rock when she was carrying her. So take things easy, all right?"

Sammy'd seen it all before—the kids. The mothers were bigtime addicts. Fetal Alcohol Syndrome, Fetal Cocaine Syndrome. They'd keep up their habit throughout the pregnancy, which debilitated the fetus' brain development. Ruined their IQs attention spans, creative- and mechanical-thought abilities. You could always tell an FCS kid: their eyes were abnormally close together, and they'd shake a lot, and stare at things. *Some sad shit*, Sammy considered, though at the same time his arousal began to glow. "I've never roughed up a kid in my life," he eventually answered his escort. Adults, sure. Street slag, crackheads—that was different. Adults were accountable for the way they chose to live. But the kids didn't have a choice. Sammy was always gentle with them, like the way he'd been with—

Kathleen, he remembered.

His mind drifted in memory.

"In here. Her name's Katie."

"Right. Katie."

The guy in the painter's pants opened the door. "Katie?" he said. "I've got a friend here who wants to see you."

Sammy peered in. *Fantastic,* he thought. *Oh, yeah, that's so sweet...* The little doe-eyed girl looked up from her perch on a bed. Cartoons chattered on a small black and white TV. She wore a smudged summer dress with flowers on it. She was barefoot. Her obsidian-dark eyes seemed immense when she looked up.

"Katie?" asked the escort. "I have a friend here who'd like to see you, okay?"

The little girl blinked; fidgeted a little.

"He's a friend of your mommy's. Okay?"

The little girl nodded.

Sammy stepped into the room. A gentle smile came to his lips. "Hi, Katie," he said. "I've heard a lot of very good things about you."

The dark gaze glittered. She twitched a little again. She had a chipped tooth. *Eight or nine,* Sammy figured. *Just the right age.* Her light brown hair was cut just above her shoulders. Just like Kathleen's when she was little.

Sammy stooped down, put his hands on his knees. "I thought that maybe you and I could have some fun together."

"Okay, Katie?" asked Sammy's escort.

She blinked again, twitched, scratched her tiny nose.

The escort's voice grew stern. "You're going to be good, right, Katie? Your mommy wants you to be nice to her friend, so you're going to be a good girl, aren't you, like all the other times?"

The little girl nodded.

"That's right, Katie," Sammy said in his well-practiced, friendly hypnotic voice. "You and I are going to have a nice time together. A real nice time."

The man in the painter's pants left the room and very quietly closed the door behind him.

(II)

"...firmly planted now in her most delusory state," Simmons claimed behind his desk. Spence noted that the psychiatrist's desk was much more expensive than his own—teak, not industrial-gray metal. Perhaps the desks metaphored their personalities, or their hearts. It was an inexplicable observation. *I'm gray,* Spence thought. *My heart feels as gray as my office desk.*

"In the killer's manuscripts she made several references to 'skulls.' 'Skulls mean death.' What's that?"

"Like 'The Cross,'" Simmons replied. "A hallucinatory embellishment of a symbol. Commonplace. Stage-psychopaths frequently see antagonistic figures, and potential victims, with delusory trimmings, to set them apart. To categorize them. She probably sees most men as death-figures. It's hallucination. I know of many, many accounts of stage-psychopaths claiming to see a person's skull or bones beneath their flesh. It's actually part of a defense mechanism, triggered by the core delusion and synaptic anomalies."

Spence felt crestfallen. The more he learned of the killer's profile, the less he understood.

"And you're still urging Shade to fake complicity with the killer?" Simmons inquired.

Spence nodded. "She pulled off a great job during the phone call. But now I'm worried about—"

"You're worried about the 'fake' complicity transforming into genuine complicity?" Simmons assumed.

"Well, yeah. Because—"

"Because now your killer has abducted Kathleen Shade's lover. Shade doesn't like you, she doesn't trust you, and she feels that your only concern is the apprehension of the killer, regardless of the cost. Maxwell Platt is now part of that cost. Shade knows that Platt is more than likely dead, or will be soon, but she will resist that fact consciously, and cling to any hope that he might still be alive. She will do anything to increase his chances of survival. It's possible that she may pursue a genuine complicity with the killer. On her own. Behind your back. And she very easily has the impetus, the motive, and the utility to do that."

"How?" Spence questioned. "We're on her phones, we've got round-the-clock surveillance on her apartment."

"Don't be stupid, Jeffrey," Simmons said. "She's an industrious, creative, and capable *woman*. You're a cold, objective *man*. Under these particular circumstances, she clearly has the power to fool you. To deceive you completely and utterly."

Spence crossed his legs, tapped a knuckle. He felt partly insulted but he knew the psychiatrist was right. *Backfire*, he thought.

"From your perspective," Simmons continued, his eyes strangely bemused, "the abduction of Platt is the worst thing that could've happened. You've now lost all control over Shade, who is your only real connection to the killer."

"I fucked up," Spence muttered.

Simmons assented, shrugged in a light, gray-plaid jacket. "You should have foreseen the potentiality, yes. But don't blame yourself. After all, you're not a soothsayer. You're not God."

I'm my own god, Spence realized. *The God of Inanities, in the Temple of Senselessness.* The muse sunk deeper, like a malignancy. "The other day on the phone…you said I still had some investigative avenues left to 'plunder.' What are they?"

Simmons' face always seemed luminous in some complacent and indecipherable joy. Or was it amusement? Spence frequently thought so. Simmons was possibly the only person in the world who liked Spence. So why did Spence, here in the doctor's office, always feel like an object of arcane mockery?

Simmons said: "Watch Kathleen Shade, Jeffrey. Watch her as closely as you can. Go to any extreme to maintain a constant monitor of her whereabouts."

Okay, okay. Spence nodded. He got the picture…

"What have I been telling you," Simmons asked, "throughout this entire ordeal?"

"Find the nascent."

"Yes." Simmons smiled. "You're boxed out now, Jeffrey. Your ploys have turned on you. That's why a rigorous surveillance of Shade is paramount."

"I don't know what you mean," Spence said.

"Given the turn of events," the psychiatrist elaborated, "I'd say it's quite possible that Shade will discover the nascent before you do."

Chapter 31

(I)

Going to sleep for a 1,000 years was what Kathleen wished for most. Reverting to a state where she didn't have to think, or feel…anything. She could not think about the killer or Spence. She could not think about Uncle Sammy. She could not think about Maxwell.

I cannot think, she thought.

She lay in her underwear on the couch, gazing up. She was drunk. She'd drunk the second large bottle of ale she'd bought at Berose, plus some wine that had been fermenting in the refrigerator for about a year, hoping the borderline inebriation would carry her senses away. To some safe place. To some demesne where nothing mattered and nothing hurt.

More lies.

"Most of every negative emotion in the psyche, especially despair, is caused by a lack of oral gratification in the formative years," claimed the radio shrink. "That is, the stage of infantile development where the infant experiences a contentedness from nursing, biting, and chewing."

Who could she ask? *Dad, did mother breastfeed me? Did you buy me plenty of teething rings when I was a baby?* She couldn't imagine asking such a thing. Nevertheless, it all sounded like mumbo-jumbo to her: excuses, psychoanalytic banalities.

The radio drifted away. *I should call in sometime,* Kathleen pondered. *Everyone else did. Who would know it was me?*

The fifth chapter of the killer's manuscript remained on her desk. She hadn't yet read it, and still refused to. Doing so felt akin to going to the morgue to identify a dead loved one. She knew she'd have to do it sometime; she simply couldn't now. Not after all she'd read thus far...

"...one big problem," a call-in listener was saying. "Whenever my boyfriend tries to make love to me, I suddenly freak out. It's like he becomes someone else, a monster, a killer. Sometimes, I actually start screaming out loud."

"Were you sexually abused as a child?" the seemingly omnipotent radio shrink asked.

"Yes. Yes," admitted the caller. "My brother had sex with me from the time I was eleven 'til I was about 16. Like...every night. Everything... He did everything to me every night..."

The pause crackled. "It's called 'hyper-dissociation,'" the radio shrink told the woman. "Your subconscious mind has been preprogrammed to think of sexual acts in a negative mode."

"But I don't know what to do!" the caller suddenly began to sob. "I can't expect my boyfriend to put up with this! Why can't I enjoy sex? Why can't I be like everyone else?"

"You can. It's simple. It takes time but it's simple. You have to fantasize. In your fantasies, you have to kill your brother. Several times a day, especially when you wake up and right before you go to bed, imagine your brother—picture him in your mind along with the scenarios of when he raped you. And kill him."

Kill him, Kathleen thought.

"Kill him?" the caller inquired. "My brother?"

"That's right: kill him. Imagine yourself killing him. With a gun, a knife—it doesn't matter. In your fantasies, in your mind, kill him. If you do this long enough, you'll eventually kill the post-traumatic effect that your brother's sexual abuse inflicted in your subconscious. You'll kill the obstructions. You'll kill the sexual dysfunction, the body-memories, and the despair..."

Kathleen's own therapists had trained her well as to the same techniques, and it had worked. *Until now,* she reminded herself. It wasn't working anymore. The recurring nightmare—of Sammy, the cigar box, and the snake—had resurfaced all that anxiety of years ago. She'd killed Sammy a thousand times in her own fantasies, but now he was back, and not merely in her dreams but in her real world as well. But Sammy's parole couldn't be the trigger; the nightmare had begun before his release...

The killer, she thought. The killer was the trigger, for the killer, too, had been sexually abused. Was that it? And if it were, what did it matter? *I'm so screwed up it's pathetic,* she thought. She squinted at the ceiling, as if trying to see fortunes.

Then she thought of Maxwell...

"...for about two years," another caller was saying.

"Yes?" bid the radio shrink.

"And then I broke up with him."

"Why?"

"I don't know. I really did love him, I guess. But I wanted to see other people, I wanted to do other things. I mean, at first I thought I wanted a serious commitment. Well…I changed my mind."

"That happens," the shrink obliged. "People change their minds all the time. They change their expectations, they change their priorities, they change their views. Change is part of what we all are. You needn't feel guilty about changing."

"I don't," insisted the caller. "What happened was, the night I broke up with him, he was killed in a car wreck."

"I…see."

"If I hadn't broken up with him, he wouldn't have been on that road. He'd still be alive…"

Those last four words seemed to turn to concrete. *He'd still be alive,* Kathleen thought. *So would Maxwell.*

"It's tragic, yes, it's a horrible, horrible thing," the radio shrink was saying, "but you can't blame yourself for fate."

Kathleen turned the radio off. It wasn't fate that had caused Maxwell to be abducted. *It was me*, she told herself. *Spence is right. I'm the one who let it happen. I was too stupid to realize the danger, and now he's…gone.*

Gone sounded better than dead; it was easier to cope with. But deep in herself, she remembered Spence's assertion: that Maxwell, by now, was most likely dead. Tortured to death.

I killed him, she thought.

She drifted in and out of sleep, lurching awake each time at obscene, atrocious images. Then the phone was ringing. Her limp hand picked it up. "Hello?"

"Kathleen?"

"Yes."

The pause seemed to struggle, a sprout desperate for light.

"Who is this?" Kathleen asked.

"It's me, Kathleen," she was told. The slippery male voice reached up, like hands groping from a grave. Then it finished: "This is your Uncle Sammy."

(II)

"I know," he whispered. "I know what you think. But there's so much you don't understand." The few simple words she'd said thus far wrung ingots of sweat from his brow. Her voice. Her words. After all this time… "Nobody understands anything."

"I understand that you're a sick piece of shit, Sam," Kathleen replied quite calmly. "I can't believe you're calling me. My phone number's unlisted. How did you get it?"

"Doesn't matter." Footsteps snapped on cement behind him; the subway closed in an hour. The turnstiles clacked. "I just wanted to hear your voice. I wanted to talk to you before—"

"I know, Sam. Before you run off with your bank roll. I know all about it. You're going to leave the country because you've got hit men coming after you."

"Something like that." But what could he say now? He wasn't even sure why he'd called at all; he just knew it was something he needed to do. "I guess I'm calling to say that I'm sorry."

"Eat shit and die," Kathleen said.

Sammy frowned. Hearing her voice, despite her rancor, aroused him. It showed him the photograph. It took him back. "All right, all right," he said. "You hate me—I know that. But back then, I was just a player, I was part of the machine. It's not my fault the world's the way it is."

"My God, you've got some audacity. You were part of a pornography ring, Sam. A lot of the stuff was *child* pornography; you were even in some of the films yourself!" Now her calm began to corrode. "I saw them at the trial. You had sex with *children*, Sam! You had sex with me from the time I was *nine years old!*"

"Did I ever hurt you, Kathleen?" Sammy asked.

"Hurt me? You devastated me! You destroyed my whole childhood! You took something away from me that I can never get back."

"That's a bunch of psychologist crap and you know it."

"You're such scum, Sam. How many kids were there? Do you know? How many innocent kids did you *fuck?*"

"You just don't understand," Sammy defended himself. "Sure, there were lots of kids, but I never hurt any of them. I loved them, just like I loved you, Kathleen."

And it was, he knew. It was love.

"And what about those other things, Sam? Are you going to justify that too? Your network or whatever the hell it was made films and magazines with women having sex with animals! Women being tied up and whipped 'til they bled, or burned with curling irons. For God's sake, Sam, I remember one magazine where men put safety pins through a woman's nipples and then defecated on her!"

Ho, boy, Sammy thought. Yeah, there'd been some pretty groaty underground, all right, and Sammy had been involved in his share of that too, not just the kp and prepubes. Scat, water sports. Wet bondage and S&M (The "wet" prefix meant blood was drawn) and the "nek" flicks. Nek wasn't like snuff: sometimes a chick would overdose on the set and die; nobody killed them, for crying out loud. He remembered one he'd worked on (—*Poke Her 'fore She's Cold*, it was called—) and he pretty much just shrugged. If some people wanted to see that sort of thing, well then... *Supply and demand*, he thought. But Kathleen needed to be straightened out on some things. "Like I said," he repeated, "it's not my fault the world's the way it is, and it's not my fault that certain people get off on watching that kind of stuff. If clients didn't order it, we wouldn't make it. Don't blame me, blame the customers. And the women in all that stuff? First off, they were all adults, and second, most of them were drug addicts. Is that my fault too? They came to *us*. We gave them what they needed, and they gave us what we needed. Of their own free will, Kathleen. Nobody forced them to be in any of it. And you want to know something? We had so many women begging to be in our productions, we had to turn some of them away." The snuff, of course, and the rape viddies were different, but Sammy thought it best not to bring it up. Hell, most of those girls were about to spin anyway, or O.D. When you lived in the fast lane, sometimes you died in the fast lane—another doctrine of real life. Hard world, hard rules. Besides, it was Vinchetti's crew that handled all the snuff. So what if Sammy had helped out with some of the other productions? At least he'd never killed any of the girls...

"Are you going to condemn me for the rest of my life?" Sammy asked. "For something that happened years ago?"

"Yes," Kathleen said.

"You ever heard of regret, Kathleen? You ever heard of forgiveness?"

"You're unforgivable." Silence. Next: "Why did you call me, Sam?"

"I—" But why had he called? Really? "Just to say...," he started to say. "...that what went on between us—I'm not talking about the films and the magazines, my job, and all that. That was something else. That had nothing to do with us. I'm talking about us. Back when I stayed with you at the house, when your father was out of town. Do you remember?"

"Yes," Kathleen more or less croaked.

"That was us. That was you and me. Those times..." The words drifted a moment. Sammy's arousal throbbed. "I'm calling to say that what went on between us, during those times, was...love."

"You're despicable. I was only a child, Sam. A child, for Christ's sake..."

He couldn't help it. Her voice over the line seemed as warm as her body had been. He couldn't help it. His pants were open. His hand was moving.

Almost, he thought.

No one could see. The metro station was nearly empty, his back to the flank of ticket machines. *No, no one can see me*, he knew.

"Say something," he begged, panting.

"My God," Kathleen croaked. "What are you d—"

Almost.

The line went dead.

"Hey!" barked a voice. "Hey, you there!"

A subway cop on the other side of the turnstiles was glaring at him at the phones.

"What the hell are you doing!"

Sammy, dotted with sweat, zipped up his fly and scooted out to the parking lot.

It wasn't fair. When he spun wheels out of the metered space, he kept the lights off; if the cop came after him, he didn't want his temp tags visible. He wheeled around the exit to Route 50, heading back for the motel.

Nobody understands anything, he thought.

Chapter 32

(I)

"Are you all right?" Spence said into the chained gap.

Kathleen let him in the apartment. She looked liked something that had fallen apart and been put back together: ragtag in her robe, her hair disheveled. She didn't answer as she padded toward the lit kitchen.

"I figured you might be upset."

"Why?"

"Well, the phone call. We picked it up on our trace. It was your uncle, right?"

"Yes," Kathleen said. "Would you like some wine?"

"No. He was calling from a pay phone at the New Carrolton subway station. I dispatched P.G. County and Cheverly police to try and pick him up, but he was gone by the time they got there."

"Forget him," Kathleen said. She hadn't yet even looked at Spence. She poured wine into a small glass and closed the refrigerator. "He doesn't matter."

"Why did he call?"

"To masturbate, I think."

Spence frowned at the reply. "Are you sure you're all right?"

The question appeared to ruffle her. "Some guy who molested me years ago calls up and you immediately assume that I'll go off the deep end?"

"Well...," Spence faltered.

Kathleen glanced at the kitchen clock like an after-thought. It was past 11 p.m. now. "What are you doing here anyway?"

"I happened to be in the area when our communications people radioed me about your uncle's phone call. So I thought I'd stop by to see how you're doing."

"How thoughtful." She slipped by him into the darkened living room and switched on a lamp. Beside her heaped desk she'd set up the rented photocopy machine. "You saved me a trip," she told him. "Here're the originals."

Spence took the manila envelope. Jonathan Duff, no doubt. Spence remembered Kohls' comments during the autopsy. "This feels thicker than the others," he observed.

"She sent two chapters this time," Kathleen said. "I haven't read the second one yet. Couldn't."

"I understand."

Suddenly Spence felt lost here; he felt awkward. What could he say to her, with Platt more than likely dead and the killer still at large? *And with me no closer to catching her now than the day I got the case?*

"It's hot in here," he said. He felt stifled in his suit, sticky. Why didn't she turn on the air-conditioning?

"Would you leave now?" she said. She lay down on the couch as if settling into a casket. Hot darkness provided her shroud. "I'm tired, and I don't feel well."

"All right. If there's anything you need, let me know." Spence frowned again. Why on earth say that? Formalities were just more lies. *What could she ever need from me?*

"Keep in touch," he said as stiffly as possible. He mustn't lose the cold tact she expected of him. When he left he made sure to lock the door behind him. *Christ, it's hotter in there than it is outside,* he realized, taking the stairs down to the parking lot. The hot night's dark struggled against sodium lamps.

Liar, he thought. *You're such a liar.* He felt he had to be, to be an honest cop. *I just happened to be in the area... A lie.* He'd just happened to be on his way over with the transponder when Central Commo radioed him about the phone trace. Larkins, the black bodybuilder, stepped out of the surveillance van, pumped up in his contractor's shirt. "Hey, Lieutenant," he gestured.

"How're things in the wasteland?"

"Hot. You know, each summer is hotter."

"You're right."

"And we haven't had any real snowfall in the last couple of years. When I was a kid we'd get several feet each winter, we even had blizzards. But not any more."

"Global warming, man. PCBs and fluorocarbons. One day the ice caps'll melt, the Potomac and Anacostia'll rise about 50 to 100 feet. D.C. will be another Atlantis."

Larkins shrugged. "No matter. Phoenix has a police department."

"Yeah, but by then the average temperature'll be around 140." Spence's gaze surveyed the parking lot: still cars ticking in heat. "Where's Shade's T-Bird?"

Larkins pointed down the front row; a big gunbutt stuck out of his belt. "What's going on?" he asked.

"Let's just say that I'm being vigilant," Spence answered as non-committally as he could. He approached the shiny black Ford's rear bumper, and got down on one knee. Following Simmons' cues was all Spence had left. *Watch Kathleen Shade, Jeffrey,* the doctor had advised. *Watch her as closely as you can.* What did Simmons fear? Maybe it was best not to know exactly what.

Yeah, I'll watch her, all right, Spence mused. The device was about the size of a pack of Lucky's: a field triangulation transponder with a selectable frequency. A special cadmium battery lasted for weeks. With this, Central Commo could monitor the location of Shade's vehicle on their direction-finding board, right down to a specific city block, sometimes even a specific plat number or address...

Spence stuck the transponder, via magnet, to the inside of Kathleen Shade's rear fender.

(II)

The cat clock's eyes switched back and forth.

tick-tick-tick-tick

Kathleen lay immobile in the familiar scape of the nightmare: splayed naked like a frozen starfish. There was such torture in sleep, such terrifying vulnerability. The ubiquitous woman-figure knelt at the bedside, a subcarnate attendant. Hands of ink-black bones displayed the dream-pictures, the Polaroids.

"No pictures anymore," whispered the soft, feminine voice. "They've changed, as *you're* changing."

Kathleen's eyes darted to the splayed Polaroids. Each square white border framed a field of shiny black. She remembered the Polaroids from the previous dreams. The photo of the snake in the cigar box. And the succeeding photos of the same snake slithering across the mattress toward her sex.

"See?" said the black abbess.

"How have the pictures changed?" Kathleen asked in night-parched voice. Her flesh trembled against her paralysis.

"They've become real, as you have become real."

What did that mean? *This is a dream,* Kathleen reminded herself.

Dreams weren't real, nor where the things in dreams. They couldn't be. Her sweat turned cold as it oozed from her hot skin, and the moon in the window lay white glare across her eyes.

"See? You're just like me," the figure said. The sound of each word skittered like a dead leaf across pavement. "You and I, we're the same."

"This is a dream," Kathleen croaked. She felt terrorized to keep reminding herself of that. "We're not the same. You're a killer."

"But so are you."

Something more than shadow, but as black, seemed to disgorge from the room's darkness. It was another figure, which brought with it a faint, indescribable fetor. Like a guillotine falling, the moonlight divested the features.

"I got out just for you, Kathy. That's all I've been living for, to come back for you."

Uncle Sammy looked down at her from the foot of the stripped bed. His eyes, tiny raven pinpoints, drank up her stark nakedness. She felt the gaze as surely she'd felt his hands, and his semen on her, for all that time so many years ago. The gaze destroyed her; it buried her deep in the past, in the grave-dirt of memory.

He stood gaunt in the cheap, soil-colored suit. He looked starved, his face merely skin stretched tight over his skull. Pasty dark curls stuck to his balding pate, and his mouth ticked like two worms pressed together, a nervous slash of flesh. "I have something," he said. "—a present."

The more Kathleen tried to squirm away, the more securely her dream-paresis lashed her down. Her skin crawled like a coat of insects when Sammy raised the gift to the moonlight. His slim, long-fingered hands held the cigar box, just one of many things booked as evidence at his trial. He opened the lid to show her its contents, not pornographic snapshots of children, but the fat triangle-headed snake. Its dry reptilian skin glistened, and its head emerged, the threadlike tongue flicking...

Then Sammy upended the box, evicting the snake onto the bed.

Kathleen's joints fused as she tremored. Her throat sealed shut against her scream, which imploded in her chest. She couldn't breathe. She couldn't close her eyes.

The snake hissed. It was huge, and its girth pulsated. Kathleen felt the pointed tip of its head running sleekly up her calf, then up her thigh.

Uncle Sammy smiled.

"We're the same," whispered her companion.

Suddenly a cold weight was pressed into Kathleen's hand.

"Embrace your hatred."

The snake slithered closer. Kathleen turned her head to see that the object placed in her hand was—

The snake's head nudged into her sex.

—a gun.

The snake began to burrow.

"Almost," Uncle Sammy whispered. "Almost. Alm—"

Kathleen—shuddering, revolted unto death—raised the gun. "Here," Uncle Sammy celebrated.

Kathleen pulled the trigger.

The report clapped like thunder.

Then came a flash like lightning.

"Yes!" whispered the abbess.

Uncle Sammy caught the slug high in the chest. He was knocked down like a hinged duck in a shooting gallery.

The snake retreated—

"Finish."

Kathleen rose, lambent now, bright-fleshed in her release. Uncle Sammy lay flat on his back. The twist of flesh that was his mouth squirmed. She stepped over him. Hot smoke made a halo about her head. The halo glowed. She calmly straddled Sammy's stomach.

"It's Sleepytime, Kathy," the voice grated under her. Black blood throbbed from the chest wound. "There are special secret things that uncles and little girls are supposed to do. That's why God made uncles, Kathy, to show little girls the special secret things."

The clammy hands groped up. Like desperate claws, they kneaded her breasts, pinched at her nipples.

"Uncle Sammy will take real good care of you while your dad's away," he promised.

Kathleen leaned over. She whispered into his drained face: "You sick...worthless...piece of...shit."

Then she pressed the gun barrel to his nostril, her thumb on the hammer grid.

"Almost," she said.

Her thumb began to slide back the hammer—

"Almost."

—further—

"Alm—"

—the hammer clicked back.

"Here," she said.

Very gently, she pulled the trigger.

First came the tiny click, then the mammoth crack and concussion. White light erupted about Sammy's face, and then the contents of his head—not brains but maggots—splattered out the back of his skull.

The corpse simmered, steaming. Soon its substance slipped away with the steam, until nothing remained for her to straddle but bones and a dry broken skull.

The snake, too, had given up all its flesh. Only a frail, tiny-boned skeleton remained on the bed, utterly harmless to her or to anyone. Kathleen stood up now, the gun smoking in her hand. Through a haze of grit, she stared at her companion. The abyss-like face gazed back from the corner of the room. It seemed to be happy, it seemed to approve. In moments the figure began to revert back into the darkness that had created it—the darkness of Kathleen Shade's mind—but before it could disappear altogether, its skittery whisper drifted up a final time:

"You're free."

What scared her most, when she awoke, was that her bedroom was the same scenario of the nightmare; for a moment, Kathleen even thought she might still be dreaming. Moonlight bathed the room in lucent slants, just like the dream. She lay naked in an ichor of sweat...

Just like the dream, she thought.

The clock glowed in luminous digits; it was just past three in the morning. You're free, the killer-figure in the dream had said. *Free*, she thought. She felt anything but free; instead, she felt enslaved by every aspect of her life. The dream, she knew, was merely her subconscious trying to purge her of her past: trying to kill the memory of Uncle Sammy. *Kill*, she baldly thought. The radio shrink had used the same word. *Kill. In your fantasies, in your mind*, the shrink had postulated, *kill him.*

All that Kathleen had killed, instead, was another night's sleep.

Sweating, she put on her robe. She switched lights on out to her work desk, and sat huddled in the chair, groggy yet not tired. The nightmare, as always, left a bad taste in her brain. *Distraction*, she pondered. Atop the typewriter lay the photocopies of the killer's latest account. *Manburger,* came the dismal recollection. But she'd only read half the submission; there was one more chapter to read. "Might as well look at it now," she mumbled to the air. She squinted in the glare of desklight and turned to the unread chapter...

CHAPTER FIVE
MORE CHILDHOOD MEMORIES

One time when your mother was still alive she told you about sick people. "There's lot of sick people around," she said to you. "Like Daddy...he's a sick person, and the people he brings to the house sometimes, they're all sick people." You didn't understand then, you were only about 10, but then your mother said, "Lots of people like to do sick things to other people." Then she injected heroin into the preferred vein in her foot. "You should always remember this. Most people are here to hurt other people, to take advantage of them, to fool them and lie to them. Like your Daddy. He fooled me. I had a good career with the electric company before I met him. But he got me strung out.

He turned me into a...." A little tear came into your mother's eye, and you ask, "Then why did you get married?" "We're not married, honey," your mother answered. "He just uses me, like he uses you. I know what he does to you in the other room. I know he makes you watch when his friends do things to me. I love it when he goes away. I love it when he's not here...." Then your mother falls into the familiar stupor. It's quiet now. Daddy's not home. Sometimes he disappears for weeks at a time. You like it when he's gone. The only problem is when he disappears sometimes he doesn't leave enough heroin for your mother. "You're going to be gone a week?" your mother once complained. You were listening from the room, looking at The Cross, right after Daddy had finished with you. "This isn't enough skag to get me through a week!" your mother yelled. Then Daddy said, "Go on the street for it. That's what your pussy's for." Once they argued about you. "How can you let your own daughter be exposed to all this?" your mother said. "You've turned me into a junkie! You bring those awful people here all the time! You rape her, for God's sake, and you let those other animals rape her! How can you do this to your own daughter?" "She probably ain't even mine," Daddy said back. "Probably a load of spunk from one of your tricks. Ain't no way that fucked up kid's mine." Then he hit her hard in the face. "Always whining, always complaining. If it weren't for me you'd be taking it up the ass for 50 cents a pop." "But this is my house, this is my life! Don't you care about anything?" your mother sobbed back. Daddy hit her in the face again and left with his suitcase. Sometimes he calls up when he's away. "Some of my friends are coming over to the house tonight. They're important friends, so tell your mother to take care of them." You knew what that meant. Lots of times when they were finished doing things to your mother, they'd come into your bedroom and they'd take you into Daddy's Room, and then they'd do things to you, too, but that was all right because all you had to do was lay there and look at The Cross in The Window, and that would make the pain go away. It gets bad again, though, when Daddy comes back home. You wonder where he goes all the time. Lots of times before he leaves you hear him saying things to your mother like "I'm going up to Jersey on another skip, I'll be gone about a week" or "I'll be staying at my brother's between runs." Once your mother replied, "Jesus Christ, what would your brother say if he knew what you really did for a living?" And "Do you do the same thing to his daughter that you do to your own?" "Just shut the fuck up and mind your own business," Daddy replied. "I gotta stay on my brother's good side, so he'll cash out my shares when the old man kicks off. When my brother's out of town, I look after his kid. I got her programmed just fine, just like that weird little retard of yours. Kids are all the same."

Kathleen stared at the paper. The words seeped into her like dark stains.

This couldn't be...

—going up to Jersey—staying at my brother's between runs—so he'll cash out my shares—when my brother's out of town, I look after his kid—

Kathleen squinted through vertigo.

—do you do the same thing to his daughter that you do to your own?—

So now you know that Daddy does the same things to other children that he does to you. He's never mean to you, like the way some of his friends are, and like the way he and his friends are mean to your mother. He always takes you into the other room and turns off the light. He does it to you from behind, and he whispers things to you, and all you can see while he's doing it is The Cross in The Window with the big light on it. And he always says the same thing, every time, jerking off on you. He always says "Almost, almost—" then he grabs your hand and makes you take hold of it and he says "Here."

Each word sunk like a nail into coffin wood; Kathleen was being interred. Tears welled, blurring the typescript. The words seemed to permute the paper until they were no longer words at all, but glyphic scrawlings etched in black blood.

Uncle Sammy, she thought.

Daddy.

Spence would make nothing of this—she hadn't told him enough details of Sammy's molestations. Nevertheless, this was exactly what Spence had been seeking all along. What had he called it?

The nascent?

This was the nascent, right here in here hands.

Her thoughts went into a slow slide like a near-death experience. She thought of the harrowing fact: Kathleen and the killer had been molested by the same man. She thought of her cruxing nightmare, and the faceless nightly words of the radio shrink. She thought of Maxwell and his dead love for her. She thought of the sad letters from her readers every month and all the energy that that sadness must possess. She thought of false prophets and broken dreams and lies. She thought of disease, despair, and deceit, of abortion, estrangement, and adultery and incest and crack dealers and stillborn babies and terrorists and war and hate. She thought of devils. She thought of death.

And then she knew, as quickly as if a bullet had struck her right between the eyes.

Yes, Kathleen thought.

She knew exactly what she was going to do.

Chapter 33

(I)

"What does Daddy do?" she asked her mother once.

"He makes movies, honey."

"Movies? You mean like *That Darn Cat* and *101 Dalmatians*?"

"No, honey. He makes movies of sick people doing sick things to other people. He makes most of them in New Jersey because that's where all the camera stuff is, and the police aren't as dangerous up there because the people Daddy works for pay the police to leave them alone. Then Daddy brings the movies back here. That's why he's gone a lot of the time. And sometimes he has to stay at other places when other kinds of police are onto them. They make movies of men doing bad things to little boys and girls."

She was so young at the time she didn't understand what her mother meant.

What kind of bad things?

Like the things Daddy did to her in Daddy's Room?

She could never understand why people would want to make movies of people doing bad things.

She remembers one night when some of Daddy's friends came to the house. She was 14 or 15 then, and she was beginning to realize that the friends Daddy brought to the house were the people he made the movies for. They'd say things like "How was the skip? Any heat?" "Word is we lay low awhile—the feds just bagged one of Vinchetti's stock mules down in San Angelo." "Christ, we never had heat like this when Carter was president. Fuckin' Reagan." "Everything'll be going video soon. Makes our job a thousand times easier." "Vinchetti's guys taking care of the equipment?" "Let's see those dupes, Sammy boy." Daddy's friends always brought money to the house. Daddy put it in cigar boxes he kept in the closet with the mirror. When she was younger, Daddy's friends would sometimes bring film projectors, and they'd always say things about "dupes" and "checking the dupes," and when she got older they'd bring over VCRs that looked different from the ones in the catalogs. They came over to watch the movies that Daddy brought back from New Jersey. One night they were all in Daddy's Room watching the movies while Daddy counted money, and she snuck into the bedroom. Her mother was unconscious because Daddy's friends had raped her earlier and then she'd injected heroin. She snuck past her mother and went into the closet where the mirror was and she could see Daddy and his friends watching the movies.

She could see the movies.

Skinny women wearing sunglasses, doing things with animals.

Men tying women up and hanging them by their arms.

Men holding women down.

Burning them with cigarettes.

Sticking pins into their breasts.

Then more movies.

Men doing things to children.

Sometimes Daddy was one of the men.

She saw him doing the same things to the other children that he did to her in Daddy's Room.

She never told anyone.

Since she was very little, like four or five, Daddy would tell her about the special secret things, a secret from God, and if she ever told anyone about the special things, then that would be like bad luck, and something very bad would happen to her mother.

She dropped out of school in 10th grade because she couldn't concentrate, and she'd missed so many days.

When she was 18 she got a job at the Wagon Wheel which was like a little convenience store.

When she was 19, her mother died.

One night two of Daddy's movie friends came over.

"Hey, Rocco, can you believe it? Sammy hot-shotted his own wife!"

"She wasn't my wife," Daddy said. "Just squeeze. Just a safe place to shack up between runs."

"Yeah," another man said. "Plus that cute kid you been plugging for the last 15 years." The man laughed. "Ain't that right, Binnie? So, Sammy, why'd you hot-shot your wife?"

"I told you assholes, she wasn't my wife. She was beat, freaking out. I turned her out on skag the first week I met her, got her on the street. Decent cash between runs, but you know junkies. I think she was getting ready to spin so I tricked up her last bang with ant poison. Dumped her dead ass way back in the woods out near Mitchellville. It'll be 10 years before somebody finds her."

"Yeah, Sam, but what about the kid? She's gettin' old now, ain't she? Nineteen, 20 she looks to me. What's to keep her from spinning to the feds?"

"You kidding?" Daddy said. "She's a retard, she's half-catatonic most of the time, hardly ever talks, stares at the wall all day. Fucked-up brain, you know. Her mother was shooting up three times a day when she was pregnant. She'll never spin. Shit, she doesn't know her ass from a hole in the ground."

She'd heard them saying these things one night when she walked home from the Wagon Wheel. One of the windows was open and before she came in, she heard it all.

Daddy had killed her mother.

But her mother came into her room every night anyway.

And told her things.

She told her that The Cross would protect her.

She told her that skulls mean death.

Several months later she overheard Daddy on the phone. He said that he'd inherited money from his family and that once it was out of probate, he'd be rich. "I'll still be making runs 'til everything's settled. Then I guess I'll off the kid and head west, start living a little of the good life."

Her mother told her she must be very careful.

Daddy was going to kill her.

You'll have to kill him, her mother said. Skulls mean death.

She could see Daddy's skull now whenever he was home.

She'd looked in the cigar boxes in the closet. Some were full of pictures. Some were full of money. But one of the boxes had the big gun in it.

But she never needed to use the gun.

Daddy left the house one day, and he never came back.

She read about it in the papers.

She was all alone now.

Daddy and some of his friends had been caught by police.

Interstate transportation of obscene materials, the papers said. Violations of Titles 17 and 18 of the United States Code. Violations of the Child Abuse Act. Violations of child pornography laws.

While Daddy was in jail awaiting trial, she had to take care of things.

Whenever a bill came to the house, she'd take some money out of one of the cigar boxes, get a money order from the Wagon Wheel, and pay the bill.

It was easy.

She was alone a lot now.
On her days off, she'd go to the library and read.
Sometimes she felt happy.
Sometimes she felt so sad she wanted to die.
But she still had her mother.
Don't be sad. I'm here.
Eventually she got hired as a custodian at the hospital.
Sometimes she felt like she could explode.
There was no one else in the world like her.
Or at least that's what she thought.
She read about the trial.
Daddy got sentenced to 11 years on a plea bargain.
One of the people who testified against him was a woman who said that Daddy had sexually abused her for years.
He'd done the same things to this woman that he'd done to her.
So that made her happy.
To know that there was someone else in the world like her.
The woman was a magazine writer named Kathleen Shade.
It made her see things.
It made her think.
Kathleen Shade had done something.
She'd risen up from the pain, and had done something to give it back.
To give the pain back...
She wanted to be like Kathleen Shade.
She wanted to do something too.
As each day passed, she felt like she would fall apart or dissolve or burst into flames from the pain if she didn't do something.
Then her mother began to talk to her a lot.

Chapter 34

THIRTY-FOUR

(I)

"Spence, MCS," Spence answered.

"Central Commo. We gotta fly line from MCS Surveillance Unit One, sir."

A fly line was the opposite of a land line; a field radio transmission relayed through Central Commo's telephone. Spence felt tired. *Almost noon*, he thought when he looked at his desk clock. "Put him on," he said.

"Lieutenant Spence? This is Larkins. I'm off shift at noon; I just wanted to let you know that Shade left her apartment at about eight this morning, and she looked like she was in a hurry."

"She back yet?"

"No."

Spence scratched his chin. Where would she be going?

Her boyfriend's abducted, probably dead. She works at home, she's got no office to go to. Where's she gone for the last four hours? "Thanks," Spence said. "Have the next shift call me the minute she gets back." He switched back to the central communications operator. "Triangulate the following prefix," he said, and gave the unit code. He heard computer keys tapping.

"Working," he was told.

Spence waited, glancing blankly down at the killer's most recent manuscript. *Manburger. More Childhood Memories.* The former was typically revolting, yet the latter seemed...arcane. He tapped the manuscript with his finger. A gold link on his cuff—from a set his mother gave him when he graduated from high school—winked like a dying star.

More Childhood Memories, he pondered. Just another account of the killer's past, her father's abuse. But this chapter didn't seem congruent at all. It seemed vague.

Had Kathleen Shade seen something in it that Spence had not? *Woman's intuition*, he thought. Women made him feel blind as a bat. *She read this shit and then went somewhere?*

Was there something in the chapter that gave a clue to the killer's whereabouts? Spence frowned. He didn't see any way that that could be.

So—

"Got it, sir," Central Commo related. "Seventeenth and Connecticut grid."

"What's on the block? Any residences?"

"No, sir. Just TA's. Stores, offices, banks. You want me to plot the exact location on the grid?"

"No," Spence whispered. "I'll be on the road—keep me posted."

Spence hung up and dug out his unmarked's keys. *TA's*, he thought. *Stores, offices...* Then:

"Banks," he muttered.

(II)

All right, all right, Sammy thought. The thoughts pulsed like fire. *Fuck 'em, fuck 'em all. Especially Kathleen.*

What did he care? He was rich now, his past buried behind him, his future bright. And of his past, he regretted none of it. He'd accepted the world for what it was—and what he was in the scheme of things. What could be more honest than that? At least he wasn't a liar. At least he wasn't phony...

He'd made a living, for years, in hard underground pornography. He'd set women up, addicted them to drugs, and had helped perpetuate the most heinous things. He'd run master tapes for probably thousands of flicks. He'd been cameraman for rape viddies. He'd tied women up for wet S&M, and had stepped back as the camera cocks had pissed on them and sunk needles into their breasts. He'd held the lights at snuff films...

And in his time he'd had sex with hundreds of children.

That was the way the world was. Period. He didn't make the world, he just lived in it. And he did what he had to do, day by motherfucking day, because if he didn't, some other snide Charlie would. Sammy had come to grips with the past. Was it his fucking fault that other people couldn't?

I did my time, and I paid my dues, and if that ain't good enough for the rest of them, then they can eat shit.

Actually, despite his emotional furor, he felt good. He'd tried to make his peace. No one else had. So that was that. He remembered his main crib back in the good old days. So what if he'd strung the bitch out on skag and used her as a kink for his people between runs? And that weirdo kid of hers? Sure, he'd put the blocks to her plenty of times, but it wasn't like he'd strung her out or anything. He'd always stuck to his rule: Never hurt the kids. Adults were different; they got what was coming to them. But never kids. Was he that bad, that absolutely awful, because he'd adjusted to the real world and the others hadn't?

The junkie had said the kid was his. Sammy didn't care. Spunk was spunk. He'd plowed the bitch big time in the early days. *Big deal. Is it my fault she was looking for a candyman and wound up getting pregnant?* Jesus, sometimes it seemed like the whole fucking universe was against him.

The junkie had made for a good, discreet crib between runs. In the business, you had to find one. You needed a place to lay low when the feds were antsy. And, yeah, down the road he'd had to hot-shot the junkie—shit, she was going nuts, she probably would've ratted them all out—but, again, it was the rule of life. You had to do what you had to do.

Sometimes, though, even now, he wondered about the junkie's kid. She'd been a good pop for years.

Where is she now? he wondered. *Shit, she must be in her mid-20s now. Did she wind up like Kathleen? A pressure-cooker of hate? An unforgiving psycho cunt?*

Again, Sammy didn't care. The way he felt now, he had no qualms whatsoever. He'd string them both out if he had the chance. He'd put the junkie's kid in some animal and scat films. See how she liked a 20-man butt-bang, then make her fletch each guy clean. The fantasy tranquilized Sammy; it was something nice to think about. Too bad the kid's mother was dead—they could do some more numbers on her too while the kid watched. It'd be even more fun to maybe set up a queer loop for his brother Jack. No sir, there was nothing like a good old all-American Crisco & Fist Party. *How's the fit, Jackie Boy? A little snug?* Then make him suck off some trade. Yeah, the fantasy was sweet.

And Kathleen? Sammy got hard pondering that one. *Yeah, I'd set up something real special for her, like maybe an animal loop. When the Dobermans were done, bring in a couple of logboys to do a scat-job. Get the camera real close. Smile and say cheese, Kathleen. My friend Roscoe here is gonna shit on your face.*

Yeah, fuck 'em all, Sammy thought. The fantasies trailed away. Time to get back to the real world. The caddie cruised down 17th. To his right stood the Old Executive Office Building, the Vice President's headquarters. Shit, Sammy didn't even know who the Vice President was. Some guy named Gore? *He's probably up there spitting on his dick.* The immense pillared edifice looked like a gothic ruins. Further down he passed the American Red Cross Building, which reminded him of a miniature White House. Right across the street a Metro cop was rousting a bum in rotten clothes, prodding him off a bus stop bench with his nightstick.

The city was a cesspool, and its bilge: contradiction, inequity, voodoo politics, and cracked asphalt. But what would the next city be like? Sammy needed to put distance between himself and Vinchetti's guns. He considered Russia, where 10 or 15 grand in U.S. paper made you a millionaire on the ruble economy. Sammy had a lot more than that, but what good was it when the stores were all empty? Mexico sounded like the best bet. Someplace way, way south, away from the tourist holes. Vinchetti's shooters would never get a line on him down there, and Sammy would live like Henry the Fucking VIII. Down there, in deep interior Mexico, a kid for the night set you back all of $10. He'd have all the young pop he ever needed for the rest of his life.

Cashing out would be the hassle, though. You didn't just walk into a bank where you had 400 large in CD's and say "Put it all in a duffle bag." He'd bite the interest penalty, take as much cash as they'd give him, and then take the rest in a lot of certified bank money orders. Then he'd cash them out along the way. By the time he made the border, he'd have the caddie's trunk full of cold, hard U.S. green.

New clothes were in order, though. And maybe a beard, a hairweave, sock on some weight. Cash never had your name written on it. He'd also need a piece. He remembered the old Webley he had, but that was back at the bitch's crib, and the kid probably didn't even live there anymore. *Probably in the nuthouse*, he considered. *Or in the ground. A schizo retard like that probably got snuffed in the first alley she ever walked past.* Sammy wasn't sentimental: the past was the past. Even if it was his spunk that made the kid, big fucking deal? He'd probably knocked up all kinds of kids along the line. What difference did it make?

At least she was a good pop.

Kind of like settling back with a good, dry 'tini after a hard day's work. The kid was always there, and he'd programmed her well. *Yeah, she'd been a good little tumble all those years.* Sammy'd lost interest in her once she got older; he preferred his squeeze young. But she had a body on her, all right. Full tilt house of bricks and a pussy tighter than a cat's. And as for copping a gun, that wouldn't be too hard either. Fucking politicians. Were they all nuts? Even with this Brady Bill shit you could walk into plenty of pawn shops all over the place where a little extra lube of the palm got you a gun without even telling them your name. *Thank God for the Right to Bear Arms,* Sammy thought. Along Connecticut he found a vacant spot. He even put money in the meter. *I'm no scofflaw,* he thought with a laugh on his lips. *I'm a rehabilitated citizen*. The bank seemed to glow across the street. Sammy turned the meter crank—

"Hello, Sam."

—and jerked around.

The sun blazed in his eyes.

"Don't do anything stupid."

His focus shifted.

A woman stood before him. A little plump but cute. Nice clothes. Plain brown hair, and a face that would be pretty if it weren't for the tense, pinpoint expression.

"Who are—"

"See that parking lot over there?"

But he didn't really hear her. By then, he knew. "Kathleen?" he said.

"We're going to walk over to that parking lot," she said, speaking so calmly her lips barely moved. "And you're going to walk ahead of me," she added. Then the back of her right hand raised, to push a few locks of hair off her hot brow.

At the same time, her left hand eased forward, over which had been folded a copy of the August issue of *'90s Woman*.

Hidden in the tent of the fold was a .38 revolver.

Chapter 35

(I)

They were doing it again.

Last night.

She'd been on her way back from the 4th-floor laundry unit.

It was her job to empty the hampers and change the drop-bags.

She liked to look at the bloody sheets.

Sometimes she'd close the door and look at the bloody sheets for a long time.

The pretty red stained into white.

And on her way back to the staff elevator, she passed the new ICU ward.

She peeked in.

Her vision swam in red.

Like the pretty red-stained sheets.

They were doing it again.

"Harder, honey."

They looked like ghosts in the dark.

Ghosts jerking.

Frantic ghostflesh slapping.

The handsome phlebotomy technician stood with his white staff pants down behind the fat charge nurse, who was bent over the elevated convalescent bend, her white skirt pushed up.

She knew the phlebotomy tech was sodomizing her because every few minutes the nurse would whisper "More spit," and the phlebotomy tech would stop and his head would tilt and she could hear him expectorate, and then he'd start again.

Yes, they looked like ghosts with the lights out in there.

She knew that if she could see their faces, she would be able to see their skulls.

Because skulls mean death.

They were all just like Daddy, all of them.

Later, right before the end of her shift, she saw him smiling at her.

PHLEBOTOMY, his plastic nametag read. WALLACE, M.

She was pushing her mop cart out of the ER.

Cherry suds floated in the mop water.

"Hi," the phlebotomy tech said to her. "I'm off in a half hour. Can I treat you to breakfast?"

She could see his skull beneath his smile.

"No thank you," she said.

She would cut all the skin off his penis.

She would inject nitric acid into his seminal vesicles and prostate.

She would lobotomize him through his sinuses.

"You sure now? They make great Spanish omelets at the Booeymonger's."

She'd do it very carefully, so he wouldn't die.

A 003-gauge autopsy pin was strong enough to break the thin nasal septum bone.

Then she'd tickle the ultra-sensitive temporal poles with the needle.

"Oh come on. Don't break my heart. I promise I won't bite."

"No, really, I have to go home. Thank you anyway, though."

The temporal poles would really get him jerking.

And then maybe she'd put Daddy's big old revolver into his anus and pull the trigger.

See how he liked people putting things up his ass.

"Well, if you change your mind, let me know."

The phlebotomy technician walked away.

Yes, Daddy's big revolver right up his ass.

It was just a fantasy.

That's why she couldn't wait to get home.

At home the fantasies are real.

When she gets home, she goes into Daddy's Room.

Where Maxwell Platt is waiting.

Blind.

Deaf.

Dumb.

But still alive and waiting.

She didn't glue his eyes shut like the others.

She used tape.

Because sometimes she wants him to see.
Now she peels the tape off.
The autopsy pin glimmers.
"Here's something I want you to see," she says.
She can see his skull beneath his face.

(II)

"Do you believe in vibes?" Spence asked.

"Of course not," Simmons replied with a smile. "I'm a psychiatrist."

Spence sat down as if exhausted. He explained to the doctor: "This morning Kathleen Shade rushed out of her apartment and took off in her car. Then she waited two and a half hours in a pay lot on Connecticut Avenue."

"How do you know? You followed her?"

"Well, no," Spence said. "I had Central Commo DF her vehicle."

"Shade doesn't sound like the kind of woman who'd give the police consent to put a DF transponder on her car."

"Well, she didn't actually give consent. I just—"

"Took it upon yourself."

"For her own safety, for Christ's sake."

"Of course," Simmons remarked. His smile settled back with him in his chair. "Be careful, Jeffrey."

"To hell with careful," Spence came back. "She's my only real link to the killer and now she's being distracted."

"Distracted by what?"

"By her fucking uncle. That parking lot? It's right across the street from her uncle's bank. She knows the guy's going to blow town soon. I think she staked out the bank. I think she kidnapped the guy."

"What makes you think—"

"Because I checked with the bank. Her uncle didn't make a withdrawal, but his car's still on the street. A ragtop Cadillac with temp tags he bought a couple days ago."

"It could be a coincidence, Jeffrey. Is Shade's car still in the parking lot?"

"No," Spence said, disgusted. "A couple of hours ago it took off down New York Avenue and drove right off the district DF grid. I got no way of knowing where she is, but I'm certain—and I mean dead certain—that she's got her uncle with her."

"Vibes?" Simmons asked.

"Yeah, vibes. All the pieces fit, at least."

"So you're angry. Shade's uncle is distracting her from your serial-killer case."

"I'm beyond angry. I'm so pissed off I feel like I'm going to have a goddamn stroke. Sooner or later the killer's going to contact Shade again, probably to arrange a meeting. And when that happens I have to know exactly where Shade is or I'll lose everything. And how can I know where the fuck she is when she's driving off the goddamn district DF grid with her goddamn uncle?"

"Don't be so vulgar, Jeffrey," Simmons advised. "It's not like you. And try not to be so selfish. There are perhaps more important things in Kathleen Shade's life than your homicide investigation. Such as resolving the traumas of her past. Put yourself in her place. It isn't her fault that her uncle happened to be paroled the same week that your killer decided to have a psychotic episode and start murdering people in your jurisdiction."

Spence smirked.

"And, really," Simmons went on. "What reason could Shade have for abducting her uncle?"

"I don't know." Spence's eyes thinned. "Shit, she's got a gun. Maybe she wants to kill him."

"That's ridiculous, Jeffrey. Kathleen Shade is a magazine writer. She's not a killer."

(III)

"I'll kill you," Kathleen asserted. She pressed the barrel of the pistol hard into Uncle Sammy's lower right side. "If you try anything funny, I'll empty this gun in you. I swear I will."

"Kathleen, please. Look, you've—"

"Be quiet and drive!" Kathleen yelled.

"Drive where?" Sammy very quietly inquired.

"Just keep going down 50. I need to be away from the city. I need to clear my head and think."

For the first hour, she'd forced him to drive obliviously about the city, then ordered him to head out New York Avenue, which had long since changed into Route 50. She seemed jittery, confused. But one thing that never wavered was the barrel of that .38, wedged into Sammy's side. If she pulled off a shot, he knew, the bullet would take out his kidney and turn his small intestine into ground meat. But—

She's not that crazy, he considered. *Or is she?*

Sammy clammed up down 50, past the Bowie and 301 exits. Then he dared to speak:

"Kathleen, think about what you're doing. I did my time, I'm a free man with civil rights. You can't just grab people off the street at gunpoint. You'll go to jail. And you say you'll *kill* me? Jesus, Kathleen. You do that and they'll put you in jail for 25 years at least."

"You think so? You're not a free man, Sam. I don't care how much time you did. You're a child pornographer and a pedophile. And you're the guy who raped me for 10 years, remember? A child? I could blow your head off right now in cold blood, tell the jury that you tried to rape me again, and that would be that. You don't think they'd believe me? You think I'd go to jail for killing a pedophile?"

"Well, I guess you got a point," Sammy conceded. *Yeah, she sure as shit does.* He changed the subject. "At least tell me what this is all about. What are you gonna do with me?"

"We're going to talk," Kathleen said. "Take this next exit."

Sammy veered the T-Bird right. The exit emptied out onto Davidsonville Road, and what faced them then was one of those PARK & RIDE commuter lots. "Pull in there," Kathleen instructed. "Drive way around the back and park."

She's not gonna snuff me, Sammy concluded. *There's no way she's got the balls...*

Sam silenced the rest of the consideration. He was sweating. He parked in the rear of the lot, between a pickup and a station wagon. Then he turned off the ignition.

Kathleen brushed damp hair out of her eyes. "In your vast experience, Sam, how many children have you had sex with?"

"Aw, Christ, Kathleen, I—"

"How many!" she lunged forward and shrieked.

The gun was poking into his side.

Sammy gulped. "I don't know—"

The gun dug deeper, her hand turning white around its grip. "All those sick films you made, you always got a piece of the action, didn't you? I'll bet you've raped hundreds of children over the years, Sam. Isn't that right? Hundreds?"

It probably had been hundreds, but what could he say? "I never hurt any of the kids, Kathleen."

"But I was your regular, wasn't I? Between 'runs,' whenever my father was out of town. Wasn't I?"

Sammy's head spun. "You don't under—"

Kathleen cocked the pistol and jammed it further. "If you don't answer me, goddamn you, I swear I'll—"

"Yes! Yes!" Sammy yelled. "You were...my...regular."

Kathleen grinned maniacally. "Yeah, your regular kiddie fuck. It takes a big man to brainwash a little kid so he can have sex with her. But I wasn't the *only* regular. I know that now."

Sammy's gaze slackened. "What are you talking about?"

"I know all about it, Sam. Your little hidey-hole. The common law wife you addicted to heroin and turned into a prostitute. A woman you brutalized for years, offered up to your degenerate film friends, debased, tortured, raped—just for kicks."

Sammy's mouth gaped.

The heat was cooking him. She insisted on keeping the windows up, the air-conditioning off. But worse even than the heat were her words...

"But she had a daughter, didn't she, Sam? A little girl just like me. And you raped her too, between your porno runs, when you weren't busy raping me. It's true, isn't it, Sam? You had a daughter, and you did the same thing to her that you did to me. Right?"

"Kathleen, I don't know where you're getting all this sh—"

"Don't lie to me, you goddamn bastard!" she screamed, "Or I'll—" The pistol jerked up. The hammer fell—

BAM!

A round went off right in front of his face: a flash like a fireball, a hellish concussion. The driver's window blew out, raining safety glass. Sammy hunkered down in the seat, his teeth gritted, flashburn on his cheeks. He urinated in his pants.

"Yes!" he admitted. "Yes, there was another girl! For God's sake, Kathleen, please don't kill me!"

"You raped your own daughter," the words croaked through particulate gunsmoke. "For—what?—10 years? Fifteen?"

Sammy could only nod, gulping.

But when the smoke spread, Kathleen's face reappeared—a total transmogrification. Calm now, not hysterical. Completely in control.

The bitter gunsmoke had changed her from a mad dervish to a complacent angel.

But the angel still wielded a gun.

And spoke profanities. "You motherfucking asshole."

She put the hot barrel to his nostril, cocked the hammer again.

"And now, Sam," she informed him. "You're going to tell me where that other girl lives."

(IV)

A wonderful brain-job.

He convulses, then dies.

The bright skull beneath his face goes out.

The autopsy pin drips dark-scarlet cranial blood.

She's so excited, she gets a little carried away.

She uncuffs him and puts him on the floor.

She slices open his abdominal wall with an Arista #22 scalpel.

She eviscerates him.

She pulls it all out, rejoicing.

She saws off his arms and legs.

She crudely cuts around his cranial dome with 15-tpi post- mortem saw.

Portrait of the Psychopath as a Young Woman

She takes his brain out of the glistening vault of bone.
Puts the brain on the floor.
And—
squish
—steps on it.
Another corrupter scourged from the earth!
But then her mother comes in, railing.
No, no, honey! What have you done!
"But, but—"
My God, what have you done?
She begins to cry like a baby.
She's a killer-baby.
"But you said skulls mean death!"
But not him! her mother shrieks. *Not him!*

Chapter 36

(I)

Spence got bored driving around, and there was nothing to do back at the office. According to his surveillance unit, Shade had not returned to her apartment. Central Communications, likewise, reported no incoming calls, nor had Shade's vehicle reappeared on the district DF table. Spence was in limbo.

My whole life, he considered, *is in limbo.*

He sat in his unmarked which he'd parked nose-out in an alley right next to Hearsay's, the singles bar where the killer had picked up Jonathan Duff. Three times city uniforms had asked him what he was doing, and he'd merely flashed his badge and stated: "Spence, Major Case Section. Get back on your beat." The officers had obliged without argument.

Rush hour came and went. The humidity rose as the temperature hovered. Across the street a panhandler with a trumpet brayed old tunes into the dusk. Spence would've run him off but he liked the music. Before him the city shifted identities: work to play. As the sun descended, revelers in droves poured out of parking garages to take their places in the surrounding bars. *Maybe I should go into one and have a drink,* Spence thought. But then he remembered that he hated alcohol. To his right was a Thai restaurant. He grabbed a carryout order of stuffed chicken wings and some weird eggroll sort of things full of curry and chopped softshell crabs. When he got out to put the empty cartons in the trash, a sign on the city wastebasket read THE POLICE ARE YOUR OPPRESSORS! *I'll show you some oppression,* Spence thought and nearly laughed. Nearly.

Back in the unmarked, he flipped through the new *'90s Woman*. The table of contents befuddled him. "10 New Surefire Ways To Tell If He's Sincere." "Fight Back! Sexuality As Your Ultimate Weapon." "Liposuction: Fact Versus Fiction." Here was a short story by someone named Thiel, an allegory depicting men as balls and chains. More articles on feminism. Eventually Spence turned to the "Verdict" column.

Kathleen Shade's picture appeared at the top: a subtle off-smile, ruminant yet suspicious eyes, brunette bangs cut blade-sharp. *If I were straight,* Spence wondered, *would I be attracted to her?* He doubted it. He knew that, on the inside, she was as unhappy as he. *Besides, I wasn't sexually abused as a child.* What would they talk about on a date, for instance? What would they do? What would she expect of him? Emotionally? Sexually?

Thank God I'm a celibate gay, he decided.

> Dear Kathleen:
> I just broke up with my eighth boyfriend. He didn't take it well. He yelled that I was making a big mistake, that I was selfish and immature, and that I had no sense of adult priority. I told him that I didn't know what I wanted, and that I couldn't stay in the relationship because I haven't yet discovered what I'm looking for in life. Then he yelled back (in public, right on the street!) "With me you were going someplace, but you're not going anywhere now but down! And if you don't know what you're looking for by now, you're never going to know!" The reason this bothers me is because I have this horrible feeling that he's right. When does a woman know what's she's looking for?
>
> —Disordered

> Dear Disordered:
> Regarding your former boyfriend, forget him. By saying such spiteful things to you he's only elucidating his own selfishness and immaturity, not to mention his lack of consideration for your honest feelings. Men like that are best left out with the garbage. And as for your current emotional perplexion, I think you need to reverse your methods of anticipation. It is no flaw for a woman to acknowledge that she doesn't know what she's looking for in life. This, instead, is an honest and very real insight. By whatever designs, influences, etc., you may be looking for things you only think you're supposed to want. The best way to deal with this sort of crisis is to do what I do. Don't try to find what you're looking for. Instead, let what you're looking for find you.

Spence could not decipher this at all. *Is it just me?* he wondered. Women's ideologies, at least to him, seemed like a foreign language. No wonder men could never understand women.

Pedestrians sauntered by, peering in through the windshield. A few laughed. *Am I funny?* he wanted to say. *You think I'm funny, huh? I'll show you funny, you bunch of overdressed yuppie punks!* He glanced back at the article, trying to apply Shade's cryptic counsel to himself. *What am I looking for?*

I'm looking for Kathleen Shade, and I ain't finding her.

At that moment the radio scratched static. "MCS Field Unit One, are you 10-8?"

"Yeah," Spence said into the Motorola mike.

"Ready for 10-89 transfer to Central Communications operator." Static crunched like potato chips. Then: "This is Central Commo. You there, Lieutenant?"

"Yeah," Spence said.

"Shade's vehicle just came back on the DF board."

Chapter 37

(I)

Kathleen had waited in the commuter lot for hours, every so often changing gun hands. "Kathleen," Sammy had asked. "What the hell are we doing?"

"We're waiting," she'd replied.

"Waiting for what?"

"Nighttime."

Sammy thought he'd go nuts sitting there in the hot car with her piece sticking in his side. She never said how she knew so much about that part of his past: the junkie whore and her little house, and the kid. Nevertheless, she knew it all. But Sammy couldn't imagine why it seemed to mean so much to her.

What's she after?

When full dark slid across the sky, she ordered him to start the car and take the interstate back towards D.C.

"How did you find out all that stuff?" Sammy asked.

"Shut up."

"Why do you want to go there?"

"Just shut up, Sam. Shut up and drive."

Sam drove.

None of it made any sense. The broad was dead, and the kid was probably dead too, either that or banging her head against a padded wall in some psych ward. There was no way Kathleen and the kid could know each other: different ages, different schools, different neighborhoods. *Different lives,* he reasoned.

Route 50 coursed on through hot darkness. New and typically disorganized road construction funneled them around split medians and jersey barricades.

The silence was killing him.

"So how's your dad?" Sam asked.

"Shut up!" Kathleen exploded. "I can't think when you're talking! You're distracting me!" The gun jammed so hard in his side he thought it would puncture him.

All right already, he thought.

Every so often he stole quick sideglances as the T-Bird glided on. The heat and humidity mussed her hair. Her lips seemed to be moving irreducibly yet they produced no words. The road wound on, tires humming over potholes.

There wasn't much time.

Exits approached. South Dakota Avenue. Earlier, Sammy had told her exactly where the little house was.

"This is our exit, isn't it?" Kathleen very quietly asked.

"Yes."

"Take it."

Just a few more miles. Sammy's palms effused sweat on the wheel. Familiar sights rose up: an auto junkyard, the old Good Will repository, Fort Lincoln Cemetery. Sammy turned right onto Bladensburg, and it got worse. The old neighborhood seemed like a haunting ground. Even the litter felt familiar, the drabness of the tar-patched streets, the grit of the cement. Off in the distance, then, against the tinted dusk, he could see the old war memorial—the Peace Cross—looming over the asphalt rise like an ancient sentinel.

"Let me talk," he whispered.

"What," she said.

"I don't know what you've got planned," he told her, "and I don't know why you'd want to go there. I haven't seen her since the week I got busted. That was over six years ago, Kathleen. She probably doesn't even live there anymore."

"Yes," Kathleen corrected. "She does."

She was commandeering him. She was forcing him back into the past.

Sammy wondered what would be waiting for him when he arrived.

Chapter 38

(I)

Cramped little cottages, like boxes. Postage-stamp yards overrun by weeds. DEAD END read a sign like a bloated yellow face. Perhaps it was Kathleen's imagination but she thought she detected a fetor in the air. Spoiled meat.

A malformed moon seemed to sit atop scrawls of trees. The street looked dead; a few of the houses must be vacant.

But one's not, she reminded herself.

"Which house?" she asked.

Sammy idled the car down the narrow street. "At the dead end. On the right."

Kathleen ordered him to go all the way down and park at the dead end. "Turn off the motor and the lights." Her hand, after all this time, now felt fused to Maxwell's revolver; her knuckles ached. She gazed at the little house, a carbon-copy of the rest, though slightly better kept. The large front window—the living room, she guessed—glowed beige behind its shades.

Maxwell's in there, she thought, chilled. *Maybe she hasn't killed him yet. Maybe he's still alive...*

It seemed like any typical hope: futile, a splendorous palace built with bricks of lies. But what else could she do?

The little house looked crushed in its solitude and moon-tinged dark. A cracked sidewalk led to the front door. Then her gaze lengthened; on the side of the house, perhaps a mile off through the trees, she noticed a massive stone cross...

The Cross. The Cross in The Window.

Kathleen knew exactly what she was going to do.
If Maxwell's still alive, I'm going to trade Sammy for him.
"Get out," she said to her uncle. She slid out right behind him on the driver's side, the revolver ever-jabbed. "It's time to pay your daughter, and my cousin, a visit."

(II)

"If you say anything, Sam, if you try anything, I'll kill you."
"I get the message."
The front door was locked. Should she knock? No, announcing herself would give the killer time to prepare. Sammy walked ahead, the gun in his back, and led them around the side to the backyard. The fetor never waned. Clumps of crabgrass sprouted from cracks in the small patio, beyond which the trees and rampant bushes seemed frozen in the hot moonlight. Ever distant, the cross remained visible from its mount at the edge of town.
The back sliding door was unlocked.
"Not one word," Kathleen whispered.
Sammy smirked.
Inside smelled musty. Tread-worn carpet passed a tiny kitchen to the faintly lit living room. Everything looked old, out of date. An old, dingy-shaded lamp. Tacky green couch and armchair, their corners patched or worn. The legged television looked like it came from the 60's. There was even a lava lamp on the end table, its blood-red glop hovering in lit oil.
But this was all Sammy needed to see; he recognized it all. *Same furniture, same place,* he realized. Then: *She still lives here.*
Kathleen seemed transfixed. A card table and chair had been set up. There was a typewriter, papers and magazines. Sammy saw several copies of the rag Kathleen wrote for, *'90s Woman.*
"My God," Kathleen whispered.
"What?"
"Your daughter's a murderer, Sam," she told him very quietly. "Did you know that? She's a serial-killer."
Sammy gaped at her. "She was a headcase, a skag-baby. What the hell are you talking about? All she ever did was stare at the wall or read books."
"When you weren't busy raping her, you mean." Kathleen almost chuckled in disgust. "You turned your own daughter into a psychopath."
Sammy's gape broadened. He didn't know what she meant. But whatever it was, one thing was clear: the kid wasn't home. The house stood silent. No lights could be seen under the doors of the extending hall.
Unless she's in the basement, he considered. But why would she be there?
Then Kathleen demanded: "Where's Daddy's Room?"

(III)

You shouldn't have killed him, honey.
"I know," she sobs.
You have to think.
I know! she wants to scream.
She's in the basement now.
To get rags and garbage bags.
To clean up the mess she made in Daddy's Room.
Her mother is standing next to the prostitute.
She's watching her daughter.
She's looking at the blood on her daughter's pretty hands.
Great stains and splatters have turned dark on her clothes.
They could catch you now, her mother says. *We're going to have to leave, go far away.*
She continues sobbing gently.
She looks up at her mother.
Her mother is beautiful.
Radiant in love and understanding.
She is smiling at her daughter.
But it's all right, honey. It'll be okay.
"I'm so sorry. I'm so stupid!"
No, you're not. You just made a mistake. It's okay.
She gathers up some bags over by the work bench.
Then her mother's ghost-hand touches her sleek shoulder.
"What's wrong?"
Her mother leans over to whisper, *Honey, there's someone in the house.*

(IV)

"Kathleen, I don't know what you're t—"
"You know what I mean, you asshole." She jabbed the gun again. "Daddy's Room. The room with the two-way mirror. The room where you watched your 'dupes.' The room where you let your porno pals rape your wife and child."

All Sammy could think was: *How the hell did she find out about all this?*

"Where is it?" Kathleen insisted.
"Down here."

She followed him to the hall. The house was so silent, he thought he must be hearing things. Nearly inaudible creaks. A distant ticking. The most tiny of sobs.

Gym equipment cluttered the first room on the left, and on the right was the room where the kid had slept. Next door down, though, was

Sammy's old party room. Whenever he brought in the masters or first dupes from Jersey, the lab guys would sample them here for resolution and quality. And, sure, as a favor Sammy would fire up the whore and let the guys have some fun with her. And if the whore was out peddling, he'd let them tear a piece off the kid while he counted his payoff. Just a favor, no big deal.

But how did Kathleen know about this room? How did she know about any of his secret past? And what was all this shit about the kid being a killer?

Fuck it, he thought. A few more silent steps. He'd worry about all that later.

Right now, he had to get ready to make his move.

Sammy turned the knob.

The door swung open.

The room stood dark.

All he could really make out was the window, which framed the far-off memorial cross.

He slid his hand up the wall and flicked on the light.

Holy motherfucking shit, he thought. *What is this? A fucking slaughterhouse?*

The room blared at them, like a shout. Handcuffs hung off the corners of a brass-framed bed. The bed's mattress looked like a sponge sodden with bright red paint. *It's blood,* he instantly realized. Guts lay in shiny piles on the wood floor. Atop the dresser was a strange wood box and things that looked like surgical instruments. Plus a hacksaw and a power drill. Before the bed lay piles of blood drenched clothes, and…pieces of things.

Body parts.

Both Sammy and Kathleen each stood staring. It seemed like they both stood there for full minute. *This is crazy,* Sammy was thinking. But the next instant, Kathleen broke and went fucking nuts…

"No, no, my God no! Not Maxwell! No no no no no!" she screamed in a shrill that didn't even sound human.

And this was Sammy's mark. *Now!* he ordered himself. The distraction only lasted a second but a second was all he needed. Kathleen, in this mysterious screaming grief, took her eyes off Sammy for a split moment. Sammy's hand chopped down.

The gun fell.

Next second his hands clamped about her throat. Kathleen kicked and flailed, and they tumbled back out into the hall. Sammy's muscles corded up like bunches of spun metal; he took her down easily, straddling her, digging his thumbs deep into the hollow of her throat. Her screams sliced right off; now, she couldn't even gasp as Sammy's grip choked off all her air.

Steady, steady now, he thought, baring down. *Yeah, this'll do the job.* She squirmed between his legs. Her tongue wagged feebly in her open mouth, and her eyes bulged forward. Despite the shock of what he'd seen—the blood and guts in his old room, and all that Kathleen had said—some tiny yet raging kernel of his spirit felt ablaze. He was getting a hard-on. His groin tingled above her thrashing hips. Part of him even thought that he wouldn't mind giving her a last pop before checking her out.

No time, he rescinded. Her throat squeezed down in his grasp. All he had time to do was finish her off and get the fuck out of this gore-hole. When her face turned blue and her flailings ceased, he let go and flipped her over. He had to make sure—who could prove that he did it? Up in Jersey he'd seen some of Vinchetti's freelance cocks do it while they were taping for a snuff flick. Just twist the head way back to one side and pull up hard: the neck would snap like a dry twig. It was a neat sound.

Harder, harder, he told himself. He twisted up, pulling, pulling, with his knee vised hard into the bone at the top of her spine.

Harder, harder, he thought. He felt glowing. He wanted to hear it. He wanted to hear that quick glass-rod snap of her neck.

And in the process of killing her, he even made the effort to whisper: "It's Sleepytime, Kathy, Sleepytime…"

Then a shadow snapped into view.

Sammy stared forward, released Kathleen's head.

Very slowly, he glanced back over his shoulder.

The sultry figure looked huge. He couldn't see her face, but then he didn't need to.

"Daddy," the figure said.

Chapter 39

(I)

Spence leaned on his car horn. *For God's sake!* he thought.

Some big beat-up white Plymouth station wagon had had a fender bender at the corner of Bladensburg and South Dakota Avenue. The drivers stood in the middle of the street yelling at each other.

"Hold on," Spence said to Central Commo in his mike. "I gotta pissant signal 9 here."

"Standing by."

Spence got out and stormed up. The guys raged, one big redneck in a T-shirt and jeans with his gut sticking out like a woman nine months pregnant, and a guy in a suit. "You guys gonna hold up traffic all night or are you gonna get your shit together and clear the goddamn road?" Spence yelled.

The redneck, already having a bad day, bulled right up. "Fuck you, dweeb! Mind your own goddamn business!" Then he put a hand on Spence's shoulder.

"Buddy," Spence said very quietly. "This jacket is a 100% Italian-wool special. It cost more than you make in a month of hanging sheetrock." Then he stuck his badge and ID in the guy's face. "If you don't take your hand off my jacket, and I mean right now, I'm gonna throw your ass in D.C. Jail for 90 days, and I'm gonna order Traffic Branch to tow this piece of shit away and have it cubed."

The redneck glared, and backed off.

"You guys settle your score *after* you clear the road," Spence continued. "You get this land yacht out of here. Now."

Spence sputtered back to his car as the redneck travailed to move his station wagon. "I'm back," Spence said into the mike. "What's the line?"

"Okay, Lieutenant, I gotta positive DF on the board now sure as shit," the dispatcher said. "Looks like about two miles west of the district line down Bladensburg."

"I'm there now."

"Gimme a second for the grid."

Spence passed the fender bender, frowning. He hit the gas and sped down Bladensburg, ignoring two municipal cops parked in the entry of the Frito-Lay factory.

Central Commo came back. "We got no plats or exact address grids, technically you're in Maryland. I'm gonna follow your bead and you turn when I tell you."

"Right," Spence said. Just when he would pass an old Scot station, and a Hungry Herman's on the right, dispatch said, "Take a left right now."

Spence turned through a red light and got a few honks. Then he was passing a town cop station and firehall that advertised BINGO! BINGO! EVERY SUNDAY NIGHT!

"Slow it down, Lieutenant. There any roads to your right?"

"Yeah, a bunch," Spence observed. "It's a residential neighborhood."

"Slow...slow..."

"How's Shade transponder signal?"

"Like Haley's Comet... Slow it down, Lieutenant."

Spence reduced his speed to a crawl. What would Shade be doing in this out-of-the-way little burg? Did she know someone here? Why the hell did she snatch her uncle and bring him *here?*

"Stop," dispatch said. "Take your next right."

Spence was right on it. Thank God for technology. He pulled a right and idled down another residential road lined with small cottage-type houses. Then he passed a sign: DEAD END.

"It's a dead-end," he complained. "It must be an adjacent road."

"No way, sir. Your signal's kissing Shade's."

"You sure?"

"Affirmative. You're there, Lieutenant."

Then Spence spotted Shade's T-Bird nosed into the dead-end. "I got it. I'm parking and getting out."

"I'll be here."

Spence unplugged his Motorola, clipped it to his belt, and stuck in his earphone. He parked right behind the T-Bird, cut his lights, and got out. Shade's car was empty. He peered stupidly back down the dark street. *Shit. How am I supposed to know which house she's in?* He could send for some uniforms and do a door-to-door, but that would be inane. What if he was wrong? What if she didn't really snatch her uncle, and was simply visiting a friend? Spence could imagine the harassment charge... *Unauthorized electronic surveillance of a district citizen. Unauthorized use of department equipment and facilities. IAD would bust my chops.*

There was nothing else he could do but go snoop.

He peeked in a window on the house on the left. An old guy and his wife watching TV. Then he quietly walked around the side of the house on the right. *County police'll probably get a peeper call any minute. Explain that to the chief's liaison...*

Dark basement windows lined the foundation. One first-floor window stood dark. He went around back.

Light, he thought.

He rose to his tiptoes, peering in. At first what he saw didn't register—how could it?

A scarlet bed.

Then more details focused.

God almighty.

Spence stepped back. He turned away to think; he closed his eyes. When he opened them again, he saw...

The great lit Peace Cross out on Bladensburg Road near the bridge. It was a war memorial or something, a landmark, probably 50-feet high and constructed of dark, pebbled stone.

The Cross, he thought.

He turned back to the window.

The Cross in The Window.

He could not imagine the link. He'd been searching for Shade to relieve her of the distraction of her uncle. But...

This was impossible.

This is the killer's house, came the blazing and equally impossible realization.

(II)

It felt like a great, wobbly bubble rising from deep water. When Kathleen awoke, she thought she was dead. She remembered in guillotine-like snatches: the room, Maxwell's entrails and limbs strew about the floor, then Sammy—

Killing me, she thought.

Pain burned at the back of her neck; her brain had winked out like a light. *But—I'm not dead,* she thought. How could she be? She lay face down in the hall. Alive.

In increments, she was able to lean up, look around.

What she saw seemed like a loud, thunking nightmare.

Two dark figures, one tall, one short, struggled behind her in the hall. "Daddy!" shrieked the taller. "You're back!" The smaller figure was but a puppet thrown to and fro against the wall. Each impact of the skinny form resounded through the house. It was like watching a dog shake a ragdoll in its jaws. THUNK...THUNK...THUNK...

Then the shorter figure collapsed.

"Aw, God, baby, please. You don't understand."

The tall figure leaned over, tremoring in some weird form of delight. "Daddy's back, Mother! Look! He's come back to us!"

"Baby, please, I love you," croaked her uncle's wasted voice. "You're my child."

"Come into Daddy's Room," he was answered.

"No, Jesus Christ *nooooooooooo—*"

"Come in with us..."

Sammy, then, was dragged into the charnel room.

The door slammed shut.

Kathleen tried to rise but then passed out again.

Chapter 40

(I)

Spence whispered into his Motorola, "I want the biggest signal 13 in the history of the law enforcement."

"What's that, Lieutenant?"

"Scramble every car, every helicopter, everything you got. I want every TAC guy in the city here in five minutes."

The pause reflected the dispatcher's confusion. "I don't get it. What's going o—"

"Just do it," Spence ordered.

"But...why?"

"Shade," Spence whispered. "I got no idea how, but Shade found out where the killer lives."

"You mean...your psycho?"

"That's right." Spence gulped. Only now was it sinking in. "This is the killer's house," he said.

"On the way."

Spence clipped the radio back to his belt. His back to the house, he checked his Smith snub in the moonlight, checked his speedloaders, and took several deep breaths. Darkness hung still in the cramped backyard. Spence wondered how many bodies were entombed here.

The window was too high to get in quietly. He didn't really want to go in that way anyhow; he remembered the quick glimpses: all the blood and entrails, sawed limbs. There'd even been something on the floor that looked like a stepped-on brain. *Poor fuckin' Platt,* he thought. *What a way to go.*

He crept back around the side. The foundation-level basement windows were dark, and one, tested by Spence's foot, was not locked. He knelt and shined his penlight in, saw nothing but blocks of scary black. *Here goes,* he thought. He ought to wait for the TAC teams but—*Shade's in the house somewhere. Every second I wait is another second she can die in.* He squeezed through the little open window, lowered himself down, and—

Good God...

—almost threw up from the stench. Meaty, dank rot. Sweat, blood, excrement. His penlight found a caged bulb hanging. He yanked the string and filled the basement with light.

And stared.

A starved, red-haired woman had been chained naked across a bench. Her skin gave off a tint like spoiled cream.

Eyes glued shut. Mouth closed by surgical stitches. She was so skinny the slats of her ribs looked like fissures.

Dead, he concluded, applying a finger to her jugular. *It was Creamy,* he realized, *'Rome's hooker. Starved to death down here.* That's how the killer had thrown him off-track. Leaving the prostitute's prints, and strands of her hair on the evidence. It seemed brilliantly macabre...

Another workbench against the cinderblock wall. Blood-encrusted tools lay in disarray. Buckets and plastic garbage bags—Spence frowned into each one. Clumped blood and sewage filled the buckets; bloody clothes filled the bags. And shoved under the bench...

A shoed foot.

Then the foot moved.

Spence dragged out a figure lashed by ropes into a fetal position. The figure trembled. *Still alive,* Spence thought in a grim rejoice. The long blond hair gave it away.

It's Platt.

Eyes glazed by terror bugged up. Spence untied the knots, peeled off the duct tape which sealed the poet's lips.

"I believe in God now," came Maxwell Platt's desiccated whisper.

"How bad are you hurt?"

"I'm all right, I think. I think she was saving me for later."

"Okay." Spence helped him up, crutched him toward the window. "Everything's gonna be all right," he said. "I want you to get out of here right now. Don't make any noise, just get out. A whole shitload of cops are on the way. Get out and start running, and don't stop."

"Kathleen," Platt whispered. "Is she—"

"She's fine," Spence lied. "She's at her apartment. Just run to the main road and call an ambulance for yourself."

"Thank you," Platt mumbled, "Thank—"

"Just shut up and get out of here, will ya?"

Spence helped the shaken poet up through the window and out. He stood a moment amid the stench and pale light. *What could be scarier than a psycho-killer's basement?* he asked himself. *Answer: a psycho-killer's basement when the psycho-killer's still in the house.* But was she? Was the killer upstairs right now? And where was Kathleen Shade?

Was that Shade's guts I saw on the floor? Was that Shade's brain?

Spence shucked his snub. Then he began to move up the stairs to the first floor.

The silence irked him. His noiseless footfalls sounded, to him, like a goon squad clamoring up the staircase.

On the landing, he peered forward. A hallway led to a faintly lit living room; he saw a typewriter on a table. An open door stood just to his left. Spence three-pointed into the room. Empty. It was a bedroom…

A veil of more light seemed to sift from an open closet.

What the fuck's this?

Gun in lead, Spence stepped into the closet.

What faced him, objectively, was a large pane of glass. But what he saw in that pane made it something else altogether.

It was an interstice. It was a portal to hell.

A tall, sleek woman leaned over a brass bed. Spence couldn't see her face. His eyes quickly cataloged the room, the same room he'd seen outside. Entrails spilled on the floor. Ribbons of gore-sodden clothing. Sawn limbs and the squashed brain. Under the window stood a dresser topped by surgical gear and power tools. A large wooden cabinet, its doors open, sat atop the dresser too, and tacked to the insides of the door were what appeared to be old newspaper clippings. In an opposing closet he saw at least half a dozen wigs on faceless mannequin heads…

His eyes darted back to the bed. A man, ankles and wrists handcuffed to the rails, tremored on the mattress. Spence remembered the mugshot.

It was Samuel Curtis Shade.

Two-way mirror, Spence realized. He was watching the killer about to start working. And— *She can't see me,* he knew.

Yet the initial horror left him rigid as a wood post driven into the ground. His eyes could not move away from their witness.

Samuel Shade looked only barely conscious. The woman had cut his clothes off and was now sewing shut his lips…

Line up, he thought. Spence assumed a firing position called The Weaver Stance, both elbows slightly flexed, his face behind his gun's tiny sights. The .38 standard-pressure round would penetrate the two-way mirror without much deflection. He decided to fire double-action rather than cock the snub's cut hammer and risk the click giving him away. *Mid-lumbars, do it now,* he thought.

Spence never heard the shot. The little gun bucked. The mirror shattered and fell like a rain of tinsel. Spence blinked cordite out of his eyes. *Sooty powder,* he managed to think despite the fact that he'd just shot a woman in the back. *Change brands.* He looked into the heinous room and saw the woman lying splayed on her stomach. The bloodspot seeped just right of the spine, a few inches. *Take some classes from the armorer,* Spence suggested to himself, still strangely calm. *You were aiming for the spine on a stationary target and you missed, you asshole.* But with a .38 wadcutter in the kidney, he doubted she'd be getting up again.

He went out into the hall, keyed his Motorola. "This is Spence, I just took down the killer. Get an ambulance here right n—"

BAM!

A chunk of wall exploded to his right. Spence urinated in his slacks and dropped the radio. The low muzzle-flash gave him the killer's position: on her belly firing up from the bottom of the doorway. But Spence was a sitting duck; he was standing in the middle of the hall with no cover. He put his back to the left wall instinctively, fired four shots left-handed at the lower doorway—

bam-bam-bam-bam!

—ejected the spent shells, popped in five fresh ones with his first speed-loader—

BAM!

—winced at the colossal concussion of the return fire, thought *This bitch must be shooting artillery at me!* then put five more .38's down toward the muzzle flash, reloaded again as his bladder continued to betray him, aimed and—

BAM!

Spence went down.

Chapter 41

(I)

Kathleen's consciousness seemed to revive like hard slaps to a tired face. She heard one of the loudest sounds she could imagine—a heavy, tonerous BAM!—then four little pops, then another BAM!

Then a thunk from down the hall.

She leaned up and saw the bedroom door creak shut.

Get out, was her first thought. She crawled forward, the back of her neck burning as if a nugget of hot glass had been embedded there. She squinted down the dark hall, saw a large figure lying before an open, black doorway.

She heard an unpleasant, wet spitting noise.

It's Spence, she thought.

She used the kitchen wall for balance. She stood up. *Get out,* the thought returned, but the wet spitting noise continued. It reminded her of someone crinkling up wrapping paper.

It's Spence, she thought again.

With all the effort she could muster, she walked past the closed bedroom door to the end of the hall and knelt before Spence.

The right side of his dress shirt, beneath his jacket, was soaked with blood. She put a hand to his cheek. His eyes bulged either in pain or outrage, and for some reason Kathleen suspected the latter. A froth of blood bubbled at his lips.

"Spence... Jesus," she uttered.

He grabbed her blouse. His voice sounded like someone talking with a chest cold: "Get out of here."

"But you're shot!" she whispered. "I've got to get you to a—"

Fluid rattled in Spence's throat as more blood bubbled up. "I'm dying, it hurts," he said inanely. "Don't waste your time." He coughed twice, and winced. "TAC team's on the way. Go downstairs, crawl out the basement window. When you get outside, put your hands up or else my people will shoot you." Even more inanely, then, he began to jabber, "Goddamn standard-pressure rounds, I knew I should have used custom loads or something, you know?" He blinked up at her. "I've never been in love, isn't that funny? Aw, Christ, I don't want to die."

"You're not dying! Shut up!" Kathleen whispered.

"I loved my mother," he rasped. "I really did. But-but I never told her that and she died."

Kathleen could not comprehend this. Her hands fumbled at his massive upper chest, loosened his tie. She didn't know what to do.

Then he squinted at her in the strangest way. "I never disliked you, Kathleen," he whispered, hitching. "It was just a game I had to play. I had to use you. I'm sorry."

"Shut up!" she whispered again.

"I'm really sorry…"

She saw now that he was crying, and the hitching, bloodspurtling coughs were backed by something close to laughter. The last thing he said before he passed out was: "Oh, and Platt's still alive. I got him out a few minutes ago. He's okay—"

(II)

It's strange.
It's nothing like she thinks it'll be.
She knows she's dying but she doesn't care.
She can feel blood pumping out of her back.
She's already sewn up Daddy's mouth.
She's already stuck dissecting pins into his ears, his sinuses, his navel, and his testicles.
He lurches with each insertion.
The smothered scream rages.
Then she opens the Bruns serrated plaster shears.
She cuts it off.
She takes it away from him.
She takes away all her pain.
She takes away all her mother's pain.
But where is her mother?
"Mother?"
She's crying and she feels strange.
She picks up the power drill.
"Mother? Where are you?"

(III)

No, Kathleen thought. She couldn't leave him here. Not here. She felt maniacal. *God, he weighs more than a piano!* she thought ludicrously. She began dragging him down the hall by his suit jacket...

Then she heard the electric whine, the drill.

She could hear its shrill from behind the closed bedroom door. *She's in there,* she thought. *With Uncle Sammy.*

Kathleen would never know what compelled her to do what she did next. She released Spence, went back down the hall, and retrieved his small revolver.

What are you doing? she wondered.

Then she opened the door and looked into Daddy's Room for the last time.

(IV)

The tall woman was drilling Uncle Sammy's Adam's apple. The body shackled to the bed arched upward, tremoring like an epileptic seizure. Then it fell limp.

Uncle Sammy was dead.

Kathleen held the gun on the woman. The woman leaned against the bed. She was dressed in a dowdy blue custodial uniform, whose right pant leg looked black from all the blood.

Still leaning against the bed, the woman turned toward Kathleen.

"I...," the woman said.

The woman's face, obscured by the wedges of fluorescent light, looked blank. It was almost as though she had no face at all.

"Don't move," Kathleen feebly commanded. But suddenly, in her mind, she saw the cat clock. *tick-tick-tick.* The eyes switching back and forth. The plastic tail roving...

tick-tick-tick

The woman slowly reached for the huge pistol which lay on the castered stand full of surgical instruments.

"Don't move!" Kathleen yelled.

The little gun in her hand was shaking. Nevertheless, the woman's hand fell away from the huge revolver.

Behind the woman's shoulder, in The Window, Kathleen could see The Cross...

The woman fell to the floor, sobbing.

"Embrace your hatred," Kathleen whispered.

She backed out of the room and closed the door.

The cat clock stopped.

• • • • •

(V)

Kathleen dragged Spence out onto the front porch. Crossing the threshold felt like exchanging tranquillity for madness. In one step she'd gone from silence to cacophony. Lights as bright as the sun glared in her face. Helicopters, sirens, and radio traffic deafened her. Kathleen released Spence on the stoop and immediately put her hands into the air.

"PUT YOUR HANDS IN THE AIR!" a megaphone-voice ordered.

My hands are in the air, you asshole! she thought. Marauding, dark shapes like dream-killers fell on her; Kathleen was tackled and dragged across the yard by a bunch of men in gas masks and vests. More men hoisted Spence and carried him off.

The street was filled with police vehicles, red and blue and white lights flashing. Dozens of crouched police aimed rifles at the house. More lights roved the yard as helicopters circled overhead. Kathleen could see more men rappelling from limp ladders. The crash of sounds was so loud she wanted to scream.

"Jesus Christ, you're going to break my arms!" she squealed as two SOD cops chicken-winged her into the back of a brightly lit ambulance. Instantly, a very rude man in SWAT utilities and a backwards blue baseball cap was in her face.

"Is the killer in the house?"

"Yes," Kathleen replied. She felt hot, dirty, and tired. "I—"

"Does the killer have accomplices?"

"No, I—"

"Is the killer armed?"

"Yes, I—"

"Does the killer have automatic weapons?"

"Would you let me talk for a second goddamn it!" Kathleen yelled.

The man grabbed her collar. "Does the killer have automatic weapons? Does she have rifles? Does she have explosives?"

Kathleen wanted to kick him. "She has a pistol, I think is all," she spat back not very grammatically. "Jesus Christ!"

"Does the killer have long hair, short, medium?"

"Short hair, dark—"

"What's the killer wearing?"

"Dark blue pants and a light blue shirt—"

The grip on her collar tightened. Slowly, softly, the rude man asked, "What room is the killer in?"

"The first room on the right, in the hall—"

The grip on her collar released. "Get her out of here," the man said and climbed out of the ambulance. Then he was talking into a portable radio. "Primary and secondary units assume your firing posts and watch for crossfire. Teams One, Two, and Three, enter the house on my mark."

(VI)

"Mother!" she cried. "Where are you?"
I'm here. Don't worry. See? I'm here.
Suddenly she was.
Her mother stood before her now.
The Cross glowed behind her.
Her mother was smiling.
She was naked and beautiful.
She was unblemished.
It's over now, honey.
She looks up at her mother.
Come with me now.
She hears footsteps on the roof.
She hears an awful chugging thunder outside.
Come with me now, honey.
With an Ethicon bivalving scalpel she cuts both sides of her throat to the bone.
She feels no pain.
She dies.

Epilogue

(I)

The next morning, Kohls identified the killer's second to last victim as an electrophoresis technician named Wallace, who worked at the hospital's phlebotomy unit. In the basement he found dozens of body parts. More body parts were detected via gas-probes in the back yard. In the killer's room, atop the dresser, was a small wooden cabinet. Tacked to the cabinet's interior door were newsclippings from several years ago, detailing the arraignment, trial, and conviction of Samuel Curtis Shade. Also detailed was the testimony of Kathleen Shade.

At the bottom of the box, congealed by karyolysis into a single mass, Kohls found close to a dozen severed male genitalia.

(II)

Spence didn't die. The .455 slug had broken his ribs and collapsed his right lung but a well-trained EMT crew managed to reinflate the lung and cessate the bleeding before the ambulance had even arrived at the hospital. Spence was promoted to the rank of captain, which didn't sit well with him because it would restrict his opportunity to work in the field. Kohls, however, who visited Spence on occasion, made an observation one evening.

"Hey, wouldn't you rather be a captain pushing fucking paperwork than a lieutenant pushing up fuckin' daisies?"

"Well, yeah," Spence reflected.

(III)

"How are you feeling?" Kathleen Shade asked.

Spence sat inclined in the hospital bed, holding the phone to his ear. "How do I feel? Like someone lowered a draw-bridge on my chest. And that bullet I took? Ruined over $800 worth of clothes."

"Buy cheaper clothes."

Spence was aghast. "Me? No way."

In the background he thought he heard a television; it sounded like a baseball game. A disgruntled male voice yelled several times, "Goddamn Yankees! You call that a pitch?"

"I read in the papers that you got promoted," Kathleen said.

"Yeah, but I might resign. I don't know if I want to be a cop anymore."

"I can't imagine you being anything else."

Spence thought about that. He wasn't sure what he wanted. He wasn't sure if he'd ever know. "How is Platt?" he asked.

"Oh, he's fine, but I think his team is losing. We're thinking about getting married."

"Good. I'm happy for you." Spence genuinely was. "Can I come to the wedding?"

"Sure, but you have to promise not to make a spectacle of yourself."

"You have my word. Just make sure no one parks in the church firelane, 'cos I'll have 'em towed."

"Somehow, I believe that."

Spence fidgeted. His chest itched. "Are you still going to write the book?"

"A militant-feminist opportunist like me? Of course."

"I never meant any of that stuff, you know."

"Don't tell me that, Spence. You'll ruin my conception of you."

Spence laughed briefly, then cringed from the pain. "You're going to mention me, aren't you?"

"You can bet your poker face and existential ass that I will."

"I told you, I'm not an existentialist. I'm a—"

"Yeah," Kathleen recalled. "A solipsist." She laughed over the line. "You've got enough crap to sink a ship."

"I know," Spence said.

"Are you really going to come to my wedding?"

"No," Spence said.

Kathleen paused. "What do you mean no?"

"The word denotes a negation, denial, or disagreement. It's an adverb. But I'm only kidding. Of course I'll come to your wedding. Oh, and I'll also say lots of good things about you when you interview me for your book."

"Get well soon, Spence. And keep in touch."
"I will," Spence said. "Good-bye."

(IV)

Simmons visited him regularly. He brought books and magazines and bantered about things of little consequence.

"You don't have to therapize me by making distracting small talk," Spence told the doctor.

"Oh, I know that. Who could ever therapize *you,* Jeffrey?" Simmons walked around the clean hospital room as if making a discreet inspection. "So when do you get to go home?"

"A couple of weeks."

Simmons looked at him. "And what then?"

Spence knew what he meant. "I don't know. I might quit."

"Fine. Start a business. Teach. Anything. You might even consider being a psychologist."

"Not likely," Spence said. "That would be even more depressing than being a cop."

Simmons turned from the window and cast Spence a reproving scowl. "It's really not that bad, you know. It really isn't."

"What?" Spence.

"If you let yourself really *look*, Jeffrey, you'll see some of the most wonderful things. It really can be wonderful."

"What?" Spence repeated.

Simmons' hand opened toward the sunlit window.

"The world, Jeffrey."

Edward Lee is the author of ten novels, 60 short stories, multiple comic scripts and novellas, and is a contributing editor for Barnes and Noble Online.

Elizabeth Steffen works for a law-enforcement agency with the Federal government. She lives on the west coast, where she spends all of her free time rescuing stray animals and wayward souls.